My Walk with Grief

Jenny,
Grace to you
in the hard
work of grief. May
love grow stronger. May
love along the way.
Elaine K Olson

Elaine K. Olson

Legacy Book Press LLC
Camanche, Iowa

ACKNOWLEDGMENTS

Thanks to those who challenged and loved me into writing and made me better—Xixuan Collins, Becky Langdon, and Terry Haru. And—readers—Lynn Batcher Robinson, Carla Tracy, Maj-Britt Johnson, and several others who read the memoir and shared their reflections.

Thank you, Lynn Batcher Robinson, for formatting the questions at the end of the book.

Thank you, Jodie Toohey, publisher of Legacy Book Press LLC, for your patience and clarity of purpose.

The 800-word, first-person narrative "feet" was published by *The Christian Century* (February 26, 2020, Vol. 127 No.5) as part of the Buechner Narrative Writing Project. A version of this narrative is written in the memoir with permission.

DEDICATION

To Brent and Sara who loved me through.
To Terry who helped me love again.

In memory of Mark A. Olson

CONTENTS

Part One: Before the Death

And life goes on,
which seems kind of strange and cruel
when you're watching someone die.
But there's a joy and an abundance of everything,
like information and laughter and summer weather
and so many stories.

— Melina Marchetta, *On the Jellicoe Road*

TOO YOUNG. TOO MUCH.

Pain and profound sorrow silently cried within the eyes of the man I loved. I sat beside him at the foot of the bed. My own eyes filled with tears in disbelief, trying to comprehend the identity of "widow." I was too young. We were both too young. I was not ready to be alone.

Mark's body held and protected me with its girth and warmth for thirty years. Now, cancer reduced this healthy body into a skeleton of honeycombed bones. Skin sagged where muscle disappeared. Translucent skin pulled taut across bones where fat melted into nothingness. Mark's beard dulled, grew grey, wire-like, shapeless. His strong hands were shaky. Tubes, through his nose, pulled the green bile from his stomach. He no longer digested the food he loved to eat, especially French fries and root beer floats. At the age of fifty-one, Mark appeared decades older.

I watched, feeling helpless and afraid. My husband had been my identity for thirty years. If he died, who would I be?

Mark reclined in a large hospital bed as he awaited his last dialysis. The room wanted to present itself as cheery on a late October day. Pale yellow paint covered the walls. A picture window on the side overlooked a wooded park. Fluorescent lights buzzed above us. Quiet, smiling technicians scurried about, extending extra kindness amid repetitive procedures. But this dialysis was not routine. This last dialysis opened the door to death.

We tried to whisper. It all seemed too loud. We worked to speak over the sounds of the machines cleaning Mark's blood. Sickening-sweet music piped through speakers above us. Our daughter Sara sat beside her dad on a metal chair near the bed, reaching toward him with her whole body. Her eyes longed to catch glimpses of his love for a few more days. She had enrolled in seminary a few weeks before, expecting her dad would mentor her along the way. They shared a love of theology along with the loving bond of a dad and his daughter.

Our son Brent had left earlier in the day to handle the preparations for hospice care before Mark arrived home. Brent and his dad shared an enthusiasm for life matched by their dark brown, wild, and curly hair. They both laughed from their bellies, imagined significant dreams, and debated ideas with arrogant assertiveness. Each admired the other's adventures, though sometimes from afar.

I sat at Mark's feet, my sacred place. The cancer diagnosis of multiple myeloma had toppled our lives only five months earlier. In these last six weeks, a mysterious infection invaded his bowels, joining the cancer that devoured his bones.

I longed to caress and hold him during this time. However, the brittle bones in his body were too sensitive to touch. His body screamed a silent caution against my desire to embrace him, warning me to stay away. Whenever I did touch him, he suffered pain. With the absence of physical contact with Mark, my body ached with loneliness. Talking was too hard. Being present was not quite enough.

Together we discovered that his feet, hanging outside the bottom of the bed, remained unscathed by the disease. I could touch his feet without causing more pain. His feet became the path for connection.

4

At the end of each day, I rubbed a lavender-scented lotion on his dry heels, soles, toes. His size-twelve, basketball-loving, hook-shot-trained, golf-putting, resting-on-the-desk-to-think feet became a home of presence. This nightly routine spoke the love we both needed, the love we lived, and the love we knew. Here we touched skin to skin, heart to heart, lovemaking of its own kind. The action calmed his soul enough for him to sleep. This touch expressed my love through a tender caress, sharing with him what I longed for but no longer received.

On this last day in the hospital, I sat at his feet, yet again. When this dialysis treatment ended, Mark would leave to die at home. He would die in our bed instead of the uncomfortable hospital version that barely fit beneath his 6'5" frame. He would die with me beside him.

I wanted to hold on to him for as long as I could. Each day the cancer consumed more of his bones, destroyed his organs, and emptied his spirit. As he slipped away, my role, my identity, my anchor, and self-understanding diminished with him.

Multiple myeloma had won the day. The doctors explained to us that in this type of cancer, the M-protein in the blood goes mad. Wildly producing itself, it overworks the bone marrow, bleaching the bones of calcium, leaving behind holes within the bones, echoing in pain. These M-proteins invaded the kidneys, intestines, and other significant organs, taking away the elasticity in the organ muscle, disabling their ability to function, allowing unknown and exotic infections to settle in their wake. The M-protein left deposits called amyloids, which destroyed Mark's kidneys in the early summer, just a few weeks after the initial diagnosis. To stay alive, Mark required dialysis three times a week. The large intestines became infected late in the summer. At the hospital, the tubes connected to Mark helped him live. Through them, he received nutrition and pain medication. Lines pulled bile from his stomach and pushed antibiotics and much-needed fluids into his veins.

During these last weeks, the monster, multiple myeloma, swallowed his physical strength. There were no more drugs to stop this enemy. In a calm acceptance of the inevitable, Mark decided to stop dialysis. He wanted to die at home, surrounded by family and friends.

Mark took charge of death, grabbing it away from the power of the myeloma, claiming death for himself. These moments in the treatment room began his empowered journey into the final ending. We expected death within seven to ten days, expedited by the poisoning of the contaminants in his blood. This death would be less painful than the continued months of suffering caused by multiple myeloma. Mark believed this was a more painless death than the agony of cancer's killing.

As he made this decision, Mark exhibited a steadfast calm and clarity of thought. He did not seek advice from our grown children or me. Instead, Mark took it upon himself to boldly lead this dance toward death. A spirit within him re-ignited.

But my spirit grieved. His singular process of deciding to die in this way only left me lonelier and more isolated. He gave me no opportunity to voice an opinion.

On the one hand, I was grateful Mark was so clear. But this exclusion hurt me deeply. During our thirty years of marriage, we made the big decisions together—decisions for education, moving, which churches to serve, when to have children, parenting, what house to buy. We shared values and beliefs. Over the years, we worked for our marriage to be a partnership where both of our voices mattered. I was working to find myself within my profession as a psychotherapist. At least that's the story I told myself.

Mark had been a charismatic leader with his body size, well-defined opinions, and strong voice, commanding the energy of any room. His charm and insights encouraged the respect that followed. My role as a pastor's wife was one of support, and it defined me. My identity, my thoughts, my life were characterized within this structure as we worked to find ways of mutuality. Yet, when Mark chose to die, he decided alone. Where did this leave me?

I swallowed my hurt. Mark was dying, and we had more significant issues to manage.

Surrounded by dialysis machines and internal musings, we sat in silence. Alone in our thoughts. I tried to stay focused on the immediate now, but my mind kept drifting toward a funeral and then into life as a widow.

"Widow." What did that mean anyway?

With each thought of his approaching death, my throat pinched shut. My gut heaved into the depths of the unknown. Panic hit with a steep headwind spiraling me into strange despair.

"Focus on the now," I breathed. "Protect these moments with your heart."

My world was quickly changing; I had to find a way to hold on. Panic would not help me manage the upcoming chaos. I needed to be a mom for my children, find a way to maintain a private practice in psychotherapy, and work with the staff and leadership of the congregation Mark served as pastor. The congregation was losing a pastor. I would also need to be strong for Mark's family, my family, our friends, and find ways to stay in touch with a network of people throughout the United States. Mark was a mentor to many. Many tasks and roles required my attention.

"Breathe," my mind interrupted. My prayer was to find a way to "breathe." It was the only prayer I could manage to do.

IS THIS A GOOD TIME?

Cancer came into our lives at just the wrong time—as if there is ever a right time.

When I married Mark, thirty years earlier, I was full of spunk and enthusiasm. We were both intense and purposeful, but different. Mark was blue-eyed and Scandinavian. I was brown-eyed and German. Mark stood 6'5", but my 5'3" personality pushed at him to maintain a sense of self. I did not want Mark's bigger-than-life character to swallow me.

One mentor from our mutual history described me as a "creative and compassionate servant of the Word and full of piss and vinegar," a Midwestern phrase about a woman of vitality and energy. I often wondered if this was a compliment or a curse. Was being a strong woman acceptable, or did it stink? Was he affirming me? Or making a patronizing statement to keep me quiet?

Mark and I met at Dana College, a small liberal arts college in Nebraska, during Freshman Move-In Day in 1969. I was a sophomore and worked as the floor leader on the top floor of a women's dorm. Because Mark was a first-year basketball player with a scholarship, the college expected him to help with move-in day. Of course, he chose to assist in the women's dorm, not the men's, and decided to carry boxes to the fourth floor to show off his athletic prowess.

I first met Mark in Julie's dorm room. Mark rested in a chair after helping her unload her belongings and carrying them to the fourth floor. His tall stature and kind smile caught my attention. I walked in, said hello, laughed, and sat on his lap.

I looked him in the eye and said, "Hello, my name's Elaine. Who are you?" We quickly became good friends, though he dated Julie during his first year at college.

I joined him and several others in a group called Youth Encounter. On weekends, we traveled to various churches in communities close to campus to sing (I played guitar), talk about Jesus, and encourage others to "love Jesus, too." With a few other friends, Mark and I met for lunch in the college cafeteria and talked theology for hours at a time. We bantered and laughed from a common purpose and joy. By the time he was a sophomore, we had added dinner to our times to meet. In time, Mark began to walk me back to my dorm in the evenings.

During the summer after his sophomore year and my junior year, Mark and two other friends received a grant to lead a summer ministry for young adults near a small country town in Nebraska. Many teenagers in the county had died from underage drinking and driving. Mark and his friends wanted to find a way to help the kids who lost friends with a message of God's grace.

For this project, Mark wanted to learn to play guitar and asked if I would teach him. Of course, I accepted. We agreed to meet in one of the rooms on the third floor of Old Main, the main classroom building on Dana's small campus. We sat down together. He held my guitar as I put my hands on his to show him how to play a D-chord, then a G- chord. He turned to me and kissed me with a passion I returned.

We were married a year later. Mark's family was not pleased, as they thought Mark should finish college before we married. Mark told them, "Elaine may be a year older, but I am wiser. Plus, Elaine has a job and a car." A marriage made sense to both of us.

I believed in Mark and his work. I believed in him and his call to be a pastor. I had grown up with the church being the center of my life, as my mom played the organ and my dad taught Bible classes. It was home, familiar, and safe. To be the wife of a pastor fit into my defined narrative. I believed God called Mark into something extraordinary. I wanted to walk beside him to support his dreams. I would not get in the way of his call. I believed in him more than I believed in myself. Being "vinegar" was not attractive.

During Mark's ordination approval interview, the leader told Mark that he would be a successful pastor because of his insight, intelligence, charisma, and wisdom beyond his years. However, the interviewer said Mark was still rough around the edges, like fresh manure on an open field. The interviewer looked at me and suggested Mark would be successful because I would soften Mark's rough edges.

"Elaine, you will bridge Mark's intense presence so others will experience a care-filled ministry."

With this statement, he clarified and commissioned my role and my purpose. The institution of the church called me to be Mark's wife, a pastor's spouse, to support his work and help others see his heart.

Blindly, I fell into the trap of an outside authority. The interviewer defined my strength as a benefit for my husband. But what did this mean for me? What would it mean as Mark was dying?

Mark led as a bold pastor. He pushed his colleagues, demanded thoughtful engagement with scripture to integrate sound theological thought, and pushed the leaders of the institutional church to a broader and more faithful vision rather than only a narrow view of entertainment for church growth. These ideas created trouble with churchwide leadership, who did not always appreciate such a challenge. Yet, when Mark worked with parishioners, he led with compassion. They loved and admired him. Beneath his height and big-boned body, he was a teddy bear at heart. He told stories as he preached, sat down with others to listen to their stories, and delighted in children.

In my role as wife, I was the number one supporter of his ministry and his public leadership. Many saw us as the perfect couple. However, I often pushed Mark at home, expecting his copious soul and body to withstand my challenges and my questions. I longed for my voice and authority to be known, too. Even as I was strong on the outside, insecurity consumed me. When I criticized him at home, Mark would initially listen but then pull away and hide within his thoughts, bury his head in a book, or get lost by watching sports on TV. I lost confidence, felt alone and confused.

I moved from career to career as he moved from parish to parish. I worked as an elementary school teacher, full-time mom, handweaver, and then director of a college program. I tried to appear confident and vibrant externally, while internally, I questioned my own worthiness. I had high expectations for myself, which amplified my self-doubt. With each career move, I hoped to escape the lack of self-esteem, shame, and perceived failures. I experienced periods of depression as I wondered where to fit and how to fit. What was my purpose? My support for Mark did not always mean support for myself. I wandered from profession to profession.

While Brent and Sara were in elementary school, I experienced severe clinical depression. I had lost myself in the role of Mark's wife. I needed to find myself again. As I started therapy, Mark and I both knew that in seeking help, I would change. In doing so, our marriage needed to change too. As the depression cleared, I found the energy to return to school. I was working with college students at the time and enrolled to earn an MA in the Counseling Program for College Student Personnel Administration. It was the counseling component that fed my soul. I loved it.

As a licensed professional counselor, I found my voice and purpose. One client told me, "You have ears that don't quit." Within this work, I found vision and direction. I did not need Mark's role to affirm me. I knew how to listen well. I learned how to challenge others carefully when they came to me for help. Because I trusted the journey of transformation, I believed I could lead others through it. The transformative change was the Passion Story in Christianity—a movement from the death and despair of Good Friday through the waiting and watching of Holy Saturday into the new life of Easter. I could accompany someone to ride the monsters deep because there is life on the other side. I was not afraid to accompany others on this journey because it was my story. I lived it.

Searching for meaning and God was part of my spiritual journey for much of my life.

I often asked, "Who is God?" "What does grace mean for me?"

At times, I only saw my unworthiness. I wrote in journals, prayed the psalms, and recited morning prayers of the liturgy. I prayed with others, finding words to accompany the stories they shared. I led workshops and book groups. Spirituality anchored my life, and I experienced God's comfort and presence. I read spiritual writers. Even as my image of God transformed from an old, bearded man of judgment in the heavens into an intimate reality of loving kindness and compassion, I pushed and pulled at God the way I pushed and pulled at Mark. Could God withstand the challenge, grow with the questions, and abide in my angst?

Mark was serving a Protestant church, which was a vibrant and challenging call. The congregation had recently completed a significant building project with an addition for a large gathering space for the community to meet and a daycare center for children called Rachel's Place. This project was Mark's pride and joy. Membership was growing. At this church, Mark's vision flourished.

13

In this ministry, Mark celebrated 25 years as an ordained pastor. I was on the way to affirming my voice and profession.

Our children were successfully on their way. Sara attended seminary at the Lutheran School of Theology at Chicago to become an ordained pastor. Brent enrolled in graduate school for a Master of Arts in Humanities. We met Brent's girlfriend Connie. We instantly liked this woman who matched our son's life-force, intellect, physical prowess, and passions.

Along with his call in the congregation, Mark continued his work to support and encourage leadership development for laypeople and clergy within the institutional church. He could integrate the current theories on leadership, theological understandings, and reflective writings for practical implementation in congregations. At the beginning of the year, a church publishing house published Mark's second book. Mark accepted invitations for the speaker's circuit to talk about his writings. He led conferences on congregational leadership, shared his well-developed ideas to support and challenge clergy and church lay leaders.

Mark agonized about the morale of pastors and wanted to find ways to help to improve it. For this purpose, he wrote a blog before it became a thing called "Notes to Eli." In the Old Testament Bible stories, Eli is a high priest who mentored the young boy Samuel. As Samuel grew to become a leader in Israel, he sought Eli's guidance as he mused and developed. In the blog, he wrote to his mentors and colleagues to share with them what it meant to be a pastor and the meaning of God's call to be a minister of the church. In these writings, Mark challenged the assumptions of the church hierarchy about leadership and church growth. The list of people who received these emails grew significantly over the six months he wrote them.

Finding our way as empty nesters, Mark and I each developed a professional role of our own. Mark had his pastoral work and writing. I created a private psychotherapy practice where 40% of my work was with clergy and clergy families. As I grew more confident in my gifts as a therapist and teacher, we began to work together at various conferences and programs.

And then multiple myeloma sped into our lives.

EXCEPT...

During the spring of 2002, Mark steadily grew more fatigued. He was so tired in May that he forgot my birthday. I was both confused and, selfishly, angry. He never forgot my birthday! I especially needed his attention because Mark pulled away from me when he grew physically and emotionally spent.

Mark was so tired he nearly collapsed as he led Sunday morning worship at his last service. He mumbled words as he read a sermon. Yet, Mark pushed to speak the words of grace at the baptism of a young child. He could barely lift his hands from the water. With an ashen face and sunken eyes, Mark was so tired he stumbled as he stood before the congregation, trying to lift his hands for the final blessing. The worshippers were fearful for his life. The staff pleaded with him to go to the doctor, but stubbornly, he went home to rest.

Mark waited for me to return from our niece's college graduation ceremony. I found this out only after the fact; he did not call me. In the midafternoon, I walked in the door. I was surprised to see Mark's subdued body reclined in front of the TV, resting, still, his face white, eyes sunken.

As I listened to the events of the morning worship, my fear grew. After much pleading on my part and both of us lying awake most of the night, Mark finally agreed to go to the doctor the next morning. From the doctor's office, they rushed him to the hospital in an ambulance because of the frightening bloodwork report.

The first test revealed Mark almost died of calcium poisoning. The abundance of calcium had shut down his organ functioning. Hours from death, his heart would have been next. The doctors treated the deadly effects of too much calcium, but they needed to discover what caused the problem.

I called the children. The guilt of wanting Mark's attention a few days earlier vanished into the fear of losing him in death.

The next morning, we heard the answer as to why – a cancer called Multiple Myeloma. This cancer had taken hold of Mark's body, intensifying quickly and dramatically bleaching the bones of calcium. I wondered what would have happened if we had waited longer?

Had we already waited too long? Anxiety ate at my memories. Eight years before this attack, doctors diagnosed Mark with Monoclonal Gammopathy of Unknown Significance (MGUS) during a routine blood test, the precursor to multiple myeloma. At that time, our family was living out the expected trajectory of a typical pattern as Brent began college and Sara finished high school. Mark had just started work as a pastor in a new parish. I was working as a therapist at a local social services agency.

At that time, Mark's doctor recommended we seek a bone marrow transplant immediately. Mark talked to the church staff. We had an intensive conversation with his siblings about the process and bone marrow donations. He bought a funky black beret to wear because he would lose his hair on his head, including his beard. Mark worried he would scare the children at church with a bare head. He planned to have the transplant during March Madness so he could watch the basketball games on TV during the healing process.

With meticulous precision, Mark planned to meet the congregation's needs. But with each detail of the plan, I grew more anxious and confused.

At the time of this first diagnosis of MGUS, the process for treatment moved very quickly, too quickly. We questioned the opinion of this young doctor. The accidental finding of the abnormal readings of his blood counts seemed too bizarre. The blood counts were high but not abundantly so. Out of growing fear, we asked more questions. Mark sought a second opinion.

After a visit to a doctor at Mayo Clinic, we stopped the process. This doctor explained we only had one snapshot of a moving train called cancer. We did not have a definite answer as to how fast the cancer train was moving. This doctor advised us to wait, to watch, and to continue regular testing. We moved forward, relieved and filled with hope.

I put all this in the back of my mind, trusting Mark would remain healthy, and our life would move forward as planned, trusting God to keep him well.

Through the next eight years, Mark had regular check-ups and urine tests. We watched, as we knew that MGUS progressed to multiple myeloma within five years in 75% of the cases. Mark was past this time. We knew that the treatment for the disease included a bone marrow transplant and trusted new procedures. If the MGUS did turn into myeloma, we had a plan. We were hopeful, pushing the idea of cancer into the very back of our brains.

None of the tests during the eight years showed any change in the blood count. Life was normal. Trusting the goodness of God, we moved to another congregation. Brent and Sara finished college.

Except.

Now, the disease moved even more quickly.

Except.

Mark's weariness in the spring should have been a sign.

Except.

I should have been more vigilant with new doctors in the move to Eau Claire.

Except.

I should have pushed Mark to see a doctor sooner.

Except.

I should have stayed vigilant.

Except, what?

Except, now it was too late.

I sat in Mark's hospital room on a sunny morning after the cancer diagnosis. I was grateful that he had lived. I was thankful the calcium poisoning did not kill him, but I was devastated. Had we waited too long?

Mistakenly, we thought Mark had made it through the crucial time. We did not expect the disease to return at such a furious pace. So fast that the previous plans would not work. Guilt flooded me. Should Mark have had the transplant while he was still healthy? Should we have worked with another doctor? Should we have stuck to the original plan? "We should have…" became the refrain in my thoughts. It fed my guilt. I felt complicit with the disease. Why didn't God intervene?

After the multiple myeloma progressed rapidly during the next weeks, Mark was no longer eligible for a bone marrow transplant. The large amounts of M-protein could not escape his system. The amyloids settled in the muscles of his major organs, making it impossible for them to work. The tissues were like the elasticity in a sock that had lost its ability to expand and contract. The muscles of Mark's kidneys stopped first and forced him on dialysis within the first month. Three months later, his large intestines sagged like a drooping old sock, allowing infections to settle in where the elasticity had been.

It had been years since the MGUS diagnosis. Now, death boldly approached. Before the final dialysis, Mark had been in a hospital bed for six weeks with infections raging in the sagging organs and despair roaring in an empty soul. I sat beside him in the hospital room, much of the time in silence. And alone. Mark struggled with what seemed to be spiritual despair. I wrestled with fear. And being alone. Now what?

We prayed for strength, answers, healing, hope. Others prayed too, many others throughout the country. They surrounded our family with petitions for health, for a cure.

Yet.

ALONE, BUT NOT ALONE

As pastor of a congregation, Mark held strong opinions of what it meant to be the leader. He understood and taught others that the leader was to care for the community of believers so they could serve the community. Mark believed if the church members turned their ministry focus internally on the care of themselves and the pastor, the congregants would lose sight of doing God's work in the world. He believed this shift would compromise the mission and work of both the congregation and the pastor. I followed his lead, thinking he knew best. But was this true? What were the consequences for me?

Maintaining some semblance of his role as a leader was utmost in Mark's mind. When Mark went on disability because of cancer, he wrote a letter to the congregation to be specific about their role as he was sick. Their purpose was to care for each other and the community surrounding the church. Mark wrote that as their pastor, he coveted their thoughts and prayers, but his care, both physical and emotional, would be the responsibility of his family and friends.

This belief belied our circumstances. Our extended family lived out of town and was only able to come on weekends. Our children lived busy lives away from home. Our close friends were mostly in other states. Overwhelmed with the immense workload, the parish staff came to visit as they had time. I sat alone, pushing my own needs aside. My role as wife and spouse buried any feelings of resentment.

During this last hospital stay, Mark appeared imprisoned in the hospital bed, bound in place by the many medical apparatus attached to his body to keep him alive. He pulled away from me, and he seemed lost, deep inside himself. The doctors and medical personnel held several meetings regarding his emotional despair. They diagnosed him with clinical depression. They wanted to medicate him with drugs to relieve the symptoms. The physical therapist thought he should get out of bed and use his body. The hospital chaplains said he was grieving the end of his life.

Most of these professionals seemed to objectify Mark as a problem to fix—an experiment for new drugs, a body in trouble, a medical diagnosis. I longed for them to see Mark as a person, a person to love, a man with a story to tell and a soul to embrace with deep compassion.

I watched Mark's attention drift further and further into himself. He stopped talking to me, either emotionally unable or physically too exhausted to speak. He lay silent, staring, haunted, blank, entirely still, disconnected from me and the world outside of himself. I watched. He seemed to be engaging in a deep inward journey. At times, his eyes opened. He pondered on some focal point in the distance. Where he wandered in his mind appeared to be difficult, as his face winced, his eyes teared, his lips quivered, and he breathed uneasily.

I wondered if Mark was engaging deep spiritual distress lost in meaninglessness and uncertainty. His very soul appeared trapped in agony beyond words and fear beyond hope. Was God absent beyond comfort, just as Mark was absent from me?

I sat alone beside Mark as he lay in the hospital bed. I could only observe and be present, helpless to respond to his walled-off being. I sat within inches from him, yet he felt miles away. I was unable to be in touch with his thoughts by talking. If I touched him, he winced.

I prayed or tried to pray using the psalms and hymns. But I experienced little comfort. God seemed far from me as well.

I explored the sky through the window on the hospital's fourth floor, watching geese play in the air, form V-lines in flight, and head south. I observed the tops of trees as summer turned to fall and greens of life changed to dying browns. A lime green recliner with a plastic cover provided refuge for me through the long ordeal, sitting alone beside his bed.

I tried to breathe into the quiet. Within the stillness, I explored memories. Remembering became my silent companion.

I remembered watching Mark walk across campus from my dorm window in college. I announced to myself I would marry him one day. I remembered musings with him over meals on plastic cafeteria trays at Dana College as we discussed Christian freedom and debated the Lutheran doctrines of grace and sacraments. I saw him hold our small children high above his head as both giggled with joy. I remembered Mark showing these toddlers how to dunk pepparkakor, a Scandinavian spice cookie, into milk to enjoy its flavor fully. He knelt beside their highchairs with a cookie in one hand and a glass of milk in the other.

"It's like this," Mark explained. With a grand gesture, he lifted the cookie into the air, then pushed it into the glass, pulling the tasty treat dripping with milk to his open mouth. He would gobble the whole thing in one bite, licking his lips in delight. Laughing, he handed Brent or Sara a cookie, saying, "Your turn."

I remembered the way he rubbed his hands together when he had an audience and prepared to speak. I pictured in my mind's eye the way Mark rubbed his nose and played with his beard. I saw Mark carry a black, zippered briefcase, stuffed heavy with books, over his shoulder wherever he went. I saw him laugh with his friend Red when they were the only ones to understand the mutual joke. The quiet of the room became filled with stories.

The quiet also spotlighted my aloneness as I sat in the green chair for hours on end. I could not focus on reading. The TV was too intrusive. Yet, I remained committed to being present and accompanying my husband, even in the silence.

I began to crochet an afghan to keep my mind and hands busy. I found an easy pattern using a large crochet hook creating soft loops and bubbles with thick white yarn to feel the accomplishment of a quick result. Each day the interlocking of stitch upon stitch lengthened and wrapped my lap and legs with warmth and security. Each stitch held feeling I could not express or even allow my mind to explore. Each pull of yarn from the ball became pleading prayers – Come. Help. Heal. Comfort.

Sitting and being present to Mark, at least in the body, became a learned practice. Initially, I understood it as part of the expectation of my role as a spouse and my stubborn-independent German self. I pushed through the lonely moments with a force of will. As the days and weeks grew long, I came to understand this quiet as a spiritual pattern. Currently, prayer was more of a practiced discipline than a thinking belief. It was what I knew to do – a body memory taking place within my being. It was a ritual, a routine, an active practice.

Yet, the deep pain of this loneliness rooted itself into my soul without acknowledgment. Denial of my internal struggles was the gift that gave me the courage to proceed.

As the hospital stay grew from one week into the next, the community's prayers were always present. With cards and written messages, many remained in contact with us from afar. As the fall program at the church began, Mark remained hospitalized. The prayers continued with more intensity. The staff at the church became the bridge for us and the congregation. They planned a prayer vigil for healing at the church with a service of prayers around the cross. With song and periods of silence, people gathered around a cross in a dimly lit church sanctuary. Each member walked forward to light candles, kneel, or sit at the feet of a cross and pray to ask for God's mercy and steadfast Love to abide.

During the evening of this service, I sat with Mark in the hospital room. From afar, we joined them praying for his healing, not for a cure. We prayed to know wholeness in the journey.

By watching the clock, we were aware of what time the service ended. Soon, we heard a surprise knock at the door. When I opened it, three members of the church staff stood with sheepish, yet cautious grins on their faces. They hurried inside and shut the door, giggling.

Although it was a cold October evening, their jackets seemed unusually voluminous. One sleeve flapped freely with no arm within it. The other hand of each person held the edge of their coat away from their bodies, hiding something held beneath within their other hand. When they opened their coats, we were astonished at the gift they presented to Mark. They each held a lit candle carried from the prayer service. They had taken these lit candles in their cars, past the hospital staff, into Mark's room, and into our hearts.

We laughed. We cried. I looked around and wondered if the oxygen tank might catch fire.

KAIROS TIME

Mark never shared his thoughts during those silent days in the hospital, so I never knew what he came to know. He had written some ideas in his blog, "Notes to Eli," in the summer. What happened within his soul on the bed in the hospital was only between him and God. After he decided to allow death to come, his eyes shifted from appearing as dark, haunted caves into lanterns, bright with a vision. Mark had a purpose—he would die well.

Five months of battling cancer, calcium poisoning, kidney failure, intestinal infections, tubes, painful bones, chemotherapy, medicines, intravenous feedings, lost dreams, spiritual searching, and no sign of future relief led Mark to this time. This time is Kairos time, holy time, the right time. The time to embrace the walk of death.

With Sara beside me, Mark opened his eyes and asked us to write as he dictated two letters. The first was to the congregation explaining the next steps. The next one was the final note for "Notes to Eli." He asked us to send this note:

> *"Sometime in August, the clocks didn't work. It was the craziest thing. Sometimes I would watch one in*

the middle of the night, and it would work just fine. Sometimes I would wake up five minutes later and be frustrated as slowly the night was trekking toward dawn. The other times I would squint my eyes to watch as the minute hand would rotate as quickly as the second hand. It was crazy. Sue, our parish administrator, commented, 'I hope they don't check your pulse by that clock.' We got a new clock, but it did not make time go slower or faster.

"I just finished spending five weeks at Luther Hospital attempting to discern and cure raging colitis and a bowel problem, which were by-products of the multiple myeloma cancer. On Sunday, October 27, we knew what time it was. It was time to go to Mayo Clinic and find out exactly what was going on. We found that cancer had taken over most of the systems of my body. At this point, no matter how the minute hand moves, there is no cure for this disease.

"We decided to return home to our house on Freedom Drive to begin hospice. The doctors indicate that the clock running correctly will offer me days and weeks, but not likely months or more.

"There is no exact time. But there is a promise. Modernity promised us a clock would work perfectly. Modernity promised us a body that would not fail after a few check-ups. Modernity promised us that a world of war, anger, famine, oppression, and abuse could be fixed by well-intended action and ideological pursuits. All of this is like a minute hand running out of control.

"Now I wait for a promise that is sure and true, 'Nothing can separate us...' [Romans 8:38-39]

"All else and all other promised ways of keeping time are empty and lead to nowhere.

"In the coming days, I will pray again and again what I prayed from the beginning of this journey, 'Lord, grant me a quiet night and peace at last.'

"Thank you for being a community of believers that has shared this prayer with me these past months. May we be shaped and molded into a people who dare to trust the vision of a quiet night for all the world and peace at last.

"Eli... I will let you know when the modern mechanical clock stops. Then you will know I rest in the promise of what is here and true and certain; Jesus Christ is our Lord.

"Mark"

Sara scribbled the words onto a notebook page as Mark dictated. My brain clouded with fear, and I asked him to repeat the words several times. Sara and I both wiped tears from our eyes, trying to stay focused on Mark's final message to the congregation. He remained calm, direct, precise.

I tried to internalize this same response. After we finished writing the letters by hand, making sure we could read our swiftly scribbled words in a notebook page for typing later, we sat again in the quiet until Mark completed the dialysis. He took great care to affirm those he served in ministry. He would be their pastor until the end of his life.

But I wondered how we might finally say goodbye. How would Mark be my husband until the end of his life? A dad? Would Mark dictate letters to us too? How would Mark affirm our love? Would he thank us for our support? Would he recognize how I remained present?

Nurses removed tubes that had cleaned his blood for the last time. They carefully attended to the wounds where the plastic tubing entered his body. Then, they quietly left the room, leaving us alone before sending us upstairs to process Mark's final discharge.

Mark thanked Sara for helping. He touched her hand and looked at her with the eyes of a father's pride. A twinkle of light danced between them. Both were grateful for the gift, a generous smile, and an abiding presence.

Mark then turned his attention to me. He asked me to come from the foot of the bed. I sat beside him. He took my hand, looked into my eyes, and gently touched my face.

"Now," he said, "When I die, it will be your turn. You will lead the widow's procession."

I stared at him for a bit, not knowing what these words meant. I was too afraid to ask.

COMING HOME

Despite the calm of a decision made, confusion hovered around in apparitions, clambering with the demands and preparations needed for Mark to go home. It was October 31, Halloween. Was this a trick or a treat?

The social workers handed me information for hospice care: pages filled with telephone numbers, needed medical supplies, instructions to set up a hospital bed, and booklets of what to expect as someone dies.

A nurse taught me how to care for the portable pump that continually pulled the green bile and gastric juices from Mark's stomach through the tubes in his nose into a clear glass jar.

"The jar will sit on the floor beside the bed, where it will be easy to see when you need to empty the drained fluids," she informed me. I wanted to gag.

Another nurse showed me how to manage the intravenous tubes through needles taped to Mark's upper arms, now only skin and bones. To these, we attached the bags of mysterious fluids to provide hydration and essential nutrition. Mark had not eaten real food for several weeks, and the constant drip of these liquids furnished the nutritional care his shrinking body needed. We joked as each new bag dripped into his body. One was a root beer float. Another was a delicious cheeseburger and French fries. And of course, the dessert bag was always banana cream pie.

Finally, the head nurse taught me how to give Mark the ultimate pain killer, morphine, through yet another IV. The thought of administrating these shots terrified me. How much? How often? If I did it wrong, I could kill him. But he was dying anyway. Would this drug make it easier for him to die? For me to live? Overwhelmed with a sense of helplessness and fear, I held power for death and life.

Bombarded with information, I tried writing a few notes and strained to remember the steps of each procedure. At the same time, I kept pushing away the thoughts of my husband's death. I put my own need to receive care aside.

I wondered about being a widow. How would I lead a procession? What did Mark mean? Who will be with me? What will be my role? Who will I become? Where was God in the walk?

Yet, during this chaos, "I can do this," became my constant mantra. "I'm not sure how, but I can do this."

The nurse touched my arm to gather my attention.

"A hospice nurse is just a phone call away," she said to reassure me. She scheduled visits for additional guidance and support for me and to check on Mark. Caregivers came for bed baths and help. Mark's digestive system did not work, so there was no need for bedpans. The stomach pump managed that.

"You will be fine," said the charge nurse as she patted my arm. I wanted to believe her.

With the discharge papers and doctor's orders in hand, an ambulance was available to drive Mark home. But again, Mark took charge.

"I will NOT ride in an ambulance again," he said in a defiant yet weak voice. "The ride to the Mayo Clinic in Rochester was dreadful. I was too big for the gurney and bounced around like a ball as the walls closed in on me. I could barely breathe. You will drive me home," he said, looking straight into my eyes with a confidence I would eventually need to discover as my own.

I walked out the hospital's front door and tried to remember where I had parked the car. My brain was racing. Tears blinded my seeing. Panic rose in my chest, cutting off my breath. My legs grew weak. My body chilled even under a warm autumn sun. I wanted to run away. Or wake up from this nightmare.

I needed to get a grip. My children, my husband, and even the caregivers of hospice required me to be resilient. "I can do this." The mantra continued as I found the car, started the ignition, and put the gear into drive.

As I approached the hospital, Mark and an attendant waited at the curb. I slowed, taking in the reality of what I saw. He boldly sat in the wheelchair, straightening his beleaguered body with all the strength and courage he could muster. His body had betrayed him, but his inner spirit, the part I most loved, remained strong.

When I arrived, we eased him into the front seat, reclined it just enough for him to rest somewhat comfortably. He placed a hospital pillow under his head and wrapped a blanket around his fragile frame. Our friend Carol, a practicing nurse, sat in the back seat to monitor his breath, pumping his stomach as needed with a simple hand pump. With an abrupt, "Good luck and goodbye," the attendant shut the door.

I drove forward from the hospital. Out of the city. Onto the highway. Watching the road and watching my life transition from the past to now. My personal autumn. Another change of season, gleaning the harvest of a thirty-year marriage.

The sun brightly beamed as we drove through the Midwest countryside from Minnesota to Wisconsin. Golden stubble covered the hilly fields empty of harvested grain. Birds gathered, flying in flowing shapes headed to warmer weather. Trees changed in hue from greens and yellows to reds and browns. Wind-blown leaves danced and rattled across the road. The autumn air, clean and fresh, let go of past promises, creating an open space for the cold to settle in. Each mile revealed an end to the growing season, the generosity of another harvest, and the waiting for another wilderness of winter.

Pondering. Watching. The silence of the miles created space for musing.

Halloween. What a strange day to begin hospice care. However, it was also All Saints' Eve, a day of ritual in the church I attended. On this day, we remembered the lives of those we loved and who had blessed our lives. We would light candles in their honor and tell stories about them. Their memories winged into our lives like the flight of a song, a bird dancing on currents of the wind. I wondered what saints were gathering with us now. Who was watching and waiting on the other side of life? Who would join us now in the mysteries on the boundary between life and death?

Mark's mom Bette had died two years earlier on All Saints' Day. Bette lived with us for several weeks while she was in hospice care dying of breast cancer. Did caring for her prepare me to care for Mark in hospice? Was this experience a practice run for helping Mark?

As we drove home, the memories of Bette grew in my mind's eye. She blessed the lives of her children and grandchildren with a quiet, gentle Scandinavian presence, which often without words, was her primary language for showing affirmation and care. Bette attended baseball games, basketball games, football games, musicals, recitals, and even dull lectures to show her support for those she loved. Her gift for us was her consistent presence. She would sit with our son Brent into the night watching David Letterman. They did not talk much, yet when she stayed awake with him until midnight, when they both laughed at the same joke, or she would gently touch his shoulder, her presence embodied her love.

From the car window, I watched a hawk gliding on the wind. Bette loved birds. She hung many feeders in the tiered gardens outside her kitchen. Cardinals, chickadees, hummingbirds, orioles, and even the simple sparrows received generous amounts of seed and suet. She wore a sweatshirt with a bird painted on the front. Perhaps these birds were her amulet.

My mind continued to wander. As Bette battled breast cancer, she revealed an inner fierceness that belied her gentle external manner. This power surprised us. Mark showed the same fierceness. As the pain of her disease gathered strength, the hospice nurse increased the dosages of morphine to make her more comfortable. Yet, with each dose of morphine, she fell into more prolonged periods of sleep and disconnection. No wonder the idea of giving Mark morphine scared me so.

What would happen as Mark weakened? As Bette grew weaker, she spent most of her time in a hospice bed. From the window, she quietly watched many birds gather in the trees and bushes, greeting her each day with their presence and song. They were a constant companion. Before falling into a deep coma, she voiced a simple longing to join them. Her last words were, "I have to find my other wing." I imagined Bette joining the birds she loved.

Within a few days after saying these words, Bette's breathing grew shallower. The family had not yet arrived. My close friend and Mark's colleague, Pastor Natalie, sat with Bette and me. Natalie was several months pregnant. We gathered as midwives, watching, waiting with a ministry of presence to accompany Bette into this journey of bridging death with the promise of new life.

As she lay dying in the afternoon of All Saints' Day, the bush outside the window of her room filled with chickadees chirping and singing. Her breath slowed, and a single bird pecked firmly at the window to bid her "come." As she breathed her last, the birds flew away. Bette had found her other wing.

During the drive home from the hospital with Mark, I wondered if Bette might join us in some way. Would her spirit presence break into the thin space between life and death? What other saints might join us during this time of dying? Which living saints, along with the dead, would bless us with their companionship and comfort?

I drove, wondered, waited, and inwardly wept. More thoughts moved through my brain as the miles passed.

How would Mark die? What would these last days be? How would God show up?

What about my children? Sara was driving back to Eau Claire, ahead of us. She wanted to be alone. I wondered what she was thinking. What about our son Brent? What did he think as he prepared for our return? What would become of them without their dad in their lives? What would they remember? What would they need? Who would they become? What would hold us together or pull us apart? So many questions with unknown answers.

What about me? Could I do this?

I prayed to God, "Where in the world are you?"

"What IS this?"

"Why?"

"How do we make it through?"

Mark was silent. What was he thinking? What did he ponder as the miles passed?

I put a disc in the CD player, needing something to quiet my racing brain. The silence in the car was too much to bear.

The three-hour drive felt like an eternity and passed by in an instant. I parked in front of our home, turned off the engine, and let out a long sigh. Mark sighed too. We looked at each other, and he smiled a weak yet affirming smile. I shared a gentle pat on his trembling hands. He turned and watched his children come to greet him.

Sara and Brent were smiling too. What else do you do when you share the love and holy moments? They walked to the car, held out their arms to their dad. Gently, Brent lifted Mark out of the vehicle, supporting his dad's body with his arms and internal strength. They slowly walked into the house, Brent carrying him along the way. I remembered the day Mark brought newborn Brent home with tender care and pride. Now Brent supported his dad with love, dignity, and tender respect as a grown man.

Inside the door, the fireplace glowed with welcome warmth. Mark's youngest brother Rich stood inside. He arrived early in the day and helped Brent prepare before our arrival. He joined Brent to assist Mark as they walked inside. The smell of baking bread greeted us. Yellow roses, a gift from my brother, Richard, graced the side table. The sun shone through the windows, creating dancing shadows of bowing trees across the floor. Mark moved into his favorite large, leather chair and put his feet up on the ottoman, letting out a long sigh. He was home.

We chatted a bit, trying to fill the awkwardness with small talk, including thanking Rich for the fresh bread, the arrival of casseroles for supper, the next steps of hospice care, the beauty of the countryside. We talked about family and discussed who was coming and when. We spoke quietly, gently, carefully into this space of an unknown journey.

TRICK OR TREAT

"It's Halloween," I proclaimed into the quiet, trying to laugh at the absurdity of it all.

Mark laughed and said, "I can just stand up and scare the treat-or-treaters. My body is scary enough." I wanted to laugh, but it was too sad, too real.

Mark remembered his mom, whose birthday was on Halloween. The day brought back memories of her dying in our home just two years before.

"What day was it?" Mark asked. Mark's pending death was close to the anniversary date of Bette's death. We shared a few stories of Mark's mom and her humor. Mark told the story about how the brothers gave her a new broom every year, along with a birthday cake. In the gentle laughter, something caught our eye. On our patio, a grey-winged mother cardinal perched on a bench—still, attentive, watching. My heart leaped in recognition. The saints were arriving. We all understood that a visit by a cardinal was a visit from someone who had died. Bette's spirit showed up.

Halloween had always been a fun family event, and we decided to make this night as normal as possible. Brent asked to leave for the evening to celebrate Connie's birthday. What a curious coincidence that his newfound love carried the same birthday as his favorite grandmother Bette. We met Connie early in the summer and were just getting to know her and her spirit. Mark said that he did not know her well, but he saw who Brent was when he was with her, which was affirmation enough.

Sara loved to trick-or-treat with younger children. She joined our friend Tom, the church organist, and his kids, Meredith, Serrie, and Ian, to go trick-or-treating and catch the excitement of the day. Carol, the nurse who rode with us on the way home, stayed with us to help settle Mark into a home routine, using her medical expertise to assure us through the next challenging expectations.

Another friend, Thomas, joined us for the evening. Thomas had called earlier in the day to see if we needed anything.

"Yes," I said on the phone. "We need treats to share for Halloween."

Mark had heard me on the phone and quickly added, "Get Snickers. I love Snickers. And get the big ones." Tom arrived soon after with dozens of full-size Snickers candy bars, laughing as he handed Mark the heavy bag.

"Just for you."

Thomas, a colleague, and his wife Audrey were friends in Eau Claire. He and Mark often played golf together. Audrey had died of cancer the autumn before. It was almost a full year since her death. He could have stayed away. I wondered if we were a reminder of his own difficult time. But Thomas often visited during Mark's illness, bringing supportive love, care, and a knowing beyond words.

I was thankful for his presence and wisdom. Seeing him reminded me that survival was possible after a spouse died. Thomas visited us a few times while Mark was still at the hospital. One day while Mark had been very distant, pulled deep into his thoughts, Thomas took me to lunch in the hospital cafeteria. We both knew Mark's death was approaching.

Thomas looked at me with kind, honest eyes over bowls of hot chili and calmly said, "Elaine, remember, resurrection is for the living as well as the dead." Thomas knew and lived its truth. This phrase became a promise I held onto with hope.

I was incredibly thankful for his presence this first night at home. After he brought the candy bars, Thomas stayed to help. With the help of Thomas and Carol, I affirmed yet again, "I can do this."

Day moved into the night, and the shadows of the moon settled around us. A parishioner delivered supper. It tasted warm and comforting. Yet we ate only a little. Mark watched, sitting silently.

The doorbell rang. Shouts of "Trick or treat!" echoed through the room. The trick-or-treaters had arrived. Mark smiled and laughed as each child grabbed candy from the large bowl of Snickers and took a quick look at a strange-looking older man in the room in the large, leather chair.

To our surprise, one of the visitors at the door was Bishop Berg, leader of the larger geographical area of which the church Mark served was a part. He and Mark saw the issues of the church from very different perspectives and shared several difficult conversations from these competing paradigms. Yet Bishop Berg remained a faithful pastor to the pastors, especially Mark. During the many days Mark was in the hospital, the Bishop visited and prayed compassionately.

On this Halloween evening, Mark's Bishop arrived carrying his prayer book and the elements of home communion—bread and wine.

Carol and Thomas moved to the door to answer the ringing bell and give candy to the many children who dropped by.

The Bishop pulled a chair close to Mark and invited me to join them. We talked about the week, the decision to seek hospice, the coming days of care, the foreshadowing of death. He read a bit of scripture. He prayed with us and asked if we might like to receive the Sacrament of Holy Communion.

"Of course," Mark said.

"Yes." I nodded, unable to speak, choked with tears.

The Bishop poured wine into a small chalice. He placed a small wafer of bread on a simple plate on the table with the yellow roses and the remains of supper. He began reading, "In the night in which he was betrayed, Our Lord Jesus Christ took bread…"

Behind us, the doorbell rang. Voices of laughing children shouted, "Trick or treat!" Thomas and Carol looked at us, concerned about the interruption.

I smiled back and whispered, "It's okay."

The Bishop continued, "And when Jesus had given thanks, He broke it and gave it to His disciples saying, this is my body given for you."

There came a softer pounding on the door from little hands. As Thomas and Carol opened the door, shy voices shouted, "Trick or treat!"

"And after supper, Jesus took the cup…" the Bishop continued.

Mark touched the wine and bread to his lips. Shouts of "trick-or-treat" joined in chorus with the blessing "given for you."

"Treat or treat."

"Given for you."

The grace of Love visited our home dressed in costumes of ghosts and princes, shriveled bodies, grieving hearts, bread, and wine.

The bowl of Snickers was now empty, so we turned out the porch light. The Bishop left. Thomas and Carol assisted me as we prepared Mark for bed. They supported Mark as he walked down the hall that ended in an angle with doors to two separate rooms.

The door on the left led to my office. In this room, Bette died. We transformed this space yet again for hospice care. Inside was the hospital bed they provided. Beside the bed was a small table with a lamp, bottles of medicine, and a notepad filled with written reminders for medical procedures. Fresh sheets and a soft blanket covered the narrow mattress. Soothing music filled the room from the CD player on the desk.

On the right side of the hallway was the door to our bedroom. The lamplight created a soft glow. Without hesitation, Mark moved right. He walked to his side of the bed, laid down, grabbed his favorite pillow to support his weary head, and sighed deeply. We covered him with a blanket. He was soon asleep.

Mark was home. Trick or treat.

DAY ONE: AN ISLAND OF REPOSE

We were at home. Mark was asleep in our bed. Our bed was now the center of all that would occur in the next few days. Friends, family, caregivers, and well-wishers would gather around this island of repose for remembering, praying, singing, wondering, laughing, crying, and saying good-bye.

This bed that previously shared our private loving was now a sacred center where a community of people gathered, an isle where life transitioned into death and love transformed into memory.

I stood in the darkened room as a single lamp created shadows in the light. Mark was hugging a pillow, sleeping. We were alone.

What I saw was not familiar.

"Who is THIS man?" I said aloud. He had grown old and frail. His hair and pale skin were as gray as his beard. His body was shaking, panting heavily to breathe. His hands, once stable and secure, were fragile tendrils extending from shrunken limbs.

Mark had disappeared. His muscles. His fire for life. His bold frame. I gazed at what remained eaten by cancer, devoured by the chemotherapy, drowned in his gastric fluids, and overpowered by amyloids and unknown, exotic infections. Only a shadow remained, as memories danced within my heart, and melancholy embraced my being.

Before cancer won, Mark was a large man, 6'5", weighing almost 300 pounds. In our marriage, I created my own place beside him to sleep. The bed was too small for both of us. I would curl within his arms, snuggled against his body. Or I pushed to the lower part of the bed to create space for his broad shoulders and arms to extend. His body covered the whole mattress, and I slipped alongside.

I missed lovemaking or even the simple act of holding hands in bed. I longed to make a physical connection. Mark's touch for me was absent since cancer became the third partner of our marriage. I turned out the light, crawled under the covers, and moved across the sheets to find him, searching for his warmth, listening for his breath. I gently touched his back. I savored what remained by remembering love. I quietly wept and fell asleep.

DAY TWO: WE ARE NOT ALONE

As the light of dawn broke into the darkness, a new determination settled into my attitude.

During the early months of Mark's illness, I swung back and forth between two reactions. In the first, I longed to be near him, to care for him, and attend to his needs. I struggled to define the difference between caring for him and caring with him. I wanted to care with him, listen to his wants, his concerns, his issues. I asked him what he wanted. It was essential for me to maintain his dignity as well as my own. I became indignant when the nurses in the hospital spoke to him in a sing-song voice of parental dismissal as if he were a child. I wanted the nursing staff to treat Mark with dignity. I wanted them to know he was a professional and thinking person, a human being of significance and influence, a man deserving of respect.

My second reaction in those early months swung into a selfish need for survival as a strong urge welled within. I needed to escape. I found reasons to run errands. I bought paint for the guest bedroom and made time to paint it to cover the aging wallpaper. I chose an orange-yellow to announce joy, but once on the walls, it appeared to be an obnoxious pretense of hope. This ugly yellow yelled disgust instead of delight. I decided I would repaint it with another color later. I bought new clothes. I smiled. I stood fast with a stiff backbone and a façade of strength.

I continued to see counseling clients. I was not sure how effective I was, but I needed the distraction. Grateful to them for their patience, I increasingly became aware that my work should not be about me. They needed more than what I could presently give, so I began the process of referring them to others who could better provide them with what they deserved.

I invited friends to coffee. I ate bag after bag of potato chips, Doritos, candy bars, and drank cans of soda to ease the emptiness inside. I took long walks through the park. I slept at home, alone, curled into a ball of fear. I held myself and my soul close, overwhelmed and frustrated about the new normal of our marriage.

I received very little back from Mark, as he had little left to give. Grief is self-focused and all-encompassing. My hunger and thirst for Mark's attention and conversation paralleled his desire for satisfying food and drink and the emptying of life from his body.

I began to smoke, though I had never done so before, not so much as even a puff. For me, this act of rebellion held my unwanted reality at bay. Virginia Slims was my choice of the day, a pack in my car's glove compartment and another hidden in the corner of the kitchen cupboard. I smoked during the drive home or in the chaos of the night to claim some semblance of power. I blew smoke into the eyes of monster death that kept creeping nearer.

But now Mark was at home preparing to die. In the light of the morning on this second day of hospice care, my resolve grew clear. I wanted to live in the now, to surrender to the present. I breathed in love and breathed out respect. I wanted to receive the love of others with gratitude and kindness. I wanted to trust God's comfort and care. It was not the time for my radical independent self to take charge. Even as I tried to run away, I would not. I wanted to be fully present to accept the truth of this sacred space.

"I can do this," I said aloud again. "I will assist Mark to die with dignity and compassion."

Mark awoke. We greeted each other with sweet, simple tenderness. I wanted to affirm the presence and the power within our mutual love. He reached out and touched my arm to assure both of us, "We can do this. We can do this together."

Waves of activity rose within the house, gathering tides of care washing onto the island Mark and I created in our bedroom. I sat beside him throughout the day. Brent and Sara joined me, sitting on top of the covers, securing a family nest. The four of us sat side by side in shared companionship. Mark rested, lying on his side of the bed, his head propped by pillows. A watercolor painting of a country cottage surrounded by flowers hung on the red wall above our bed. The long windows on the west side of the room allowed light to enter. The family positioned chairs around the room for people to gather, to bid welcome, to be present, and to hold vigil.

Medicines, bottles of pills, bags of fluids, and notes of procedures filled the top of the dresser. Vials of morphine stacked one on top of the other. Brent mused this batch of drugs had enough street value to pay off his and his sister's college loans.

All of this pushed aside the many family pictures that had sat on the dresser. These photographs were no longer necessary because the loved ones in those frames were present with us in our room. Within this space, we lived Mark's final days.

Members of the congregation arranged for meals to arrive throughout the day. Smells of goodness filled the house as people in a Scandinavian reserved character and kindness brought baskets of food—homemade cinnamon rolls, apple pie, lasagna, stew, soup, cookies, Jell-O, and salads. People knew my children ate vegetarian food and tried to accommodate this desire. One person made a beef noodle casserole using ground turkey instead of beef. She did not understand what vegetarian meant. Sara, Brent, and Connie took turns greeting the many visitors with care and hospitality. Fresh coffee was always available.

Mark's best friend Red had arrived from Seattle in the morning. Red could speak the truth with compassion and bring hilarity into the most unusual moments. As he entered any room, his red hair announced his fiery spirit and enthusiasm for life. He and Mark had been friends since seminary, each pushing the other to a deeper level of understanding. The intensity created moments of conflict, but the commitment and respect they had for each other remained constant. He companioned us to the end.

Wayne, Mark's mentor, joined us with a bottle of 94-dollar scotch and the spirit of a pastoral heart. He was the church leader who described me as filled with "piss and vinegar." He knew us both since college days. Wayne reminded us of the grace of God's presence and years of loving connection. Wayne, small in stature with a greying beard, sat with us as the wise elder with the compassion of his own grieving heart and sadness of losing a man he mentored for years like a beloved son.

Mark's brother Barry and his family arrived. Barry carried the Olson character both in his physical stature and his commitment to family and friends. Friends called him "bear" to reveal his kind heart, strength, and conviction for integrity, a competitive spirit, and a sturdy, lumbering body. He did not smile often and could project a misunderstood scowl in what we have come to know as the "Olson look." His stable soul would become the anchor within the changing structure of the Olson family, as his elder brother's death would pass this role on to him.

Members of the church staff, colleagues, my brother Rich, and even some pastors who read "Notes to Eli" visited. The house was busy.

The angled bands of an autumn sun lightened the living room to warm the friends gathered on the couches and chairs. Quiet conversations with bursts of laughter echoed throughout the house. A second cardinal joined the first on the patio. The old oaks surrounding the house dropped an abundance of leaves, piled in drifts throughout the yard. Wild deer nibbled on the bushes in the backyard. The autumn chill had not yet arrived. Someone occasionally played the piano. A small fire crackled in the fireplace.

The hospice care nurses joined in the activities of the house, bringing lifeboats of supplies. They checked Mark's vitals. They affirmed my actions of care to ensure I was following the directions for the meds and painkillers. They answered the many questions we asked yet again because we forgot their answers in the chaos. One gentlewoman washed Mark's body in an old-fashioned sponge bath with warm water and a washcloth rather than with quick antiseptic wipes torn from pre-packaged envelopes. She brushed his teeth, cleaning his mouth of ugly smelling rot.

Always thirsty, Mark drank bottled lemonade to soothe his dry tongue. But this bit of relief was pumped out of his non-functioning stomach by the tube that ran from there to his nose. Without dialysis, Mark's blood grew more toxic, causing his skin to be dry and itchy. These caregivers rubbed his limbs with lotion to offer some relief. All of us kept checking the tube, the pump, and the glass container of fluids. When it was too full, Mark gagged and vomited the overflow.

Together we read the pamphlets describing the process of death. What were the steps? Where was Mark now? I checked his feet. Were they getting blotchy? Blackening? Was his breath shallower? Was death close? The clocks ticked forward. The vigil extended.

I ended this day with a grateful heart. The many affirmations and the outpourings of love we received kept the approaching death at bay. Mark remained responsive and engaged with us.

We were not alone. God's presence showed up in the company of others.

DAY THREE: INTERRUPTIONS

The day began in a hurry with the energy of many people knocking, interrupting the silent abode of the bed. More food arrived. Questions poured into our space about out-of-town visitors. Would it be okay if they dropped by? How long could they stay? Who did Mark want to see? Who would he turn away? Connecting with others consumed his limited energy. Mark asked me to help him set limits. When I was unsure about whom to allow in, I would check with Mark and he would nod yay or nay.

One couple called seeking a moment of reconnection and reconciliation. Through some unknown past hurt, this couple had distanced themselves from us for several years. Mark was too exhausted for this hard work of reunion.

He said, "No, not now." I was surprised, curious, and confused about the disconnect yet again. I was learning that having only a little time demanded hard limits. I prayed for the grace that this couple might grow to understand Mark's response and eventually receive forgiveness through me.

April and Judd arrived for a morning visit. April's and Mark's mothers were best friends since their childhood in

Minnesota. They shared memories of chickens, farms, and playing games in the northern woods as well as professional connections in the church. This goodbye embodied the fullness of life integrated with family and vocation.

I was friends with them because of Mark. I wondered what would become of these friendships and other friends I had because of Mark. Would our connections end after his death? Or would their companionship remain after Mark was gone?

The nieces and nephews arrived. After sharing brief greetings with Mark in the bedroom, they gathered in the dining room and connected in the one way that bridged their many differences in age and experiences. Finding several decks of cards, it was time for a familiar game of Nertz. Each cousin shuffled individual decks of cards and counted thirteen cards for the Nertz pile. Each person handed the Nertz stack and the remaining deck to the cousin on the right. The quick announcement of "go" turned a personal solitaire card game into a group battle of speed and persistence, the slapping of aces sequencing to kings, an occasional "damn it" or worse with a lost chance to play. Each cousin pushed the speed of the others, playing cards quickly, driven by the Olsons' competitive spirit to win. Hilarity offered to heal as we lived forward through this generation, ringing joy toward Mark's bed from the dining room table where they gathered, challenging each other as they stood. Mark laughed, cheering on Brent or Sara to win. Conversations grew louder. I marveled at how the power of living held its ground within the movements of death.

Red took charge, creating intentional connections with Mark's mentors. Without our knowing it, he had made several phone calls to significant people in Mark's life who were not able to attend on short notice. Yet they remained on the line waiting for an opportunity to speak with Mark briefly. With a smile as radiant as his hair, eyes beaming, a chuckle in his voice, he handed Mark the portable phone with yet another well-loved mentor on the line.

"Douglas John Hall is calling you," he said, though we all knew it was Red who arranged the call.

Conversations with other mentors, professors, previous parishioners, and other people whose writings Mark read and admired continued throughout the day. With each person, Red, in a gracious and heedful voice, reported, "They want to talk with you." My gratitude for these selfless actions expanded with each call, each greeting, each connection.

My eldest brother Larry, his wife Kathy, and my dad arrived in the afternoon. My eldest brother always brought a source of calm. Kathy spread a spirit of happiness wherever she went, making friends with strangers in quick fashion. She held me in her arms and whispered in my ear the joy she felt that Mark was on his way to Heaven. Kathy's words were sincere and heartfelt, revealing her faith as a devoted Christian. This joy, however, was not part of my journey. I only knew the pain of letting go.

I could only reply, "And it's very sad. Mark's death is very sad." She agreed.

Dad sat with Mark in quiet conversation in the late afternoon. Mark had never fully lived up to Dad's expectations of the man his only daughter had married. Dad had always wanted to be a pastor, but the demands of the family farm did not allow him even to get a high school education. Dad had a vision of how to be a pastor, and Mark did not fit. He thought Mark read too many books, was disappointed Mark didn't help on the farm and considered Mark's theology and political ideas too liberal. I often felt trapped in the middle of their relationship. But in these final moments, Dad was generous and affirming, letting go of his stubborn German pride. I did not hear the words, but I watched his body language as he leaned into Mark's space with a loving heart.

My brother Rich and his wife Valerie also joined us for the week. During Mark's hospital stay in Rochester, they sent us the yellow roses, which now graced the living room in full bloom. Rich and Valerie showed this same kindness and offered hospitality as they stayed to help.

These activities felt outside of me. People came and went. The rooms outside the bedroom disappeared into a far distance like other countries. I did not know who arrived and who stayed. Or who left, when and why. I did not know where the many family members slept or what they ate or who answered the door.

The energy of the house was outside of me. The relationships from the many visitors were outside of me. Dying was outside of me. Even the presence of Spirit was outside of me. I did not feel alone so much as distant. I watched as from a high balcony, my soul silent in response to the comings and goings of others.

Mark's soul lingered outside of him, active, silent. His spirit hovered around him and engaged the energy of the friends and family who visited his body. For a moment, both powers moved together in the dance of death. A vitality moved from inside his being into vibrant energy around his body, preparing to leave his flesh and bones. His soul haloed him, glowing into others, visibly active in its movement of leaving his body.

I watched for a time, useless to any other action.

Interruptions interrupted interruptions throughout the day— people, food, phone calls, laughter, goodbyes, morphine shots, fluid pumping, naps, family, more friends, hospice. Yet, it was Mark who created the most extraordinary interruption.

Late in the afternoon, when calm began to settle around us like the setting of the sun through the bedroom window, Mark asked for his administrative assistant Sue and me to join him in a private conversation.

Mark expressed concern. He was pleased with the way he was active in saying goodbye to family and close friends. Yet, he was disappointed in himself for his lack of attention to the needs of people at Hope Lutheran Church. He loved these members of the congregation he served. He had a plan and needed the two of us to make it happen.

The next day was Sunday, All Saints' Day—this timely reminder of his mom and loved ones who had died and the great crowd of witnesses living and dead surrounding our lives with love. This Sunday would be the perfect day to affirm this community of saints by the pastor who loved them.

First, he wanted John Ylvisaker to sing for the congregation during church. John and his wife Fern were dear family friends and had arrived in the afternoon to say a final farewell. John wrote a well-loved Lutheran hymn, "Borning Cry." Mark wanted John to sing a new song John had written at church the following day as a gift from him to those he loved. And second, he wanted to invite the members of the congregation to our home for an open house on Sunday afternoon. Whoever wanted to come to say goodbye was welcome.

Sue and I looked at each other in disbelief. "Really, Mark, you must be out of your mind." We tried to discourage him, but his earnest plea and longing eyes won us over.

John and Fern had not planned to stay the night, as John was eager to go back home. He was to introduce a newly written song for All Saints' Day, "Shine like the Sun," at his home church.

"But how do you ignore the plea of a dying friend?" John replied. He made phone calls to cancel those plans and created new ones. To prepare for the unexpected overnight stay, John and Fern went to Target to buy toothbrushes. The generosity of others paid for the room at a nearby hotel.

The household quickly shifted its focus. Tom, the church musician, reordered the worship service for John to sing the new song at our church. Sue prepared the announcement to invite the congregation members during worship the next morning. The family and friends staying in our home mused in disbelief, cleaned, and bought cookies in preparations for the open house the following afternoon.

Mark believed his role as pastor needed a final action. My role as the pastor's wife still carried responsibilities. This island of repose opened its harbor, creating a bittersweet moment—one filled with gratitude, and to be honest, resentment.

DAY FOUR: THE VISIT

"Buzzzzz." Alarms started the day. I found it odd to hear this push to wake up when I just wanted to be alone with Mark and not share these last days with so many people! Wake up. Get up. Clean up. Hurry up. Look up. Cheer up. Hold up. Give up. Up and at 'em. Another Sunday morning.

Everyone who stayed in our home, including my brother and brothers-in-law, their families, my dad, and friends, had gone to church to hear John sing. They wanted to be part of the community at the church on All Saints' Sunday. I watched Mark through the morning as he paid attention to the movement of time, following it closely with the rhythm of the Sunday morning ritual he had led for twenty-five years as pastor. Together we worshiped in our memory as we followed the timeline of the service alone in our bedroom.

10:30 - Announcements and Confession of Sins.

10:40 - Prayer of the Day and reading of the Scriptures. Mark voiced the words he memorized early in the week. He spoke the words coordinated with the congregation within his memory timeline:

"Almighty God, you have knit your people together in one communion in the mystical body of your Son, Jesus Christ, our Lord. Grant us grace to follow your blessed saints in lives of faith and commitment, and to know the inexpressible joys you have prepared for those who love you, through Jesus Christ, our Savior and Lord, who lives and reigns with you and the Holy Spirit, one God, now and forever. Amen."

10:50 - A sermon.

11:10 - The singing of John's song, "Shine Like the Sun."

11:15 – Communion.

11:30 - Final Benediction. When Mark led worship, he stood in front of the congregation, putting down his books. He would open his arms wide to the assembly to bless those he loved.

At this moment, Mark's arms opened in response. "The Lord bless you and keep you…"

He sighed. I sighed in sadness as so much was changing.

The family returned from church with a large cardboard box for Mark, a gift from the children. Inside were hundreds of carefully folded paper cranes, strung one after another on long lengths on yarn, each sending a prayer for healing. We hung them around the house. Deeper in the box were piles of craft paper with crayon-colored pictures and simple letters sending blessings to their pastor. The cards depicted hand-drawn images of a bearded man with angel wings and a halo, stick figures with outstretched arms, drawn crosses and red hearts; circle faces with blue tears, smiles, rainbows, and birds; and names printed in large misshapen letters. Mark and I sat on the bed looking at each card, remembering each child, receiving love in return. The children's greetings and prayers confronted my selfish resentments and transformed them into gratitude.

Several young adults were the first to arrive for the afternoon open house. They walked up the street like an army of gardeners, carrying rakes and bags with their self-appointed tasks to clean the leaves in our yard, emboldened to greet their dying pastor with a mission of service. They did not spend a lot of time talking with Mark, yet each spent a moment in his presence before they hurried outside to complete their tasks.

The family and friends staying in our home were gracious to all who arrived. They greeted the visitors at the door, guiding them through the hall. Dozens of men, women, and children whispered to each other as they waited patiently in line for their turn to greet Mark.

Mark positioned himself on the left side of the bed, propped up by pillows. Though frail in body, dressed in casual navy-blue gym shorts and a T-shirt, he remained faithful in his call to greet each visitor. We opened the blinds on the windows by the bed and turned on the lamps for soft afternoon light. A towel discreetly covered the medications lined atop the dresser. The CD player sat in front of the pump to hide the bile it contained and cover the sounds of the pump with easy listening music. Mark remained connected to the IV and tubes in his nose while he crossed his legs, focused his eyes, and placed his arms across his chest.

I stood at the door, observing, allowing each visitor to have a private moment with their pastor. I received hugs, gentle words, and greetings of care. Red stood beside me, monitoring the line to allow each parishioner enough time to connect but not so much as to dominate space from others.

The procession continued. A man knelt with his children beside the bed, allowing the little ones to say hello as they giggled in shyness. Mark touched their heads. An elderly couple bent over to touch Mark's arm lightly, saying in concert, "Our Father, who art in heaven…" Another woman reached to touch his hand, saying thank you. A young man simply handed Mark a note and walked away. Person after person quietly walked into the softly lit room, seeking a way to say goodbye and say thank you with a prayer, a word, a story, a laugh, a touch, or just a smile.

Movement after movement, moment after moment, word after word, Mark found the energy of grace through a community surrounding him to attend and be present. A force grew within all of us, making it easier to embrace death together rather than walking into it alone.

Not only did grace and care surround Mark in the bedroom, but they also filled our home. Many people stayed throughout the afternoon. My family provided hospitality, conversation, coffee, and cookies. The church staff managed the coordination of parking in a crowded neighborhood to standing in line in the hall and providing calm in the waiting. Friends offered guidance, kindness, comfort, and tissues and listened to the stories each parishioner told. Some wept quietly in the presence of another. Others laughed in the lightness of connectedness.

My heart ached as each family walked into the room to gather by Mark's side. The men stood holding hats with their arms around their families. Couples walked hand in hand. I did not know the stories of the people who talked with him. I was not aware of the information they shared in the privilege of a pastor's care, but I could see the importance of each to be in Mark's presence. Some people appeared stunned at his skeletal appearance. Others wiped tears. And a few talked too loudly in nervous connections.

I did not know how to offer comfort to so many when my resources were empty. I remembered the words in scripture, "To weep with those who weep." Together, we could weep. Together, we could not forget. Together, we could tell stories.

I watched that last couple leave and walk down the sidewalk. I closed the door and sat on the edge of the bed, this sacred island where Mark lay, exhausted. I touched his feet. We smiled, sighed, deeply touched by the affirmation of so many.

On this day, I experienced the gift of a community. I was not alone. Nor were Mark and I alone. We were not an isolated island. The care of these parishioners embraced us. Together, we experienced embodied Divine Love, one for another. We were all saints, a communion of saints. Today we lived the day we observed, All Saints' Day.

He fell asleep as I massaged his feet. I was Mark's wife, but also a pastor's wife. This day reminded me of that yet again. I sometimes mused that being a pastor's wife was like being part of a marriage and an affair because Mark spent so much time away from home and because of the many people who desired his attention. I was not always sure if I was the wife or the mistress. Sometimes I resented this duality.

Yet, on this day, I affirmed the blessings I received in this role. This day reminded me of the many people who showed their love and care with visits, prayers, cards, food, and kind words. As members of the congregation waited in line to visit with their pastor one last time, they also took my hand and held it with tender care. They hugged me and shared stories about me to thank me for my presence in their lives, not just Mark's. They remembered the times I listened to their pain; the hospitality I showed when I invited them into our home; the classes I taught on relationship and prayer. They honored the way I loved Mark. They loved me, too.

As I fell asleep beside Mark, I breathed in and out. I mused at how my life was "both/and." Resentment and admiration. Life and death. Greetings and goodbyes. Roles and authenticity. Wife and lover. Like my breath, in and out, all these parts created my wholeness.

DAY FIVE: PRAYING

Sunday was the day of visiting. Monday was a day of study and prayer. With so many pastors in the house, one would not imagine anything different. Red (a pastor in Seattle), Wayne, (a mentor, retired bishop, and pastor in Denver), John (songwriter and muse of theology) and Sara (daughter, in seminary), and Pastor Roger (interim pastor at Hope) gathered at Mark's bed for a typical Monday morning text study.

Together they read the assigned biblical texts of the *Revised Common Lectionary* (an international guide for studying scripture during a church year). As was typical for this group, they read the gospel text and proceeded to help each other memorize the words. They believed that knowing it by heart helped to discern "what the text then has to say in our now." The pastors consistently challenged each other about the meaning of the scripture text. I told Mark it was a pastor's version of "roostering" – looking to see which rooster crowed louder to show his importance.

Today was no different, but this time they included Sara for a chance to share this experience with her father. Today was her time to study with her dad. There would not be another, ever.

I sat at the dining room table, wanting to be involved, yet knowing the importance for these pastors to be together and claiming a bit of time for myself. I tried to claim as many moments as I could with Mark in these last days, but so did many others. The time of hospice care was so complicated - the push and pull of selfish wishes and the desire to show generous hospitality.

Mark's energy was reasonably vital after the prior day's blessings. Voices exchanged various perspectives in vigorous discussion. Their time ended with Mark and Wayne praying the prayers they had shared for years.

> *"I give myself to you this day—*
> *All that I am,*
> *All that I have—*
> *to be totally, unconditionally yours*
> *for your using.*
> *Take me away from myself,*
> *and use me up,*
> *as you will,*
> *where you will,*
> *with whom you will,*
> *and I will give you all the praise and the glory.*
> *Amen"*

During some of the difficult periods over the past months, I had contacted Wayne on my own. I shared with him my confusion about God and lack of trust in prayer. Mark's body did not heal. The cancer was winning. I wondered with Wayne how to pray.

Wayne's response was, "Pray the ancient prayers and let them do their work." Wayne invited to me pray hymns, psalms, liturgies.

I said the words, but I did not always feel them in my heart.

On this same morning of prayers, the doorbell rang. A woman from the community who knew Mark through his work greeted me at the front door. She handed me a note. Having been unable to attend the open house, she stood awkward and emotionless with a painted smile on her face, saying the letter would reveal her message. As she left, I quietly closed the door with a bit of suspicion, looking at the handwritten note on a folded piece of paper in my hand.

It began with several quotes of scripture and concluded with a statement of reprimand. It said Mark must have committed some awful sin in his past. If he confessed and asked forgiveness for this sin, whatever it was, the disease destroying his body would end its destruction, and God would restore his health. She asked us to pray for the confession of his sin, the cure of his body, and his future salvation.

I began to shake with fury. Why such a judgment? Why such rebuke? Mark was not perfect. Neither was I. We had hurt others. We made mistakes, significant mistakes. Yet, I knew in an instant that I would never let him see the note. I jammed the paper into my pocket. I listened to the conversation coming from the bedroom in which faith-filled people trusted a loving God. God's grace embraced the room. No one in our home questioned Mark's faith. Her judgment was not the final word. We trusted a Divine Love that abided with the suffering of the world, forgave along the way, offered the healing of the soul and peace of mind.

I wanted to believe this woman deeply understood her message to be one of loving concern. I wanted to affirm the importance of salvation for Mark's soul as he died. I, however, experienced it as a confusing message filled with condemnation. This intrusion into the last days of Mark's life hurt deeply. As Pastor Roger left for the morning, I gave him the note and asked him to take the words out of the house and destroy them. I stood firm on the belief in grace and its abiding presence in our home.

More notes arrived as well. But these were different. They were emails from friends unable to be with us in person but offering words of comfort, gratitude, and affirmation. Sara, Brent, and I sat cross-legged, side by side on the bed with Mark reading these notes aloud. The youth leader reported how Mark taught him "a come to Jesus" talk was not necessarily about evangelism. Another pastor thanked Mark for the affirmation he received during a lonely time in ministry. A parishioner expressed gratitude for Mark's visits when the man was homebound. Others thanked Mark for the writings and reflections he shared in "Notes to Eli" about ministry in a postmodern era. Each email told a personal story about an experience with Mark. Each email surrounded Mark's shrinking world with an air of affection. Each email embraced the four of us with comfort, goodness, and peace—an abiding presence of grace.

Mark's niece Kari needed to head back to school. She came to the bed to say goodbye. As Kari came near, they both smiled with a twinkle of shared laughter from years of playful banter.

Mark said, "I have one last request for you."

Kari replied, "Sure, whatever you want, Uncle Mark." With a wide grin, he rubbed his hands together, as he often did before some significant event.

"I need you to let Brent and Sara win at the card game Nertz."

Kari laughed loudly. "I can't do that, Uncle Mark. Sorry." They hugged in mutual admiration, upholding the competitive spirit of the Olson tribe.

The day ended with prayer, as it had every evening for the last several weeks, using the liturgy of Compline or Holden Evening Prayer, a family favorite. Tonight, we sang Holden Evening Prayer. Mark found the strength to walk into the living room and sit in his large leather chair. We gathered around him. The darkened room glowed with the light of several candles placed on side tables and the piano. Sara sat on the arm of his chair, Brent on the floor by his father's feet. Friends and family found places around the room, couches, chairs, cushions, and the floor. We passed the booklets to all who gathered.

Into the quiet and the darkness and with a clear voice, Sara began the opening notes of the service, "Jesus Christ, you are the light of the world."

We joined her in singing, "The light no darkness can overcome."

She continued, "Stay with us for it is evening."

We responded, "And the day is almost over."

At the place in the service for the reading of scripture, Mark raised his hand to call our attention. He wanted to speak. In a soft, shaking voice, he recited the memorized verses from the morning study. As his voice grew weaker, the other pastors joined with the words they remembered and practiced together. Mark took on the role of pastor and spoke a few words of reflection about these texts. Being a pastor was his call and identity. This identity would die with him, but not just yet. I watched as others listened.

The service continued. Together we sang and prayed the ancient prayers, longing for them to do their work—their work of comfort, of presence, of healing for the soul if not for the body— their sacred work of hope ringing into the dying of the night.

As the prayers ended, we sat together. Quiet, but not disheartened. Grateful in the comfort of each other's company and the presence of Holy Light.

As Brent, Sara, and I helped Mark back to bed, the others in the room blessed us with the words taken from the prayers of Compline, "God grant us a quiet night and peace at last."

DAY SIX: "ONCE ON THIS ISLAND"

The night had been rough.

My sister-in-law stayed with me in our room while Mark slept. As we rested into the night, Mark's breathing was erratic and heavy. Concerned, both Diane and I paid closer attention. Was this the end?

He inhaled loudly. We waited. No sound came out. We waited. Wide-eyed, we held our own breaths.

Mark let out a loud snore. Diane and I relaxed. Relieved, we laughed, quietly trying not to wake Mark.

But then, the gasping grew louder as Mark began choking from the fluids in his stomach. Something in the night had fallen on the jar, breaking the suction and stopping the NG tube's pumping action. Mark coughed, vomited. We called hospice for help after aspirating what we could. The nurse came quickly and provided the care needed.

My exhaustion grew. The family made assignments to take turns keeping vigil through the night.

I slept on the hospital bed in the side room or on the floor of the spacious walk-in closet off the master bedroom. The closet became my favorite place as a private sanctuary, hidden within the comforting scent on Mark's clothes. Here, alone, I let myself cry. On the floor, I did not need to model bravery or stand with a strong backbone for others. Here I was free to name the fears of living alone after Mark's death. Here I let go, surrendered, and melted onto the carpeted floor. I hid under a blanket where prayers seemed absent and hope diminished.

But in the morning or after a "nap," I found the courage to leave the closet. I reached out to connect with the family and friends who visited. I dressed and put on a "company face," as my mother taught me to engage yet another day.

Mark's determination to lead all of us into his death remained. So did the itching of his skin from the poisons generated by his malfunctioning kidneys. The never-ending desire to quench his thirst did not leave. The painful fury of deteriorating bones never ceased.

Seeking a distraction, Mark asked to listen to music, specifically to the soundtrack of *Once on This Island*. During a visit to New York several years earlier, Mark had attended this Broadway musical and loved it. For him, the story was the message of God's love and promise of this Divine Love to remain in the world.

The musical takes place on an island like Haiti, telling the story of life, pain, love, grief, faith, and hope. A fearless peasant girl, Ti Moune, falls in love with a wealthy boy, Daniel, from the other side of the island. When their divided cultures keep them apart, the powerful island gods guide her in her desire to reunite with the man who has captured her heart. Rhythms, drums, dancing, and the power of love to bring together people of different cultures rang within the music. The destructive forces of the cultures pulled this love apart. Yet, love lives on through the life of a tree and the children who play beneath it. The play ends with a pledge of the gods to tell the story of love just one more time.

This story built a special bond between Sara and her dad. They listened to the CD often. Mark wanted to hear it one more time, this time on his island bed beside those he loved. Brent, Sara, and I took our places, nesting cross-legged beside Mark, who propped himself up with pillows, NG tube in his nose, surrounded by all who were still in the house. Mark insisted that everyone needed to listen to the music. And of course, at the request of a dying man, they stayed—sitting on chairs and the floor around Mark's bed. His brother Rich sat on the floor, holding Mark's foot.

The CD player sat at the end of the bed, the volume turned too high, and the story began. The drums beat loudly. We moved our bodies, dancing to the music. We listened closely to the legend of love found, love forbidden, and love conquering yet again. We wept when the lovers separated. We laughed with the singing children.

Everyone stayed in place, mesmerized by the melodies bursting through the bedroom and drum sounds echoing off the walls. The musical ended with these words:

> *"And this is why*
> *We tell the story*
> *Why we tell the story*
> *Life is why / We tell the story*
> *Pain is why / We tell the story*
> *Love is why / We tell the story*
> *Grief is why*
> *We tell the story*
> *Hope is why*
> *We tell the story*
> *Faith is why*
> *We tell the story*
> *You are why*
> *We tell the story*
> *Why we tell the story*
> *Why we tell the story*
> *Why we tell the story*

So I hope that you will tell this tale tomorrow
It will help your heart remember and relive
It will help you feel the anger and the sorrow
And forgive"

As the song ended and the CD turned itself off, the room grew silent. The melodies and verses echoed into the quiet. The message within the music was the same message Mark preached his whole life. Divine Love will never leave the world. Mark was no longer able to preach, but the music proclaimed for him. I wept for the telling of it. I knew I would not hear Mark tell any gospel story again.

Breaking the silence, Mark looked at Wayne and then me. "Now is the time for scotch." I caught Brent's eye. Having a scotch with his dad had become a meaningful time for him as they drank and mused about the world. This one would be the last. My heart broke for them.

Brent, Wayne, and Red walked to the kitchen, found enough glasses for all the people who gathered in the room, and got the bottle of expensive scotch. Red and Brent gave each person a glass. Wayne opened the bottle and poured a bit of gold liquid for each one—the young nephews, people who never drank scotch, people who hated its taste, those who wanted more. A communion of all who gathered.

When the bottle was empty and every glass in the room held enough liquid to swallow, we held up our drinks and looked at Mark, anticipating a response. My husband lifted the glass high above his head.

First, he looked at me and said, "I love you."

Mark looked lovingly at Brent, then Sara. "I love you."

And then around the room, he looked into the face of each one - children, brothers, their wives, my family, dear friends, the cousins, and the staff members. He looked at each one, and with a last bit of energy, said, "I love you all."

We drank the bitter liquid. Some coughed, overpowered by its taste, while other people in the room smiled from its smooth warmth.

Mark spoke again, "It's getting close," and then fell silent, spent. He closed his eyes, letting out a sigh. The NG tube pumped the scotch from his stomach. Mark moved deeper into his island of dying.

After the scotch, silence. A long silence. If we were in a movie, the background music would have swelled, and we would have gathered holding hands around the bed. Mark would have breathed his last. A heavenly glow would have filled the room.

But this was not a movie. Mark did not die yet.

Everyone quietly left the room, each seemingly lost in their thoughts. I remained, sitting beside my husband. No longer in charge of the process, Mark's energy shifted. He was surrendering for death to take its turn.

Final beams of daylight nestled through the bedroom's window as dusk approached. Hushed voices drifted through the quiet outside the room. Serenity stilled around us.

Mark touched my hand, asking me to come close. In a soft voice, he wondered, "When did my mom, Bette, die? What day?"

"The anniversary date is today," I said. "November 5, two years ago."

Mark sighed, closing his eyes, his spirit moved further away.

Time passed. I remained alert, keeping attuned to the subtle shifts of Mark's body, his breath, his essence.

Watching. Listening. Being. Waiting.

A bit later, he stirred again. He opened his eyes and looked into my eyes.

Pleading, he said in a broken voice, "Could you get Wayne to pray with me?"

It was time. Wayne, his trusted mentor, spoke the words of commendation. Wayne opened his well-worn prayer book, repeating the prayers he had shared with many others, making the sign of the cross on Mark's furrowed brow.

"Into your hands, O merciful Savior, we commend your servant." The scented oil wafted into the room, filling the space with the ancient longing for peace at last.

Night descended yet again, readying the vigil for the final hours of life. Breath. Then another breath. Again. Again. Mine. Then his. For me, sleep remained far away.

I held fast by waiting, wondering, and experiencing the presence of others gathered in small groups around me.

Brent and Sara moved in and out of the room. I felt the gentle touch of care caressing my back from those sitting alongside.

I held firm in my resolve that Mark would not die alone. Someone would be nearby. We kept vigil into the grey of the morning.

DAY SEVEN: FINAL WORDS

The darkness of night turned into the morning light. Mark again opened his eyes, bidding me come near, asking for a favor. With a genuine immediacy, he wanted to know the Prayer of the Day for next Sunday, engaging in the weekly discipline of his role as pastor, memorizing the prayer for each week. Mark did not have the energy to learn anything more. But he wanted to know the prayer used on Sunday and think about it.

With the hymnbook in my hand, I walked to his bedside. I pondered his commitment and life as a pastor. Even as he died, his last thoughts would focus on the prayers of the church.

I read the prayer slowly. Then Mark asked me to repeat it line after line as he recited each word aloud with me. Again, I read the same phrases, and he repeated them until they were well-rooted in his mind.

"Thanks," he said and closed his eyes.

These were his last spoken words, his final exchange with me, his wife. I sighed with bittersweetness. How I longed to hear, "I love you," one last time. I longed to be within his arms one last time. I longed for my lonely heart to be the center for these ending moments! Yet, Mark remained faithful to this profound trust of his soul, living into the faith he professed.

Disappointment grew, but I was powerless to change who he was, who he had been his whole life. Mark was Mark. I decided I could not think about this now. I pushed the hurt down, told myself to be grateful I could support him again. Support was what I did, what I knew, how our marriage worked.

The day before, Brent and Sara were reading emails of affirmation to their dad. He stopped them in the middle of reading one of them. Mark commented on how helpful it was that we, as a family, did not need to do this now because we had affirmed our love often throughout our family time together. It was true. We had shared words and gifts of affirmation through the years, in "special Christmas gifts," birthday cards, the baptismal remembrance dinners. But I wanted one more expression of love and appreciation. Just one more.

I wondered if it was too difficult for him to say goodbye. Was it too hard for this large man with a gentle heart to share the last farewell to those who were most dear to him? Was this the only thing he had the power to do? Did he only have the strength to hold onto the more effortless action to learn a prayer?

Wayne and others in the house told me how much Mark voiced his love for me to them. They said to me that Mark was grieving for me and deeply sad. But Mark did not say any of this to me.

I wondered why. I was sad, brokenhearted in the wondering. I felt disappointed, yet I pushed any glimpse of frustration deep into my core. I loved Mark. Mark loved me. We lived it. I knew it even though I wanted to hear the words one more time.

Mark was dying, and now was not the time to fix my hurt. I had to let go of this longing. This was the way it was.

"I can do this," I said again. But this time, the words were about me.

Waiting remained. I breathed in rhythm to the NG tube pumping fluids from his stomach, still green in the throes of death.

Mark stirred, restless with pain. I gave him yet another dose of morphine. I pushed its relief into his veins, remaining fearful of its power. How much was too much?

Mark's spirit quieted into stillness, no longer active around him, no longer demanding the attention in the room. The household was calming too. Family and friends began to leave. They needed to return to work and their everyday routines after pausing their lives to say goodbye.

Yet, I remained. The circles of care around us grew smaller. The sadness within me grew deeper.

Many who left had projects to complete before the funeral in the next week. Much was already in place, especially the critical pieces Mark insisted on having. Wayne would preach. Susan, Red's wife, would preside. Red would share the life story. Megan, Red's daughter, would sing along with the choir. We chose the hymns. John would again share "Shine Like the Sun."

At New Melleray Abbey, a monk was making Mark's casket from the wood harvested from the surrounding forest. Simple. Carefully crafted. Pine. Plain cotton cloth. Straw. All elements of the earth. A reminder of the grave. A reminder of the words, "Dust to dust. Ashes to ashes."

Details of next steps, well planned and dutifully programmed, stirred the quiet or embraced it, depending on where my mind drifted. Anticipating the funeral overwhelmed me. Members of the congregation would be watching me, and my family needed me to model the way. Mark needed me to lead the way, a widow's procession.

The morning moved into the afternoon. The Bishop visited. More prayers. So many ancient blessings. So many God words. So many sacred readings written to provide comfort, embracing the quiet. These words voiced my understanding and beliefs, the core of convictions I trusted.

Yet, at the same time, these words stirred me into restlessness. They were also empty, shallow in their promises, and incomplete in truth. These ancient prayers silenced the laments lying in wait, pushing my grief cries into the recesses of my soul, where they were unknowingly gathering strength.

Into the hollow echo of hope, I looked for touch. The touch from someone was concrete. Each contact was real. Now. Immediate. Through touch, I felt the stability of another holding on and not wanting to let go. I held Sara's hands. I felt the warmth of Brent's strong arms around my shoulders. I sat near Mark into the hours of the night. Others sat near me. Their presence held onto me as my grip on Mark was slipping away. Touch was real in its receiving. And in its leaving.

Time kept moving. Hour after hour. Minute after minute. Another night. Another prayer. "God grant us a quiet night. And peace at the last." Would this be the last night of our vigil? When would peace come?

I longed for sleep, but no sleep came. Others provided many things in their care for us, but no one could sleep for me. I envied those who could sleep as time kept moving, one moment into the next.

DAY 8: A SINGLE TEAR

As the dark of night finally lifted into the morning light, I found myself sighing. Loudly. Heavily. The weight of it all bearing down on me. My shoulders hurt. My head swirled in confusion. My heart weary, numb.

Mark had come home only a few days ago, yet it seemed like forever. I drank more coffee. Someone brought me toast. Breathe in. Breathe out. The NG tube kept pumping. The stillness around him grew louder as the busyness of care slowed down. Brent, Sara, and I remained present at his side.

The day was rainy, dark, haunting.

By noon, Mark's breathing changed. Each breath grew shallower than the one before, spaced further apart. I did not notice who came, who sat, who gathered, how long they remained. I do not remember any thoughts. I only watched. Noticing. Watching Mark's face. Mindful of each movement, holding onto each stir of muscle, flitter of an eye, a twitch of the lips.

Breath… Pause… Breath.

Quiet.

Breath.

I reached and drew Brent and Sara near.
Breath.
Quiet.
And a single tear.
A single tear
moved
slowly
from the corner of Mark's eye
onto his cheek
into his greying beard.
Breath stopped.
Quiet.
Peace at last.

THE WALK BEGINS

Time: 2:20. Precisely. I wanted it noted, exactly. Mark died.

His life was over as his breath stopped. His eyes opened in a hollow stare. Compelled to free his body and his soul, I pulled the plug on the suction and removed the tubes from his nose. No more, I thought. No more intrusion from pumps. No more medication. No more morphine. No more demands to live. I gently closed his eyes.

Brent, Sara, and I stood beside his lifeless, empty body. No prayers. No tears. No words. Only silence. Complete and utter silence. Only the reality of the last. Only the calm of peace. Peace at last for Mark's soul.

The news of Mark's death moved throughout the house, and others joined us. Someone phoned hospice and asked them to come and bear witness to his passing for the sake of legal notification. Someone else called the funeral home to retrieve the body.

Step by step, we moved away from the immediacy of Mark's death. But my life did not stop. Surprisingly, my heart kept beating. I continued to pull air into my lungs after each heavy sigh. Each breath reminded me that this time was not my last. It was only my now, my life. How would it move forward?

The bedroom held a holy space between life and death. The four walls embraced the presence of the Holy. Mark's spirit left his body but had not yet left the room. I sensed it hovering near, welcoming those of us gathered there with an essence of warmth and love. The room seemed to glow within a soft light.

Sue, the church administrator, did not allow Mark's body to be alone while he lay where he died. She understood the holy role of presence. As we waited for other members of the family to pay their last respects, Sue sat on a chair beside the bed with Mark's lifeless body. She sat bathed in the soft lamplight in a gentle quiet, attending the mystery, accompanying the Spirit in death. Sue left her chair as others came to the room to say a final farewell but always returned to her hallowed spot, honoring the remaining Holy presence.

One by one, each person in our home visited Mark's body to say goodbye. Family, friends, staff each walked into the room alone. The rest of us understood and respected this personal time and its importance in allowing an opportunity for a word or gesture of goodbye. The afternoon morphed into dusk, and light crept from the room. A longer night emerged with each farewell.

When the mortician arrived, I knew it was my turn to attend this sacred ritual.

Sue acknowledged me with a nod and a loving hug as I entered the bedroom and moved toward Mark's body. She closed the door behind her as she left. I was alone, enfolded within a glowing Love.

I stood at the foot of the bed staring at Mark's body, so still, so wounded, devastated by cancer. So thin. Yet his face, haloed by a wiry grey beard and thinning hair, appeared at peace. Energy surrounded me, held me, invited me to come. How would I say goodbye?

I looked around the room and noticed the hospice staff had removed the drugs and medical equipment. The bottle of moistening cream remained on the dresser, the only reminder of the constant care Mark's body needed. It beckoned me. I took the bottle, instinctively knowing what to do. I did what I had done for months on end at the close of the day. I wanted to rub his feet for one last time.

I opened the bottle, placed some lotion into my hands, and began to massage his feet. From there, I connected to his body one last time, rubbing the sweet-smelling salve into his legs, caressing his hands, soothing the skin of his arms, and then anointing his face. Each touch was a gesture of farewell. I prepared the body of the dead with the love of the living. With each stroke, I felt the warmth leaving his body, the waxy turning of his skin.

Within each touch, I heard the echo of his gentle voice and imagined the twinkle in his eye. My hands released his body to the Holy. Mark's being, once united with me, now moved into the universe.

I kissed Mark's brow, caressed his face, smoothed his beard, and whispered into the quiet, "I love you."

With one final loving look, I turned and walked away from the room. Toward what? Fear? Loneliness? Anger? No, I walked into numbness.

I entered the living room and was surprised by the number of people sitting there—friends who came to share their respects. I was surprised at how quickly they arrived. I sat in Mark's comforting leather chair as a place of refuge in their midst. The chair cushions, molded in the shape of his body, carried the scent of his being. Overshadowed by the chair's size, I knew a silent comfort held within its security.

As I looked up, I saw the mortician push a gurney toward the front door with a black body bag lying on top of the dark red plastic cushion. I swallowed hard, pushing against the image embedded in my brain. There went Love out the door.

Sue walked behind the entourage as they left the house and then sat on the floor beside me. She took my hand. Her role of presence was now with me as my widow's walk began.

Other friends arrived. Sandwiches showed up from somewhere within the house. A cacophony battered around the room; laughter, tears, stories, and remembrances echoed through the words of condolence.

Pressure grew inside me to complete the funeral arrangements. But this need competed with the sadness and the desire just to sit a while. Through the chaos, internal and external, I knew I had to connect with Tom, the organist; Wayne, the preacher; Sue, the administrator; and Brent and Sara to make the final arrangements for the funeral before Wayne flew home to Colorado in the morning.

An awkward moment of dueling agendas added to my numbness and confusion. I so wanted to bask in the gentle care of the many well-wishers and let their love soothe my heart. Yet, it was essential to me to complete the planning while these critical leaders for the funeral were with me in person.

With a large voice, I spoke, "Thank you for coming and for your care and love for Mark and my family. You are welcome to listen in, but we must get the funeral planning done before Wayne leaves."

The planning of Mark's funeral was now communal. As the pastor's wife, even the intimate reflections of planning a funeral were open to all who sat in this room. *So be it*, I thought with a heavy heart. My role remained even as Mark was dead.

Planning ensued, and we checked the various tasks off the list. Visitation. Hospitality. Hymns. Special music. Communion. Wayne's preaching.

I looked Wayne directly in the eye. We had known him since college, and Mark was like a son to him. Wayne longed to memorialize Mark's image as a servant of the church, remembering the man he mentored, honoring the years of mutual service, the hours of shared theological study, the moments of intimate prayer, the glasses of scotch, and the times of laughter and laments. Yet I understood that the funeral needed a different purpose than this.

"Wayne," I said with all strength I could muster, "I need you to preach a sermon of pastoral care for a congregation who lost their pastor. Mark would want you to preach words of hope for them."

"But," Wayne interrupted, "what about you, your kids, your dear friends, and family. What about your loss? My loss? What about..."

"We will find a later time for that. Now it is about the members of Hope Lutheran. They loved him too. I think Mark would have wanted this for them."

Wayne quieted and nodded in understanding, but not necessarily in agreement.

The people who had gathered with us began to leave, wrapping their coats around their bodies to enter the dark and cold November night. They left with a wave, a pantomimed hug, or mouthed words of sympathy. We talked a few minutes more to agree on the final decisions.

Quiet settled into the house. My children headed to their own places, to engage their own thoughts, wondering within their own sorrow, resting upon their own beds. Wayne escaped into the guest room to pack his belongings to fly out in the morning and to attend to his own grief.

I wandered into Mark's office, touching the bindings of the books he read, flipping through the pages of recent writings he created, running my hand over the computer he used. I finally sat in the molded desk chair, looking into the backyard of barren woods with leafless trees on a moonless night. Too quiet. Too calm. I sat inside Mark's private office, the home for his creative heart. The numbness of my heart broke open, and the tears finally came. I sobbed into the emptiness of the room once filled with the fullness of Mark's life.

Sue followed me into the room and sat yet again on the floor at my feet. Fully present, she allowed my heartache to spill into her and listened as I reviewed the funeral plans, remembered the feel of Mark's body, shared images of saying goodbye. She heard my plea yet again for the funeral to be for the people of the church. Sue listened with her heart. How do I help my children grieve the death of their dad? How do I manage my sadness and hurt? Her stillness held the rambling chaos of my thoughts.

In time, Sue stood and took my hand. "You need to sleep." She walked me up the stairs, down the hall, and into my bedroom. I was surprised. I had not thought about where I would sleep. Earlier in the evening, Sue and others thoroughly cleaned the room, washed all the bedding, and prepared the space for me to go back to this place of Mark's death. This room was no longer a caring place for the dying. It was now a lodging place for my journey ahead. Their care for me touched me profoundly, and I wept.

I initially resisted. How could I sleep in this bed? In this room? In this place of death?

Yet, with Sue's encouragement, I realized I needed to start here. I needed to sleep in this bed, surrounded by these memories. Sue excused herself, shutting the bedroom door behind her as she left, just as she had done earlier in the day. I heard the front door close as she quietly left the house.

Sitting alone on the bed, touching the pillow where Mark's head had rested, I breathed in the scent of his essence. The room remained filled with Mark's spirit.

I looked around. I saw the faces of those who kept vigil with us and felt the comfort of their care. After I changed into an old pair of pajamas, I turned off the light and moved into the darkness. What now?

I lifted the sheets on my side of the bed and crawled inside, feeling the coolness against my skin. I turned to face the emptiness beside me and closed my tear-filled eyes. Sleep came more straightforward than I imagined. In the dreaming of the night, I was not alone. I felt a weight on the bed, a stir of the sheets, a presence of loving.

I rested in the remembrance of the past. The unknowns of tomorrow would come soon enough.

A MESSAGE

Safe. The bedroom was safe. In the past days, I had spent hours sitting in this quiet space, rocking in this chair, staring at these walls, surrounded by the remaining presence of Mark's life. He breathed this air. I wanted to breathe it in before it escaped and before the safety was gone. I wanted to sit where no one required anything of me. A completely numb feeling held me captive with inaction.

I stared at the clock. It is time. "Put on your clothes," I told myself. We had to leave for Mark's funeral in less than an hour. It was time to dress. "Get up. Get moving," I told myself. At the same time, the clock hands moved quickly and not at all.

I listened to the others' voices in the house through the closed bedroom door, but I did not want to hear them. I turned on the radio to my favorite station. Perhaps the soothing sounds of classical music would help me start moving.

I wanted to be alone. I did not want to look into my grieving children's eyes. It hurt too deeply. Their father was dead. Nor did I want to see the face of Barry, whose brother was dead. Red, whose best friend was dead. Wayne, whose beloved apprentice was dead. The members of Hope Lutheran Church, whose pastor was dead.

My eyes moved back and forth from the clock to the black suit hanging on the back of the door. I was unwilling to move as panic grabbed me at my throat, fear cracked open the numbness. I could barely breathe, breaking into a sweat. Throughout the week of hospice care, I repeated the mantra, "I can do this." This prayer empowered me, but now those words were completely absent. "I can't do this. I do not want to do this. God, I don't want to do this." I tried to scream, yet nothing escaped from my throat.

I reached for the phone to call the one person who might help. I needed someone to pray for me because I could not. I wanted someone to listen to me, who did not need me to be resilient. I needed someone to help me get up and move. I dialed the phone number for Sister Michaela, my spiritual guide, who knew me and knew pain. I had met with her at the Benedictine monastery regularly since Mark and I moved to Eau Claire years earlier. I visited her each month, reflecting on God and my life. Michaela listened as I explored my role in the church. She heard my thoughts as I explored the changing patterns in my life with my family, to wondering about my dreams and writing, and to praying. She listened to my heart. Sister Michaela was my touchstone of care through Mark's illness. She was a constant, embodying compassion and a loving presence. I visited her often. Now I needed her to help me breathe. I needed her to help me find courage.

When I heard her voice on the phone, I could barely speak. But somehow, she understood as we both listened to my panic, my breath, and the few words I could express while so many stuck in my throat. I wept bitterly, "I can't do this. It's too hard."

I heard the kindness in her voice. I was grateful for her compassionate presence as she prayed for me a prayer of the saints. I do not remember the ancient words, but they helped to calm me.

"I'll be there," she affirmed. "Allow others to love you, Elaine. You are not alone. Others see the hurt in your eyes too. Open yourself and let them love you."

"Okay." I tried to allow myself to be open and vulnerable to receive her love. I hung up the phone.

I stood, ready to put on my clothes when a song began to play on the radio. "Jesu, Joy of Man's Desiring" by Bach.

I stopped and stared at the radio. I could not believe what I heard. Bach's "Jesu, Joy of Man's Desiring" was the music that accompanied me as I walked down the aisle when I married Mark thirty years before. It was a song of promise, of love, of hope. On the day of Mark's funeral, it became a hymn of presence. Was this a message from Mark? Was this a word from beyond? This music from my wedding procession was the one to accompany me on my widow's walk. I breathed the melodies into my heart. Yes, I believed it to be so. Amazing. I smiled. "I will do this."

I put on my black suit and remembered the time of stepping into a white gown. Combing my hair, I remembered a white veil I had secured on my head years earlier. That day, I imagined a different covering, one of love draped around me. I put on a gold, heart-shaped necklace with a small diamond - an engagement gift Mark gave me to affirm the beginning of love. Now, staring into the mirror, this token announced a love that ended, yet did not leave. I placed the gold wedding band on my left hand and remembered a promise of fidelity.

"Wear it today, Elaine," I told myself. "May it bless you with Holy Presence."

A wedding. Now a funeral. Odes for joy at odds with sighs of loss. Not a competition, but rather a completion. The music had been at the beginning. Today, it was the ending—a full circle. Today this music carried a message as well. Love remained.

I slipped on my black heels and walked out of the bedroom door.

Brent and Sara were waiting for me in the kitchen. When we saw each other, I had no words. I hugged them tightly and looked into their faces. We had each other.

"Let's go."

FOR WHOM THE BELL TOLLS

The crowd was gathering as we arrived at the church. Smells of lunch wafted from the fellowship hall. The chef was preparing a meal of Swedish meatballs and mashed potatoes with a dessert of root beer floats, all the foods Mark craved while he was connected to feeding tubes. We would not be eating ham and scalloped potatoes, a regular funeral fare of which Mark had his fill as a pastor.

Like a statue in a park, Mark's closed casket anchored the center of the gathering space. A Christ candle on one side. A large cross on the other. The pine box was surrounded only by the room's emptiness.

But yesterday, the scene was so different. Was it only yesterday that I stood by this open casket for hours greeting the many well-wishers who had come to pay last respects at the open casket?

Yesterday, I welcomed hundreds of people for the visitation. Hundreds of people shook my hand with a firm grip trying to embody their love and support for me. Their hold was so strong it felt like the power of a vise grip bending the simple ring I wore on that hand into an oval shape. My hand still hurt that day, the funeral day.

But yesterday, many of the mourners gasped as they approached the coffin. They saw Mark's emaciated body dressed in a black suit with a clerical collar. I wondered if the people were shocked to see a powerful man so diminished.

Was it only yesterday when I was surprised at the number of children who wanted to see his body, who gently touched his beard in a familiar greeting as they had often done when he was alive? They did not seem afraid, but merely curious within the safety of their parents and the remembered delight of their pastor who had told them stories and made them laugh.

Was it only yesterday when my family, friends, and people of the community gathered in the sanctuary for prayer? After closing the casket, the ushers rolled it into the church, placing it before the altar. The room darkened, illuminated only with candlelight. The youth leader carried the lit Christ candle into the sanctuary through the quiet, announcing it was time to begin Evening Prayer. The music and readings eased our grieving hearts, gently moving in tone and tenor, proclaiming God's presence. The congregation's singing gave voice to what no one could speak on their own but found comfort in mutual melody.

Was it only last night that Mark's casket remained in the darkened room with only the lit Christ candle beside it? It seemed an appropriate ritual for a man's life defined as "pastor."

After the service, one small child remained in the church as most everyone left. The six-year-old girl sat in a pew just to the right of his casket, quietly, patiently, alone. As her father was preparing to leave, he realized she was still sitting in the same place. He entered the sanctuary and sat beside his waiting daughter.

"Why are you here?" he asked gently.

"I don't want Pastor Mark to be alone," the little one said. "It's scary to be alone in the dark. I don't want him to be scared."

Her father gently pulled her into his arms and whispered, "Pastor Mark will be okay. God is with him." They left the sanctuary, walking hand in hand.

I envied her. I longed for someone to hold my hand and walk me home. I needed reassurance too. I feared the darkness of the unknown, in the aloneness of grief, in the process of saying goodbye.

But that was yesterday. Today was the day of the funeral. Congregants and friends filled the church pews again. The ushers added chairs to accommodate the large crowd. The balcony was standing room only.

I was not alone, though I felt alone even as caring people surrounded me. I felt too numb to notice. I reminded myself of Sister Michaela's words. "Allow others to love you." Many "others" filled the church, including family who came from afar; Mark's friends and colleagues who argued with him and loved him still; church leaders who implemented his thoughtful insights into their own ministries; congregants from this church and from the other parishes Mark had served in Iowa and Colorado; my children's friends; and national church leaders. Many were people I never knew. Yet, we gathered at the funeral together to remember one man, Mark Alan Olson.

Perhaps I was not as alone as I felt.

The assisting minister lifted the bell bowl high into the air and struck it boldly. With each strike, the bell rang the call to worship, and the congregation quieted in reverent respect. Dong. Dong. Dong.

The widow's procession began. In silence, Brent, Sara, and I walked together behind the casket, behind the pastor, behind the bishop, behind the acolytes, behind the cross, behind the candle. The widow's walk continued behind death. Death led the way.

I watched myself from an internal place far away, present in my body but distant in observation. Following the pastor's directions, I saw my hands and Brent's and Sara's as we placed the

97

handwoven funeral pall on the wooden box, straightened the folds of the white and golden cloth I wove years before. The congregation's voices carried us in song as we walked down the aisle toward the front pews. Sitting with my family, I stared at the space between us and the altar. The service unfolded before me — Red's eulogy, Wayne's sermon of God's promised Love to a beloved community, John Ylvisaker's singing "Shine Like the Sun." I ate the bread and wine during the Eucharist but tasted nothing. Noticing the touch of care on my shoulder as others walked past me to receive communion, I felt nothing. Numb. Senseless.

I watched myself, the service, and the actions around me. I felt the eyes of others watching me. I wanted to curl up into an invisible ball, but I was the wife of the pastor. I was sitting in the front pew. My husband's casket was to my right. My children were on my left. The congregation was behind me, caring for me but watching.

I believed Mark wanted me to be a model of strength, faith, and leadership. Perhaps Mark was watching too. I put on my professional face, squared my shoulders, looked up, and contained my sorrow from behind a mask of confidence.

The funeral continued—commendation of the dead, the prayers of the church, and a final hymn. An usher touched my arm and extended his hand to invite me to walk behind the worship leaders as we processed out of the church. Mark's casket remained in the sanctuary while we joined the community for the funeral dinner.

The energy shifted from one of reverence and reflection to one of a clamoring community connecting in conversation and remembrance. A feast waited for us in the fellowship hall. People formed long lines at the banquet table, eager to fill their plates with food. Friends, family, and colleagues met each other with memories of Mark. Every grouping of people told stories about Mark. The conversation united the people from one table to the next. People laughed, cried, and mused within a community grieving together.

Could this ritual of feasting and fellowship embody love for me? Perhaps it might become fuel for the future strength I would need.

I tried to eat, but the greetings from so many different people interrupted too often. I needed to move. Wasn't I expected to greet those who attended the funeral?

"Thank you for coming."

"Thank you for remembering Mark."

"Thank you for your care."

"Yes, Mark was a gifted man."

"Yes, Mark challenged and loved the church."

"Thank you."

Again, I repeated these words. With person after person, with group after group, I reassured others in their loss and felt the presence of their love in return.

The large room quieted as many took their leave to go home. The concentric circles of those who attended the funeral dropped off at the edges with just the rings of the closest friends and family remaining, waiting for the next step of the ritual. The chatter softened. The many helpers carried platters of leftover food into the kitchen. The scraping of plates and the stacking of dishes for the dishwasher rattled in the distance.

I sat in a chair at a table in a corner to rest. Sighing, I wondered, what next? The processions were not yet finished. These final circles of family and friends were to process to the funeral home for the final prayers of internment. Mark wanted his ashes buried at the family cabin. There would be no grave-site service. Instead, the burial ritual would take place at the mortuary.

With the sound of the bell, the pastor invited us to gather again in the sanctuary around the pall-draped coffin. Tom, the music director, picked up the processional cross. Another leader lifted the Christ candle from its stand. The pallbearers of older men who had mentored Mark raised the coffin. April, Mark's childhood friend, walked behind the casket holding the bell bowl high in the air.

In yet another procession, Brent, Sara, and I walked side by side behind the leaders. Everyone else walked behind us. I turned to look at each of these good people. I wanted to remember their presence, their care, their faces, their love of Mark, their love of me, and my kids. I saw Connie, Red, Susan, Wayne, Roger, Tom, Carol, Sue, Thomas, Barry, Diane, Larry, Kathy, Richard, Valerie, my dad, Rich, Denise, Joanne, Tim, John, Fern, April, Judd, and many family members, including nieces and nephews, so many friends from so many places. With tears, I acknowledged each person, looking eye to eye. The people fell in line into the widow's procession behind me.

In the silence, we walked. April struck the bell bowl.

Dong. One ring. Two. Three. Four. Five. Six.

Each strike at the tolling bell represented one year of Mark's life.

Twelve. Thirteen. Fourteen.

The toll accompanied each step as we walked through the church doors, placed the coffin into the hearse, and moved toward the cars.

Thirty. Thirty-one. Thirty-two.

The sound rang in my ears. I remembered the toll of the church bell at my mother's funeral—the toll of the bell at the funerals of neighbors when I was a child.

Forty-seven. Forty-eight.

Each strike affirmed a life lived.

Forty-nine. Fifty.

Each ring affirmed a love shared.

Fifty-one.

Silence. The sound stopped. The toll ended.

Startled, I stared at the bell. It ended too soon.

Fifty-one strikes were not enough.

The pallbearers placed the coffin in the back of the hearse and shut the door. The thud broke the silence. An eagle circled the church several times, flying high in the sky above.

In my car, my children and I followed the hearse carrying Mark's remains. The driver started the car's engine, and we left, driving through the city to the funeral home. A simple, black flag attached to the side of each vehicle rippled in the wind, announcing our presence to all we passed. A few pedestrians and other cars stopped to watch the procession snaking through the streets of Eau Claire.

We stopped in the funeral home drive and walked into the cold afternoon sun. The pallbearers again gathered at the hearse to lift Mark's coffin and carry it inside the funeral home. These six men loved Mark into leadership and mentored him for years with time, teaching, wisdom, and glasses of scotch. I am sure they never imagined they would carry his remains at a funeral.

Taking our place, Brent, Sara, and I sat in the front row. Our friends and family sat in the chairs behind us, arranged in simple rows within the solemn, closed room with bare walls, low lighting, and quiet music in the background. I stared at a white cloth draping a wooden casket, a cross on one side, a lit candle on the other.

There was no open grave in front of me. No hole in the ground to bury the dead. No reminders of life in nearby trees. No grass, flowers, birds. No open sky. No wind in my face. Nor were outdoor cemetery or headstones naming the complexities of other lives—only a walled room with florescent lights and chairs lined in rows facing death.

Instead of the earth, a fire awaited—an all-consuming fire. One I would not see, but a fire that transformed Mark's body into ashes. The remains would fill a small box.

The room felt like a small box. The walled room, barren of any organic reminders of life, was also a simple box. How can death be transformed into life here? This room felt like a coffin, too.

I watched the pastor open a prayer book. He spoke a few words. Said prayers. I did not hear them.

I waited for the bit of dirt to be dropped on the casket.

"You are dust. To dust you shall return."

I watched for the sign of the cross.

I saw the pastor's hands extended in a final blessing.

I heard, "Amen. It shall be so."

What do I do now? I waited, and everyone else waited for me. People watched me.

I stood. Maybe too quickly after these final prayers. I was screaming inside and had to get moving. I had to get out. I needed to leave the casket behind me. I had to see life. I had to exit death.

I walked out the door to stand under the light of the sun, to get some fresh air. I led the way.

To where? To what? I did not know.

I had to get out of the widow's procession.

I had to leave it behind.

I needed to walk into life.

Part Two: Beyond the Grave

"But grief is a walk alone. Others can be there and listen.
But you will walk alone down your own path, at your own pace,
with your sheared-off pain, your raw wounds, your denial, anger, and bitter loss.
You'll come to your own peace, hopefully, but it will be on your own, in your own time."

—Cathy Lamb, *The First Day of the Rest of My Life*

IS THERE TIME FOR TEA?

A few days after the funeral, the house was quiet, too quiet. Everyone had returned to their lives and routines—Sara at the seminary, Brent and Connie in Minnesota, family members and friends to work. I assumed Hope Lutheran was doing well under the leadership of Pastor Roger, Tom, Sue, and active lay leaders.

I stood at the kitchen counter, holding a cup of freshly brewed tea. I wrapped a tattered, forest green flannel robe (one Mark gave me years before) tightly around my body and tied it firmly with the cincture at my waist. My hands peeked out of the rolled-up sleeves. My feet warmed within a pair of slippers too large for my feet. I stared out the window and watched bare trees wave hello as they stood against a grey sky. Clouds were heavy with a forecast of snow.

I wanted to feel sorry for myself.

"Just for one day," I repeated the words, resigning myself into the emptiness of the house and the void in my soul. "Just for one day."

Exhaling slowly, I recognized sighing as a constant companion. My tears seemed locked beneath a numbing survival. I cried when Mark was sick. Now, after his death, I just was.

My whole body hurt, working to hold myself together. My stomach was still queasy from a significant bout with stomach flu the day after the funeral. My abdomen muscles were still sore from the wrenching.

My mood mirrored the sky. Grey. Heavy. Weary. Blank. I waved back at the trees, bidding hello, beckoning their bare limbs and the bleakness to join me for the day.

As I poured hot water into my cup for a second serving of tea, the phone rang. I didn't want to answer it, but thinking it might be one of my children checking in, I picked up the wall phone receiver.

"Hello?"

A young, unfamiliar male voice was on the other end. "Hello, Mrs. Olson. I'm a reporter from the Eau Claire paper. We would like to run a story about your late husband, Mark Olson. Can I ask you a few questions?"

Shit, I thought. (I do not swear often.) So much for a few hours of quiet and feeling sorry for myself. I swallowed hard. My role as a pastor's wife remained, even in death.

"Sure. What do you want to know?"

Resigned, I put down the cup of tea, placed it in the center of the counter, untied my robe, pulled the receiver with its long cord across the room, and sat in Mark's leather chair. Resting my feet on the ottoman, I turned my back to the day's grey companion and responded to the various questions. I told stories about his work as a pastor and shared the names of a few national church leaders for the reporter to call to complete the written description of Mark's life.

When I hung up the phone, I turned around. With a weary body, I gazed into the barren sky. The cup of tea was now cold. I got up and walked to the bedroom to dress for the day.

Leaving the cup on the counter was an intentional act. The phone call demanded a new resolve. I would not feel sorry for myself. I had to keep moving. I looked into the mirror as I brushed my teeth. A German-stubborn-independent-self stared back from within the reflection.

"Get going," she commanded.

As a child, I feared being alone. My mom battled depression and anxiety and was often physically ill. My dad worked long hours as the owner of a feed mill in rural Nebraska. As the youngest child and only daughter, my family adored me. However, I was often alone with my imagination and projects. I would wake in the night and listen for my mom's heavy breathing, afraid she'd died. As a young child, I instilled a self-imposed independence to survive. The image in the mirror reminded me of this young, stubborn girl of German heritage. Her sad yet demanding soul talked to me again, "Do what you know. You are a radical, independent spirit. You will survive."

I walked to the kitchen, dumped the tea in the sink, washed the cup, put it on the cupboard shelf, and closed the door. "Get going," echoed in my head.

I pushed forward. I longed to go through, to drive grief away quickly. "I can do this," became the words for my survival. These were once the words of care for Mark as he died. Now they were the words for my walk forward.

I called clients to reschedule appointments, cleaned closets, scrubbed floors, wrote in my journal page after page. I shopped, overate as I tried to fill an internal void.

Days moved forward into more days.

IT WOULD HAVE BEEN ENOUGH

Wayne, Mark's mentor, called from Colorado. He was planning another memorial service for Mark for some time before Thanksgiving at a large congregation Mark had served in Denver. Wayne quickly arranged for Sara, Brent, and me to fly to Colorado for the weekend and the evening memorial service.

When I stepped off the plane in Denver, my breath caught in my throat. I realized this was another experience of my new life. But it was also strangely familiar. The dry air, the shadow of the Rocky Mountains, and the deep blue sky reminded me of the thirteen years we lived in Colorado.

Our children grew up there. These were the years of children's theater, music programs, youth mission trips, school projects, and youth handbell choir. This was also the place I struggled for my voice. It was in Denver I practiced the art of handweaving, created liturgical art, and left to travel across the Midwest to show and sell the weavings to clergy and churches. In Denver, Mark and I, along with several alums, developed a program for a small liberal arts college in Iowa. In the program I directed for five years, students lived and worked in an urban setting for one semester. Colorado was where I returned to college, received my MA in Counseling, and started a practice as a psychotherapist.

In this city, I spent many days alone as Mark traveled in his work as an assistant to Wayne, then bishop of our church's area governance and the national Lutheran church. Mark usually traveled from Thursday through the weekend and into Tuesday. I worked, cared for the children, and held the home-front intact as Mark traveled, wrote his first book, and became recognized as a leader within the national church of our denomination, developing controversial ideas about evangelism.

Mark and I supported each other's work, but we worked separately, in parallel lives. How strange as I returned, widowed. I was alone again.

Early the next morning, I sat at the hotel restaurant, pen in hand, my journal opened to a blank page, a cup of tea beside me with steam rising into my musings. Wayne asked each of us, Brent and Sara and me, to share a few thoughts at the service. These were to be our reflections on who Mark was for us.

Quietly musing, the Jewish song, "*Dayenu*," began to dwell in my head. *Dayenu* is a Hebrew word meaning "it would have been enough." I understood that Jewish families sang this song of praise to God for God's steadfast love at the Hebrew Passover. My family sang this song each year at the Easter Vigil service shared by our friends Red and Susan while we lived in Denver. The words and melody fed my reflection.

I wrote quickly. Words flowed onto the page, gratitude for Mark's role in my life. *Dayenu.* "It would have been enough."

The evening, the Colorado night sky cleared as winds blew the smog away. The moon and stars shone into the darkness as faint images of the mountains disappeared on the western horizon. I stared at their beauty through the sanctuary window. More than 250 people arrived at the church.

Those who attended the service greeted me with smiles, stories, tears, and more numbing handshakes. I felt oddly at home, reconnecting to so many who loved Mark. The years we lived in Denver were productive years for him and me. Greeting these beloved friends warmed my heart in the late November chill.

The service began with music, songs of celebration, and continued with prayers and Bible readings. Numerous friends and colleagues shared personal musings of Mark's laughter, wisdom and challenge, horse backpack adventures, scotch, and his enormous personality that matched his broad frame. Brent and Sara told stories of Christmas and the "special gifts" they received from their father.

As the last to speak, I confidently walked up the stairs into the large pulpit. I stopped to take a breath before I began. I stood alone and looked into the faces of people who knew me as Mark's wife. Yet these people also knew me as Elaine, significant within my own right. I was alone, but not apart. I was alone, but not voiceless. I was alone, but not powerless. "I can do this. I have done this." I cleared my throat and read:

"It would have been enough
to be married to a gentle man who encouraged me to be all I could be. Whose entrepreneurial spirit spoke the words 'sell' in my ear after I learned to weave liturgical art. Who opened a way for me to explore who I was, who taught me to risk and to love.

It would have been enough
to be married to my own personal cheerleader, who boldly applauded my growing and reflecting.

It would have been enough
to have married a man who fathered our two children who grew up to see the world with eyes of honest critique, speak with voices of hope and live lives of compassion yet still laugh, play, cry, question, and believe.

It would have been enough

to have partnered with a man who pulled me into the unknown worlds of yurts, church hierarchy, and conversation with extraordinary thinkers. Inviting me into the experiences of missionaries to South Africa; justice, peace, and poverty in Guatemala; theologians from North American, theater; voices of hope in San Luis; congregations in Iowa, Colorado, and Wisconsin. Each experience expanded my worldview, opening me more deeply to others.

It would have been enough
to have married a man who taught me to love, to read, and now to carry five books in a bag for a weekend visit in Colorado.

It would have been enough
to laugh, to cry, to fight, to love within 30 years of a good marriage.

It would have been enough
to learn about the grace of a loving God from a man who knew it deeply within his spirit and was able to integrate this grace into all he spoke, lived, and wrote.

It would have been enough.

It would have been enough
to be held close by a man who loved many and was loved by many.

It would have been enough.
Yes, God.
It would have been enough."

BURYING THE DEAD

When I returned to Wisconsin, a clear sky wrapped the air with bitter cold. The weather shifted to a barren existence, holding both stillness and survival.

Mark wanted his ashes buried at the Olson family cabin in northern Minnesota. He loved this northern land, the lake, the quiet, the time he spent there. At the lake, he read and mused, watching the water.

Mark's siblings and their families, along with colleagues from Hope Lutheran, gathered Thanksgiving weekend for the burial. Everyone joined in the potluck and brought the food for the feasting. Brent and Connie drove from Minneapolis with the beer. Tom, the organist, carried the processional cross for the praying. I brought the ashes.

Sara arrived in Eau Claire from the seminary in Chicago to ride with me to the cabin. But first, we drove to the funeral home in the late afternoon to pick up a small, sealed wooden box. Imprinted on the bronze plaque on the lid were the words, "Mark A. Olson, 1951 – 2002." The contents rattled gently against the wooden sides; a simple echo of a full life now ended. I carefully placed the box behind the front seat. I motioned for Sara to drive the three hours into the night for this final time to say goodbye.

The night air was clear and cold. The stars shone into the darkness with distant reminders of light and hope. As I opened the sunroof, cold air rushed above our heads, breaking into the dead silence, proclaiming a mindful presence, affirming, and uniting all of life. I turned up the heat and played CDs with songs I loved. I turned the volume up as high as I could. We heard the moans of bagpipes, the melodies of guitars, and the musing of Christian ballads. I touched Sara on the arm, looked up into the heavens through the open car roof, and smiled.

"We can do this."

When I woke up the next morning, I heard voices outside the cabin and the smell of burning wood. I put on my coat, hat, gloves, and walked outside. Barry and my brother-in-law Tim were standing on the side of the steep, slanted hill stirring a small fire just above the lake. Each leaned against a tree to keep from sliding down the embankment. They waited and watched with shovels in hand for the fire's heat to thaw the frozen ground. When the ground thawed, they would dig a single hole, a few feet down, big enough for the wooden box.

"This'll take a while," Barry said, lifting a beer in greeting, a familiar Olson gesture often received on the lake's banks, even in the morning on a cold, winter's day.

I grabbed a cup of coffee and walked down the steep set of stairs to the water's edge with my journal in my gloved hand. Despite the cold, I wanted to think, write, and wonder. I needed to maintain a long-established habit of cabin life.

It had been three weeks since Mark died. On this day, it was three weeks exactly. It had been so much time with so little. Yet, it was also too short a time with so much.

While I sat on a rock near the water, unfamiliar sounds interrupted the silence. The frozen lake sang in waves of sound, zinging off the sky, reverberating, resonating across the ice into the heavens and my soul. I sat still, held captive in the unearthly interruption of heavenly rhythms created by cracking ice. I wrote...

Your spirit now waves
through the cosmos
sounding on the lake weaving through the air.

Whistles, whips, and winds
twisting, echoing, and etching
through the space around me.

Your spirit sings across the deep,
connecting to an ancient cadence
released and unbound.

Your spirit now free
penetrating me deep within
reminding me not to forget.

Free to move,
to fly across
to move beyond.

Free to bend and whip, curl
to echo, crack, twist, dance
out into the wholeness.

You dance on the frozen water.
You dance into the brilliant sky.
You dance for us, singing and
waving goodbye.

When I walked back up the stairs, Barry quickly reported that the fire had thawed the earth, and they dug a hole for the ashes.

We gathered, standing close to each other to stay warm and to hold on to each other so as to not fall down the steep hill. Tom read a few prayers. We each told a memory of Mark and then placed stones around the sacred gravesite. Finally, I reached deep into the earth and set the wooden box with Mark's ashes at the bottom.

As I stood, the lake's images spoke to my heart. Mark's spirit was not held captive in the dirt. It was set free at this lake. Mark's soul found freedom in this place he loved.

Barry and Tim filled the hole with dirt and stamped the ground in place. We quickly returned to the cabin to warm our bodies, to eat turkey and pumpkin pie, and to feast and show love for each other.

It was time to laugh and a time for the family to have another beer. Brent and Connie had the gift to bring play and build community in almost any situation, and it was no different on this day. Brent teased his sister with his own version of "hide and seek," continuously hiding her silverware throughout the cabin, making it almost impossible for her to eat. He and Connie often said, "Have more fun." And we did. I believe Mark smiled into the hilarity of the day.

Overnight, the northern Minnesota winter winds blew against the cabin. The windows in the bedroom rattled with each gust. My calm shifted with each blast. I curled into myself under the heavy blanket on the bed Mark and I had once shared. I knew others were sleeping in rooms near me. I loved these people, and they loved me. We walked together in grief. We needed each other.

Yet, within the darkness of night, I felt more isolated and afraid. Grief is a lonely experience. The work of mourning was a selfish task. Its energy consumed me. My family and friends surrounded me, but I had little compassion to share for others. I wanted to talk about what it was like for me. It was hard to hear that others hurt too. Self-absorbed, I could only focus on what I did not have. What would I do? What was next? Where should I go?

Each of us who stayed at the cabin that night lost the person of Mark when he died. Yet we each grieved someone different. I lost a husband. Brent and Sara lost their dad. Barry lost a brother. Tom lost a friend and mentor. Sue lost a guide. Each of us grieved in common. But at the same time, we each mourned apart. The space between us expanded. I wondered if they were awake too. Alone, too.

TRADITIONS BECOME HOPE

Thanksgiving opened the way to the liturgical season of Advent, the beginning of the church year for Christians throughout the world. The four weeks before Christmas are a time of waiting in preparation for the coming of Christ. In the Western church, it was a seasonal time of remembering the light of Christ during the shortest days and the longest night of the year. The church proclaimed Christ, the Divine Love, came to shine into the darkness. *The light shines in the darkness, and the darkness does not overcome it. (John 1:5)*

It was my first Advent without Mark. It was time to wait and watch in the darkness. Longing for the light, my mood matched the season. Will I even know a Christmas when it finally gets here?

I waited, sitting in a foreign land called "widow," feeding only anger and impatience. I made a list of all the losses I experienced in that last decade and checked it twice to affirm the truth of the emptiness:

- *We moved three times, twice in Eau Claire*
- *Mark left a conflicted congregation*

- *Bud, Mark's dad, died of a heart attack*
- *Bette, Mark's mom, was diagnosed with breast cancer*
- *My dad suffered a heart attack*
- *My mom died*
- *I had an emergency hysterectomy after heavy bleeding*
- *Bette, Mark's mom, died in our home*
- *Brent, diagnosed with testicular cancer, was okay now*
- *A dear friend Audrey died*
- *Mark died*

December brought despair. I experienced the gloom of the day, the pain of loss, the pressures of change, and the hard work of transitions. Life moved on and stopped at the same time.

Hope seemed distant, useless. If I had faith, I would imagine something new, a glimpse of light in the darkness. In these bleak days, all I experienced was darkness.

Many theologians say, "Go into the darkness because this is where you will see the light." But the darkness of this December held me captive in disorienting fear. I read scripture, hoping for words or images to free me from the gloom. I was unable to pray— no words captured how I felt.

I drifted into melancholy. Visiting Sister Michaela, my spiritual director, became a lifeline. She encouraged me to pray prayers of gratitude.

"Prayers of despair without gratitude," she taught, "lead to bitterness. Prayers of praise without acknowledging the despair lead to empty sweetness." Life was not sweet these days. Bitterness grew instead.

In my efforts to ward off this darkness, I lit candles—many, many candles. I lit tall pillar candles at the kitchen table when I ate breakfast, peering into the grey sky and tops of the barren trees, hoping to brighten my day.

I lit lavender scented candles in the bedroom where I tried to rest in quiet. But deep angst wrestled within, and darkness nearly smothered the flickering light. During the day and into the night, the candles filled the rooms in my home with soft light.

Perhaps, if I did not have hope or light or joy inside my heart, these lit candles would surround me and hold the light of hope for me. "A light in the darkness," as they say. I longed to see any ray of hope.

I drank cups of hot tea and coffee, swallowing its warmth into my sorrow, tasting the bitter/sweetness on my tongue, waiting for the light. I knew deep within my heart I would survive until life came. But this feeling was not "hope." It was only a simple resignation.

In my journal, I wrote four words, "Wait. Rest. Walk. Water." While I sat in the December darkness, I waited, rested, walked, and drank water to move me from one day to the next. I drank a lot of water.

Days passed, and my movements stilled to a sullen stop. I spent most days staring out the window into the bland winter day, sitting in the large leather chair that had been Mark's refuge. His cushions molded to the shape of his body. Now it held mine in quiet solace. I wrapped a knitted afghan my mother made around my body to cocoon myself within a hint of warmth and safety. Even though my body remained motionless, my mind wandered into memories of Christmas.

Images danced in my head. I saw my children as toddlers standing at the kitchen stove with their dad. They anticipated with wide eyes as he poured a buttermilk batter into the rounds of the cast iron ebleskiver pan, giggling as he flipped over the cooked edges in the bubbling oil to make balls of the tasty Scandinavian pancake. I joined them in the car as we traveled into the woods to cut a fresh tree a few days before Christmas. With the fresh smell of new pines, the children reached high above their heads, trying to hold up the limbs of an oversized fresh-cut tree as their dad secured it with twine to the top of the family van.

When we returned, Mark stretched his football-player-sized body on the floor to secure the tree in the stand, grunting with each movement. He stayed there, grinning from ear to ear as the kids decorated the tree. Brent, and then Sara, told the story of each unique ornament as they placed it on the tree—a German pickle, a hand-crocheted candle my family thought looked like a condom, and ancient ornaments made from a used flashcube hung with purple beads.

I watched in my memory as I turned off all the lights in the house on Christmas Eve. Our children gazed in wonder as I carefully lit twenty small, white candles clipped to the fresh tree's boughs. We sat in the quiet darkness in awe of the candlelight as Mark recited the Christmas story. I stood guard beside the tree with a bucket of water. Together we sang, "Away in the Manger." After a few moments, the children eagerly blew out the candles, excited to open the gifts found under the branches.

Most importantly, we shared "special gifts." We each gave a gift to the other members of our family to show our love for them by affirming something we loved about them or something we wished for them. These gifts were not to cost a lot of money but were reflections of our hearts. I saw gifts of picture books, poetry, Kermit, keys, Eveready batteries, words, and songs.

A gust of wind at the window shattered my reverie. I shook my head as I returned to reality and reminded myself that this Christmas was different. Mark had died. Our family changed, forever it seemed. What should I do? How strange it was to anticipate Christmas amid deep grief!

Tree limbs clattered against the window as the wind outside rattled open something within my heart. I had to do something to break this internal malaise.

I pushed myself out of the chair and hurried to the basement to search for the boxes labeled, "Christmas." I carried them into the living room to explore within each one and decide what to keep and what to throw away. What memories do I hold, and which ones do I let go? My body needed to act, to engage with something I could control.

First, I unpacked the boxes of green artificial boughs, thinking I would throw them out. But instead, something inside my heart begged me to drape them around the living room windows, bringing color into the bleakness of the day.

"Now what?" I said aloud. I opened the boxes of ornaments marked "Brent," "Sara," and "Family." First, I unwrapped a ceramic ballet dancer and ran my finger across the crack at the base of the head, broken in the excitement of a young girl's hand.

"Where do I put her?"

I had no tree, no fresh smell of pine. But, from the corner of my eye, I saw the twelve-inch Norfolk Pine, a gift from Sara to her dad, sitting on a side table.

"This will work. This plant will be my Christmas tree."

I smiled and hung the dancing girl on the little tree. Then my son's wooden Norwegian jumping jack, the croqueted candle, and finally, the flashcube ornament on a purpled-plastic-beaded-string.

Completing each task led me to another. I unwrapped the crèches I collected, touching their essence to ground me in the now-carved wood from Germany, soapstone from Africa, tiny painted sculptors created for toddler's hands. When I placed each creche on a shelf or a table, I prayed for joy to be born in the manger of my hollowed heart.

As I emptied the boxes, life grew again inside me. Their contents invited me into the present reality.

I had last touched them a year ago and had packed them carefully for use this Christmas. I would repack these same sacred objects in the same boxes to use yet again next year. There would be another Christmas even after this one. From the past, there was now. From this present, there would be a future.

My melancholy quieted. A glimpse of hope slipped within. These reminders of the past grounded me within the now. They illuminated the light of Christmas past and penetrated my weariness to lighten the burden of the present.

At the bottom of the last box lay the mugs Mark and I used each Christmas morning – one with a Santa and the other with a picture of Mary holding baby Jesus. As I lifted the Mary cup in my hands, I remembered the joy of waking on Christmas morning after church services the night before, the smell of freshly brewed coffee, and Mark's smiling face as he handed me this cup filled with coffee and sweet cream saying, "Merry Christmas."

I walked into the kitchen, washed the cup, and heated a pot of water—renewed.

WHOM DO I TRUST?

The anxiety over money joined the survival frenzy of eating and shopping. I did not make enough money in my private psychotherapy practice to fully support myself. Mark's full-time work and benefits made it possible for me to follow a dream of opening a private practice as a psychotherapist. He often teased me about being my muse. In the early days as a widow, this was no longer amusing.

The widow's benefit from the national church's pension fund, as well as Mark's insurance benefits, helped bridge the gap. The amount was significant enough to pay for the funeral expenses and the first few months of living on my own. I put the rest in my personal savings account, but the amount was too large to stay in this account for too long.

My brain ruminated on various questions about what to do with the remainder. I needed to invest it in some way. But how? Do I pay off the house mortgage? Do I buy stock? Do I put it in an annuity? Do I cash it all out and hide it in my underwear drawer? Many questions swarmed in my head as I did not know whom to trust for help. My dad criticized me one too many times about my lack of financial savvy. My brothers had their own financial concerns.

I soon received a call from the investor at my bank. He stated in an overly friendly voice, "I see you have a large amount of money in your accounts. Let us set up an appointment so I can help you with this." Naively, I thought this would help. Gratefully, I made an appointment.

The receptionist graciously greeted me at the front desk and told me the financial officer was waiting for me. In his office, I sat down in a burgundy leather armchair at a large mahogany desk with a thin, grey-haired man dressed in an elegant black suit on the other side.

A bit too eagerly, he began, "Well, dear lady."

The hairs on the back of my neck stood on end. The words, "dear lady," hit a nerve.

I introduced myself as indignation slowly edged into my voice. "Give this bank officer a chance," I told myself. He continued to overexplain in simple language and a patronizing voice. He summarized his titles, his background in finance, and the firm belief that he was the one to help me. He approached me in a fatherly voice and spoke with full confidence.

"All this money should not be sitting in an account, especially now that you're widowed. I can make it work for you." He seemed to salivate at the thought of getting his hands on a pile of dough. "What are your questions?"

I crossed my legs and arms, wary of this too evident enthusiasm. I started with a question about the mortgage, believing it a safe place to begin.

"Do I pay off the mortgage to free myself of debt?"

He smiled a wide, patronizing grin, looking down at me through the top of his glasses. "Oh, that's a no-brainer," he explained. "I'll figure it out. Don't worry your pretty little head about it."

It was then I stopped talking. I stood to thank the investor for his time and left the bank. As I walked to the car, I broke into tears, sobbing, furious at his diminishment of my brain. Angry that I had to ask for help. Mad that I had to discern whom to trust. Furious that Mark left me alone to figure this out. I was college-educated, owned a therapy practice, acquired a counseling license, and raised two children. I was lonely and widowed, but I was no dummy. I had a brain. I just needed good advice. At once, I willed that I would not be a sucker to someone else's power. My stubbornness retook control.

Yet, somewhere deep within my radical independence and desire to be in charge, I also knew I needed help. I called Lois. She worked as the financial secretary at the church for several years and was wise in her understanding of money. She also was widowed, so she knew my story. Not only did she have a good head on her shoulders, but she also embodied a compassionate heart. And she made great cookies.

I decided to call her and ask for help. When she answered, my voice still shook in anger. I was barely able to get the words out, "I need some help."

Lois responded by inviting me to tea. Another cup of tea. I knew I needed to sit and slow down. I needed to be quiet and heal. I needed help from someone I trusted. And perhaps, I also needed to drink more tea with someone who loved me enough to help.

Over a cup of chamomile and a plate of homemade cookies, Lois listened. She cried with me and remembered Mark too. She gently sat with my anxiety and my pain, my broken heart, and my fears. At the end of the afternoon, Lois handed me a card with the name of her financial planner. "He has been with me for years," she said. "I don't need to know your affairs, but I will refer you to someone I trust."

I wondered how it might be possible to integrate vulnerability and strength. There was so much to learn within this new life called "widow." What did it mean? In scripture, the widow was the marginalized, voiceless one. But I was neither voiceless nor marginalized.

I did not want the title, "widow." Yet, I had to live in this new way of being. A fog of unknowns hid the path ahead. I pushed through with competing necessities—time, quiet, rest, independence, assistance, vulnerability, friends, family, decisions, expectations. All of this was calling for attention. All of this required me to move forward. All of this overwhelmed me.

When I went to bed at night, I was restless, agitated, tossing, turning. When I finally slept, I dreamt. In one dream, I rearranged the furniture in the house, particularly in the kitchen. But nothing fit. Where would I put the stove? The table? The chairs? Newspapers were everywhere. My head spun with the confusion of it all. When I woke into the darkness, I realized nothing worked in my life either.

Several days later, I received notice from the social security office to present a copy of Mark's death certificate to obtain the widow's benefit from his account. I dressed in a black suit yet again, a bit overdressed perhaps, but I needed the external empowerment to mask the fear. I might have to deal with yet another patronizing male.

The woman at the reception desk called my name and led me through a maze of desks and room dividers. At one small cubical, a petite, middle-aged woman greeted me with a smile. I sat in a green, fake leather chair with aluminum arms at a grey-metal desk. A crack in the plastic seat bit me in the back of my leg. She asked to see Mark's death certificate, social security numbers, and other documents and then began to fill in the empty spaces on the official forms.

"Marriage began?" she questioned.

"June 17, 1972," I replied, clearing my throat.

"Marriage ended?"

Ended? My brain scrambled to make sense of this. What? The marriage ended? Yes, Mark died, but I saw myself as married. I still wore my wedding band. Mark's life defined each day—his life, his memory, his smell. Mark's presence was ever before me, beside me, with me wherever I went. I was still married. When did it end? How did it end?

The woman looked at me and then at the papers before her. In time she cleared her throat and looked back up. I was sure she walked through this process many times before.

She spoke softly, looking at me with kind eyes. "I need the date Mark died to complete the information. What day did he die? Your marriage officially ended on that day."

"Oh... November 7, 2002," I replied, holding back the tears, believing the marriage was not over, not yet anyway.

After completing the final information, grateful for the woman's kindness and clarity, I walked out the door with a $250 check, the full extent of the Social Security Death benefit. Do not spend it all in one place. I tucked the paper into my purse.

When I sat in the car in the parking lot, the words hit me again. Had the marriage ended? What ended? What did not?

A confusing fog grew thick within my brain.

ROAD TRIP FOR A SOUL'S JOURNEY

The Volkswagen bug headed west under the blue Colorado sky. The chilly winter air of eastern Colorado rushed across the open sunroof, joining the sun's rays as my only companions on my journey. Black pavement spun the car's wheels, a treadmill turning mile after mile in automatic succession. The CD player blared in my ears. Tears ran down my cheeks while I smiled into the freedom of the road.

While he was sick, Mark encouraged me to travel. "Update your passport. Go see the world I will never see," he advised. A road trip to Colorado compelled me, even though I did not need the passport for this trip.

Men's voices filled the car with the haunting melodies and choruses of lament. Refrains of sadness played from a recently released CD, *Against the Dying of the Light*. Brent's friend was a member of the group called Cantus. Brent gave me the CD, reminding me, "Art can speak when our hearts cannot find the words." The melodies played a drama of dying and hope. The music danced on the stage of my mind. Each song pulled me more deeply into feelings I could not voice. As the songs grew louder, they liberated my sadness into anger. Minor chords changed into dissonant harmonies. I screamed in unison when a gong clamored loudly into a raging climax. The wind of the western plains rushed in my windows. With a balm of sweetness, the music calmed, creating a quiet ending with relief. With a single note, the CD concluded with hope. The music led me through pain into peace and finished with a promise. I listened to it repeatedly—mile after mile. Crying each time and screaming with each replay. I allowed the refrains to reveal glimpses of renewal. The road and the music moved me forward.

The road led to San Luis, Colorado. Mark and I had visited this community often while we lived in Littleton. Part of Mark's portfolio as the assistant to the bishop was to lead trips for white suburban church members to gain a cultural understanding of the Hispanic communities in this region of the country. We traveled to this small town in the southwestern part of the state to learn about the culture and the importance of transformational leadership from the people who lived there. San Luis was one of the most impoverished areas in the United States, yet with the guidance of the local priest, Father Pat, and other organizations, the people of this community discovered a path toward economic growth.

The town commissioned a local artist, Humberto Maestas, to create bronze statues for the Stations of the Cross placed on a nearby mountain trail with a resurrection statue on the top of the ascending path. The residence that provided housing for the nuns became a bed and breakfast. In town, Maria's restaurant served the best green chili I ever tasted. It warmed my tongue and throat to the point of sweat dropping off my forehead. Maria grew the chili peppers in her backyard and stirred her love of the people into each new batch with the heat of her compassionate heart.

Neither Mark nor I had any Catholic background or had much understanding of the Stations of the Cross when we first visited. However, each time we went, we shared a spiritual presence and an awestruck knowing of God's compassion within pain. White stones and mountain brush marked the paved walk as it ascended gradually. The view expanded the valley's depth with each step forward. The statues at each station were one-third human size. However, the bronze figures fully captured the human expressions in a snapshot of the time through each scene of Christ's passion.

The presence of humanity within the art captivated our imaginations. Each face, each body meticulously embodied a depth of soul. The soldiers' faces conveyed disdain and hatred. Jesus expressed calm, hurt, agony, or compassion as demanded by the scene. The watchers gasped, cried, shouted at what their structured eyes envisioned. The structured muscles tensed, ached, withdrew, or attacked.

The statues revealed what my body knew, what humanity knew of suffering. We saw within the frozen faces captured in bronze the pain I had witnessed in my vocation as counselor and Mark's role as pastor. As Brent said, "Art can speak when our voices cannot find the words."

Mark and I visited often to be reminded again of this passion story of Jesus and to meet people who lived hope amid their own passion stories. We had accompanied groups there to bear witness to their stories. Mark and I traveled to San Luis on our twenty-fifth wedding anniversary, met with Humberto Maestas, and bought a miniature of the resurrection station. This place was a sacred center for me. It named a holy presence affirming life and love in, with, under, and through overwhelming pain.

After Mark's death, I longed to travel there, drawn by its energy. I could not explain it, but I was open to discovering why. Before I left home, I wrote in my journal:

The first few weeks after Mark's death, I felt hollow, not deep in despair, but just empty inside. I longed to be away and longed to be home at the same time. I am aware that I cannot run away to some place to get over the grief. I know I must just live in it. Live through it. The process cannot be hurried or pushed, either back or forward. I just have to be in it, day by day, event by event. The emptiness will just be empty. The hollowness will just echo into itself. I will only be. The longing for it to be different will remain. The longing, in fact, will grow bigger, or it will wane in being busy, but it remains a constant in my heart. This trip to San Luis will not fix this but rather be a time to pray, to cry, to wonder, and to be. To walk open to a vision if it comes. To trust the Spirit as it leads.

I arrived in San Luis in the late afternoon and stopped at the Catholic church to get the keys to my room. I walked up the steps to the simple building, surrounded by a white picket fence, built of reddish stucco, and topped with a plain, white cross on its steeple. I had called ahead so Mary Jo, the assistant to Father Pat, expected my arrival. When she opened the door, she wrapped her arms around me in a huge hug. Red hair blossomed around her face. Her brown eyes carried the warmth of Maria's chili. After a few tears, we shared stories of Mark, our many visits, and updated information on the people we knew from the village.

When I finally got to my room, I fell asleep quickly. Mary Jo remembered me. I needed to be known and seen after the long road trip. Her kindness wrapped my sad soul in love.

The morning sun shone into the chill of the next day, and I dressed warmly to walk the Stations of the Cross up the mountainside.

I walked from station to station in awe of the art, acknowledging sorrow, and open to the messages revealed through it. That day, it was the station of Veronica that gave me pause. The legend taught Veronica met Jesus as he carried the cross to Calvary. Out of compassion, she stopped to wipe his face with the veil of her clothing. This action left an imprint of Jesus's face within the cloth's fibers. The statue of Veronica's face embodied compassion, tenderness, and sadness with eyes of profound kindness. I could not take my eyes off her. It was like looking in a mirror. I wept.

Step by step, I walked. I stopped at the full-size statue of the crucifixion, the pieta, and finally, the resurrection where the artist depicted Jesus's arm raised upward as if pulled off the cross. I imagined God drawing Jesus from the depths of the sea of the dead into the heavens for the living.

But something different captured my attention. Within the valley below, two ravens soared into the wind. I sat on a nearby rock to rest and watch. Initially, they flew together, swaying on the currents, playing, weaving back and forth, calling in response, one to another. As one dove into the horizon, the other stayed, dancing. Black feathers reflected beams of light as she glided on the lifts of the breeze, diving deep into the ravine, and flying upward toward the clouds. She called again, but the sound drifted into the distance. The bird flew, twisted, and turned with calm and freedom held within the wind's grace, dancing for me.

As I began to walk down the mountain, I stopped at the pieta created by Humberto. Jesus' lifeless body lay across his mother's lap, cradled in her arms, limp, twisted. Mary's eyes were downcast, looking at her son, his head resting against her breast with a tear falling along the side of her cheek. "A woman of sorrows," they said of her. "A teacher of sorrow," they proclaimed of her. I stared into her face memorialized in stone, wondering about Bette, Mark's mom. How would she feel if she were still alive as Mark died? Would Bette's face carry this same expression of grief? What did a weeping mother teach us? Teach me?

I took these thoughts with me as I began to walk the labyrinth that had recently been created beside this Station of the Cross. With an open heart, I wondered, what will be affirmed? Challenged? What will I learn? With each step, I mused about the morning—the walk up the hill, the faces capturing human emotions, Veronica, the dance of the raven, breathing in the clean mountain air, the sun sitting low into the sky. Following the path, I walked into the center of the guided maze to breathe and pray.

As I began to walk the path out, the image of Mary holding her dead son appeared vividly in my mind. I felt panic in the pit of my being, seeing a vision hauntingly clear. Would I hold a dead son in my arms, just as I held my deceased husband?

The fear grew as I remembered the dream I had the night we moved into the house in Eau Claire. In the vision, a spirit-woman came to warn me this house would hold sadness and great pain. Two years later, we provided hospice care for Bette, and she died in this house. Two years afterward, Mark died in this same house. Was this a similar warning? How many mothers must grieve the death of their sons? Would I? How many women must mourn the end of those they love?

Or was it a vision of presence, the presence of mothering God holding my own pierced and pain-filled heart, holding me as Her own? Was it a blessing or an omen?

Perplexed and troubled, I exited the worn, rocky, defined path of the labyrinth trying to breathe and calm my heart. This journey of the soul calmed yet clanged in confusion.

In the late afternoon, I met with Father Pat. I did not share the story of the labyrinth, as it was still too raw. Instead, I told him about the birds in the valley and other birds I had encountered on the journey: the hawk perched on the top of a tree standing sentry as I drove into San Luis and the mourning dove that nestled in a tree outside my window. He graciously told me about a family of birds who created a home for their babies. The baby birds loved the house so much they never flew away into their own lives. The parent birds then tore the nest apart, so that the baby birds had to go and find a way of their own.

"We have to move on too," he said. "You have the gift of thirty years of marriage with Mark, and now you need to move on and fly on your own." He prayed with me, blessing me as I walked out the door.

Two friends, Juanita and Audrey, also widowed within the last year, invited me to dinner. I remember their husbands as strong, faithful men, filled with life and love. Juanita's husband was blind yet had been a leader in the Farm Workers strike in the 1970s in California. With great patience, he taught a young adolescent girl in one of our group visits how to use a chainsaw. Audrey's husband, strong in stature, was a gentle leader within the parish. As we ate together, I discovered a unity of shared story even though we had not talked in years. Our common bond needed no words to explain. In the laughter and mutual journey, I found renewed courage to go home. I was not alone.

Back on the road, headed east, my mind bounced between both the journey's haunting and healing images. The external work of driving the car shifted into an internal drive to find the answers to the questions bombarding me from the future. What was next for me? What do I do, vocationally? Do I stay at the church where Mark was the pastor? Do I move from my home? Where? Do I stay in Eau Claire? What vocation is next? Do I go back to school? Others demanded much from me. What did God want? How would I get there?

An internal resolve to discover the answers linked arms with a compulsive determination to push and get it done. The drive continued, but without a car.

ON THE RUN

On the first Sunday, after I returned, I worshiped at Hope Church. Members of the congregation greeted me with kindness. Many seemed at ease, reassured in seeing a sense of calm about me. They said I appeared confident, and radiant, with a glow of joy on my face. But I did not feel calm on the inside. My internal mantra of "fake it till you make it" must have been working.

Later in the week, I talked with Sister Michaela about the journey to San Luis. She invited me to gently hold my experiences in my heart—the images of Mary, the flight of the raven, the message from the priest, and the companionship of the widows.

"Don't hurry," she said. "Gently ponder within the presence of Holy Compassion and the heart of Veronica. Move forward slowly, and the truth of it all will be revealed when you are ready."

However, anxiety and a self-obsessed need for survival pushed me into intense action. My mind drifted from task to task, seeking to anchor the stirrings within me.

Before Mark faced the onslaught of the myeloma and its effects, I enrolled in classes in a graduate program in St. Paul, Minnesota, to acquire a certification in spiritual direction. At the time, clergy and clergy families composed forty percent of my private practice. Many faced depression, anxiety, or grief. Often, they mourned the death of a vision of a church they had imagined but never experienced, as the institutional church was often more focused on success rather than compassion. They knew the loss of time with those they loved. Entangled within the business of God and the demands of the institutional church, many pastors experienced distance from God within their souls. The more I listened, the more I recognized a spiritual hunger within my clients, and I wanted to find ways to assist them. A certification in spiritual formation fulfilled the professional training I desired.

Just weeks after Mark died, I enrolled again in a theology class, a program requirement. This class provided a way to put my life back together and to interrupt the obsessive thinking about my grief.

In the push to survive, my internal drive to find a new path loomed large. Each week compelled me to press forward. Each week took me into the longings of my soul.

I moved my practice from Hope Church to work as a therapist under contract with another counseling center.

I saw a posting for a position as a director of spiritual formation at the small liberal arts school where I worked several years before. I convinced myself the job was perfect for me, believing this to be God's call and an invitation for the next stage in my life. The process of applying for the job consumed me for weeks. I wrote a resume pushing a vocational identity I sought to attain but had not yet achieved. I asked friends to network in the system for me. When the school hired a different person, another loss intermingled with Mark's death.

I obsessively watched videos of Mark—one as he presided at a friend's wedding or another of him presenting at a theological conference. I craved hearing his voice and intently listened for the gentle way he said my name.

I planned a final meeting of the Center for Congregational Leadership, a gathering of like-minded clergy Mark had established and led over the years. I struggled with the idea that I might be the one to carry his legacy into the future.

Keep moving. Do not stop. My mind and body raced forward.

I wondered how to integrate Mark's identity into my work even as I searched for my own identity. Who was I? What were my gifts?

I knew I listened attentively. Clients told me I had "ears that did not quit." I taught with clarity and enthusiasm. Several bishops affirmed the depth and energy I brought to the workshops on boundary training, team building, and relationships. Was this my next role?

I wore my radical independence as a coat of armor, imagining myself as a warrior woman holding a raised sword in my hand, striking out into the world to survive. Nothing would stop me.

People annoyed me. I recoiled at connecting with others who got in the way of my path forward, especially as they asked challenging questions or made demands on my time.

I felt like a stranger in a foreign land and escaped by pulling more deeply into myself. I read, wrote, pushed, and studied, demanding a new life to begin.

Was this healing? Or protection? Was it realistic? Or a diversion from the heartache?

I dreamt anxious dreams. In them, I balanced on a high balcony or the edge of a cliff or the top of a tall building, peering at the bottom far below. There was no way to get down. In another, I walked onto the theater stage in front of an attentive audience and had no idea what to say or what lines I should have memorized. I dreamt Mark divorced me for another woman. In another dream, I gave birth to a huge baby girl who cried a lot. I knew I did not want her in my life.

As the loneliness grew, I began to look at other men. With curiosity, I searched the hand of each new acquaintance to see if he wore a wedding band. I wondered how to attract his attention. Was anyone available? I realized I was paying closer attention to my friends' husbands. Feeling guilty and ashamed of what I believed to be an inappropriate desire, I pushed the feelings away. And sometimes I pushed friends away too.

Days went by and then weeks. I kept moving.

One night, I walked into Mark's office, searching through his books for information I needed for a theological class. A book with a black pen holding the page within its closed cover sat on a lower shelf. I settled into the desk chair to examine the book more closely. The pen marked the page where Mark stopped before cancer stopped him from reading further. The book, *Between Cross and Resurrection: A Theology of Holy Saturday,* by Alan E. Lewis, was as unread as Mark's life was unfinished.

Careful not to lose the marked page, I quickly skimmed the book. Mark highlighted two key messages. First, the author said our society and our churches were in a Holy Saturday time. Their culture and identity ended (Good Friday), but the future (Easter) had not yet revealed itself. And second, the central emotion of this time was anxiety.

Catching my breath in its revelation, I saw myself within Lewis's words. My life was also in an "in-between"—a Holy Saturday between Mark's death and my own new life. Anxiety held me within its grasp and spewed out of me.

Confidence disguised my anxiety. In the last months, I had pushed forward with unease and worry. I kept a fretful pace to find the other side, to find a new life.

Holding Lewis's book, I realized how tired I was. I wanted to be a warrior fighting a war of unknowns. However, the most challenging part of being a widow was to stop fighting and abide in the now.

Was healing found within the present moment? I was too busy to notice. My lived anxiety blinded me to any real possibility.

I saw Mark's pen pushed between the pages of the book he did not finish. I wanted to stop too, to put a pin into the in-between. At least for now.

Several weeks after his death, three packages arrived in the mail. The first was my renewed passport; the second, the itinerary for the trip to South Africa. I served on the Board of Directors for the seminary Sara attended. As a board member, I invited myself to join the seminary's gospel choir to travel to the townships of South Africa for a cultural exchange goodwill trip. Thankfully, they agreed to have me come if I would join the choir. I hoped the trip, planned weeks ago, would help me stop or at least slow the intensive push into the future. The third package was a new camera. I spent the entire Social Security Widow's Benefit in one place after all.

I hoped travel would put a stick in the spinning wheels of anxiety. Would the journey to South Africa put an end to my running from me? Would it provide time for me to recognize myself and affirm my soul?

THOSE ON A PILGRIM JOURNEY EXPECT SPECIAL INSIGHTS. THAT IS WHY THEY FIND THEM.
~UNKNOWN

Clapping hands and deep, resonant singing surrounded me as I stood in a line between Agnus and Edna, my arms lifted high in the air. I stared at their feet, moving forward and backward in complicated steps to the syncopated drumbeats. Struggling to follow their lead in the dance, I laughed at my clumsy, failed attempts. My feet seemed stuck to the floor, even as I smiled in gratitude for their generous openness, hospitality, and patience.

Our carry-on bags sat beside wooden tables covered in red plastic in the back of a small, wood-framed church. Glass plates held only the crumbs of sugary biscuits. Empty cups stood next to pots containing the last of the rooibos African red tea growing cold. The warmth of music and kindness surrounded me. Side-by-side, the members of the two choirs, one from America and the other from a South African township, bridged the difference in language and culture with song, dance, and laughter.

On this night in South Africa, we danced to reassure ourselves. The first forty-eight hours of travel exhausted us. The adventure included a 24-hour layover at the London airport because of an airport workers' strike, lost luggage, a wayward trailer that broke loose from our van, and last-minute shopping to buy a few personal items needed until our luggage arrived. We arrived late at this destination, a pattern that haunted us throughout the trip.

I began this first leg, exhausted from the travel and the chaotic gospel choir group dynamics. Nineteen Americans of different cultural backgrounds and religions and a wide span of ages formed the group. We fumbled into an unstructured process to know each other at the very same time we visited the South African townships. Most of us joined the choir only to travel to South Africa. The director personally invited some people to participate because of a unique musical talent they brought to the choir to sing, play piano, or play the drums.

I was not one of those. I invited myself. Five of us identified as white, including me. Four men. One adolescent boy. Students from the seminar. A social worker. A couple of teachers. A few Southern Baptists. More Lutherans. Rural folk. Urban dwellers. Administrators. Two widows, of which I was one. Lovers of Jesus. Lovers of books. Lovers of music. And just lonely lovers.

Each one of us joined the choir for various personal reasons but with one common theme—to sing in Africa. I tried to leave my radical, independent self behind, hoping to be open to learning, to see through another's eyes, and try to understand what I might not otherwise comprehend on my own. I wondered what message I might receive in South Africa. Would a spiritual encounter greet me in this foreign land?

As the evening ended, I sat alongside my traveling partners on a wooden pew. Worn out, I listened to a few final announcements and the housing assignments for the evening. The local pastor called the choir members' names. Two-by-two they found their host, picked up whatever bags they had (those not lost by the airlines).

Each grouping walked into the night on the dusty road into the South African township toward their host's home for a night's rest.

As part of the adventure, I agreed to be a single guest for home visits. The pastor called my name last. Soon after he spoke, Tsidi, a tall, proud woman, dressed in a skirt and thick sweater, walked up to me and hugged me warmly. She communicated with me in broken English, gesturing her hands with a kind smile. She invited me to sit as she and the other event organizers stayed to finish washing the dishes, do a final clean-up before we left, and lock the church door. She picked up my backpack (my large suitcase was also one of the lost) and walked beside me into the street.

The cold air of a mild winter's night in the southern hemisphere chilled me quickly. I pulled my jacket closer around my body. Scattered streetlights dimly illuminated the dark, graveled road. We walked past each home. Cement block walls with broken glass on the top for added protection surrounded a few buildings. Only a simple, gated wire fence protected others.

Tsidi walked close to my side, cautious, eyes alert, acutely aware of her need to keep me safe as we walked through the neighborhood. We stopped at the gate of a home. It looked exactly like each of the other houses we passed and all the others down the road. The mining companies built the "matchbox" houses, a rectangular box with a slanted roof and red bricks, to provide cheap accommodations for the black workers during apartheid. A stone path led to the front door with a single window on each side.

As we entered, the room's warmth enfolded me. I felt safe. About the size of a two-car garage, the house was divided into four chambers—a living room and bedroom in the front, with a door from the living area opening to a kitchen, and a second bedroom in the back. A single light bulb hung from each room's ceiling.

Two young boys eagerly hurried to meet me and politely shook my hand in hello. Each, in turn, told me their name as they giggled with excitement. Tsidi's husband also extended a welcome hand and invited me to sit on one of the four chairs in the kitchen for yet another cup of African tea.

Tsidi left the room through the back door into the backyard to fill a bucket with water from the single-handled water pump. After heating some of the water in an electric pot, she made tea for us all in simple white cups while I talked with the boys about their studies and school.

After about 30 minutes, Tsidi rose to explain it was time for bed. She cautioned that it was not safe for me to use the toilet and bath located outside in the backyard and motioned for me to go to the front bedroom. Just inside the bedroom door, she pointed to a large bucket covered with a towel—the toilet. She placed a plastic basin filled with warm water, a bar of soap, and another towel on the bed for me to wash. The room glowed in the yellow light from a single lamp on the bedside table.

Tsidi motioned me to go inside. She shut the door behind her as she left. Luckily, I packed one change of clothes in my backpack and changed into a t-shirt to sleep. After I carefully washed my body and refolded the towel, I moved the basin to the side table, turned out the lamp, and crawled into the soft bed under a dense layer of blankets. I was thankful to finally be alone to reflect on the day, and I looked forward to a good night's rest.

Within minutes, I heard the bedroom door open and listened as Tsidi walked into the room. I laid motionless, curious. The covers lifted as she crawled into bed and moved close beside me. Without saying any words, her body relaxed into stillness. Her breathing drifted into sleep, warmed by the presence of our bodies side by side. Wide awake, I tried to convince myself that this must be a cultural thing and urged my body to relax. But I was too tired to be overly anxious and fell into a restful sleep.

I awoke the next morning to the sound of a gentle knock at the bedroom door, alone in bed. Fully dressed, Tsidi entered carrying a tray of freshly brewed tea and a simple breakfast of juice and a sweet biscuit. As I sat up in bed, she placed a small towel around my shoulders for warmth, put the tray of food on my lap, wished me a good morning with a smile, and then left. I look around the cluttered room, filled with mementos of Tsidi's family, a washbasin with fresh warm water, and the plastic bucket. Within this simple home, I experienced the embrace of hospitality and protection. I felt as honored as if I had stayed in a five-star hotel.

Throughout the next two weeks, the people of South Africa shared the gift of hospitality in abundance within the poverty and struggle of life in the townships.

"It is what makes us wealthy," many told us. "Rather than dwelling in pain or joy, it is a gift to be in community and to be forgiving. Hospitality is what we can share."

The choir traveled from congregation to congregation in the various townships. Singing and ample time for tea and biscuits greeted us at each visit. The communities formed relationships with us first. After tea, we heard the people's stories. We heard about the devastation of AIDS, the cruelty of apartheid, the struggles of poverty, and the high unemployment and crime.

Their resilience through profound grief astounded me. My personal sadness welled deep as I heard of the suffering caused by the hatred and evil humans afflicted on one another through apartheid. Some of the people we met were able to move through the trauma with resilience. Yet, others stayed stuck in revenge, brutalized in spirit, shrunken into more profound despair and unimaginable poverty.

Curiously, many of my experiences reminded me of my youth in Nebraska. Several of the women I met at the churches had Christian names like my own aunts—Edna, Agnes, Dora, Doris, Lillian. Much of the food we ate was like that of my German roots— notably, the potato salad and sweet rolls, which tasted just like my grandmother's. Just like home, the women in the church kitchens heated water in large pots to make coffee with an egg in the grounds. Just like my mom, they wrapped their casserole dishes in kitchen towels. The experiences in the township churches paralleled that of my Nebraska home, where my dad's family immigrated from northern Germany, close to the Netherlands.

Then the realization hit me hard. The Dutch settled in South Africa and took the land away from the indigenous and instituted Dutch language, culture, and religion with absolute power over the native peoples. The land grab also happened in America, as the Europeans took the land from the Native Americans. The Dutch ancestry linked South Africa with my home in Nebraska. The familiarity was one of oppression. I had much to learn.

Most of the singers in the choir were people of color. As I traveled with them, I learned they saw parts of themselves among the peoples of the townships. I listened as best I could. I tried to remain mindful as I heard their reflections about the trip. I was curious, but I was also afraid to ask too many questions for fear of revealing my ignorance about race and difference.

Several of the women from our choir cried when we stepped off the plane onto the red dirt of this distant land. "This is home," they explained. When these choir members investigated the faces of the people who lived in the townships, they saw the faces of their aunts and uncles, cousins, and friends. I heard only names; they recognized family. As we sang, the music resonated in their bones. Each time we entered a township congregation church, we heard the words, "Welcome home." My friends in the choir planted their hearts within this truth.

As much as I wanted to identify with them in our common humanity and say, "Me too," I also knew my skin was white. I knew enough about my white privilege to stay quiet and listen to my fellow travelers' stories. I did not know how or did not trust myself enough to engage in any meaningful dialogue. I reminded myself to listen and learn, to observe and be mindful. I longed to live with compassion for my fellow travelers, for they had as much to teach me as did the people of South Africa.

I did not know what to do. I struggled with how to engage in a conversation about race and difference. I did not want my cultural racism to get in the way. Afraid I would embarrass myself in my ignorance, I remained quiet and tried to learn by observing my fellow travelers, as well as our gracious hosts.

But I wondered, was this process only a matter of trust and listening? And I was afraid. Afraid of what? Looking stupid? Looking racist? Being ignorant? I listened because I was uncomfortable with my thoughts, confusion, guilt, and power— even my own racism. I listened because listening was what I knew; it was what I did. This was what I trusted as a trained counselor. But I also came to realize that listening was not enough. I longed to engage more deeply. But in not knowing how, I regret that I missed a significant opportunity.

I had much to learn about how to engage in challenging conversations. I needed to know how to address my discomfort and how to be with others different from myself. I wrestled with the questions in South Africa, but I did not find many answers. My fear got in the way.

I did learn to eat boiled cow's lung, at least three small pieces when there was a glass of water to wash down each bite. I learned to love taking time for tea, especially the taste of rooibos tea and cookies. After I relaxed and laughed, I learned to dance—okay, sort of. I learned that Africans were allergic to time, or at least that was how they described it here, meaning the time to begin any gathering was when everyone finally showed up, often hours after the established time. I learned to love the sounds of the song, the click of the tongue in speech, the complicated rhythms of drums, the bounty of colors surrounding me. I learned to receive the gift of hospitality and graciously say thank you.

The longer we spent with Edna, Agnes, and Dora, and the other leaders, I learned they, along with their families in South Africa, spoke four to five languages of their indigenous histories. I also discovered that each person I met had another name—a name they preferred, a name they held in pride, a name with the integrity of their full identity. Pits, Pales, Homs, Mpho. For those controlled by apartheid, these African names embraced them with dignity.

I learned about poverty and power. One afternoon, our hosts escorted us to a nearby squatters' camp. The rented bus tipped and swayed as it moved through the ruts on the main road into the valley. A mosaic of tin roofs, cardboard boxes, barbed wire, rotted wooden planks, and blanketed canopies bonded with mud, human waste, and smoke pasted itself on the hillside. Fires built inside barrels warmed individual camps. As we drove, a child waved a greeting of hello. He stood barefoot in the entrance to the one-room shack, wearing a torn T-shirt with the Nike label, "Just do it."

Earnest "Mona" Makwala stood in the front of our bus as he described the camp, the poverty, the need for jobs, and the resulting crimes.

"Mona," he explained, "means to look without judgment. We are in the land of promise. Especially after apartheid ended. Much needs to be done. In Africa, we understand the strength of a man is determined through his ability to withstand difficulty and to venture into the dark."

The bus drove us through the camp, but I stayed inside my head. This trip pulled me into my venture into the dark, my private grief, and my confusion about race, power, poverty, and privilege. This darkness became my common touchstone to engage with others.

At the third church we visited, the host asked our choir to sit in chairs in the front of the room.

"We have a surprise for you," he said. He introduced himself. "My name is Takalani." Something changed. He spoke his African name as a symbol of trust. The use of his African name removed a barrier between our cultures. Speaking their names with us was a sign of being a part of the community.

Takalani graciously invited each of us to stand and speak for a few minutes to describe what work we did in the United States. Using this information, members chose an African name for each of us. I relaxed and rejoiced, as I knew this was an essential affirmation of trust and inclusion.

My friend Dona began. Dona, petite with a beautiful smile, described her work as a social worker seeking to bring new life to difficult places. After she spoke, the room buzzed in conversation as the South Africans talked among themselves. After reaching a consensus, the leader stood, looked at Dona with a broad smile, and proclaimed, "You will be called 'Palesa,' which means 'little flower.'"

When it became my turn, I stood and described my vocation. "I am a counselor, and I talk with people who are hurting or grieving. I listen and try to help them heal." I chose not to tell them that I was recently widowed. I felt too vulnerable within the crowd of people I had just met.

The host, Takalani, spoke up quickly. "I will give you my name," he said, "You will be called 'Takalani.' It means 'finding joy while knowing great pain'. It is from Bible verse Philippians 4:4, 'Rejoice in the Lord always. Again, I say rejoice.'"

I said the name to myself several times. "Takalani." "Takalani." Dumbfounded, I received a gift, a spirit message from beyond. It has been said, "Pilgrims who journey on a spirit quest expect special insights. And because they travel with expectation, they find insight." As I began this journey, I prayed to be open. I longed to hear a message to integrate into my life. I wanted to be open to receive something. It happened. I received a new name.

"Takalani" rang in my head. "Look for the joy in the now." I heard these words within my soul. I heard them at each gathering until the end of the trip.

"Hello," I would say. "My African name is 'Takalani.'" People responded with a smile.

I traveled to South Africa on a spirit quest because much of my life had fallen apart. Mark had died, and I longed to find a way to put myself back together again.

While in South Africa, I often cried myself to sleep at night, missing Mark. I became confused by all I saw and experienced. The stories I heard troubled me. And yet, I was profoundly blessed by a stranger's hospitality. I was often afraid to speak because I did not want to embarrass myself or others.

And I longed to share the stories with Mark—the joy, the food I tried, the dancing. I thought that he would help me sort out my confusion and disorientation when I faced racism, both within a culture that hurt others and within myself. I longed for someone to talk with about how vulnerable I felt within this different culture.

I wanted to hear Mark say my new name, "Takalani," in the same gentle way he said, "Elaine."

Did I set out on a world adventure too soon after Mark's death?

I traveled to South Africa to engage in the broader world, to learn and to wonder, to receive. I visited as a pilgrim on yet another spirit quest, and in return, I met many people and a culture that embraced suffering. And many survived with amazing strength. I ventured into the many unknowns, listened, looked, learned. I was afraid and often confused. I realized I had much more to learn.

I traveled on a spirit quest and came home from South African with gifts I never expected to receive. A new name—"Takalani." A vision—"to find joy in great pain." And a deepened desire – to reach beyond my fears and learn from others.

I was glad I took the journey.

A PROMISE

I sat in the warmth of the sun shining through windows into my living room, revealing the smudge and residue of a long winter. I stared at the spring flowers already in full bloom and the azalea blossoms that were breakfast for the deer. The fresh smell of spring bidding new growth from deeply planted seeds buried beneath the remains of the cold hung in the air. I felt restless as my grief moved through the first year after Mark's death.

On these kinds of days when I was a child, my mom and I would begin the deep cleaning of our home—emptying closets, sorting clothes, cleaning drawers, throwing out junk, washing walls, scrubbing windows. As I walked through the house, all my stuff overwhelmed me. Books packed tightly into shelves in both Mark's and my office, in the family room, and beside the bed. Boxes of forgotten importance cluttered the storage room, along with a table needing repair, an array of tools, financial records for thirty years of marriage, my mom's quilting supplies and buttons, professional magazines, weaving looms, and yarn. Photographs jammed into shoeboxes, Brent and Sara's grade school masterpieces and cross-country skis, a toy boat. Cardboard boxes held the various parts of my life—a baptismal blanket, my favorite doll, a prom dress, a graduation cap and gown, pregnant pants, running shoes, a business suit now too small. Boxes of cards and letters, keepsakes of the funeral, mementos of my travels, and whatever I needed to push out of sight filled the extra bedroom. I wandered from room to room and looked at all that surrounded me. I explored the props left behind from the various roles I lived throughout the past fifty years.

Though I was never an actor, I felt like I had been in various theatrical plays throughout my whole life, living defined roles—a dutiful daughter, pastor's wife, mother, teacher, therapist, weaver. I acted with diverse parts and memorized lines. Even as I longed to be a free and independent spirit, I worked to please others within these roles, too afraid of rejection and loneliness. I played these roles since childhood because I was scared to challenge the authority of the church or my parents. I feared hurting others with my power.

My house held the props, masks, and memories of the drama, comedy, or tragedy. I played one after the other. I wrote in my journal:

All these identities, actors of my past.
Clothed in costumes of place, time,
Expectations, commitments, honor.
Hung in this strange costume shop
Packed inside boxes.

The stage now empty, lights lowered,
I stand in the wings, wondering
What role is next? What costumes are needed?
What are the lines to be learned?
Waiting for a script, a director,
A part, a title, a place.
Who will I be?

I looked in the bedroom closet. One half was nearly empty. I gave most of Mark's clothes to a men's homeless shelter during the cold months of winter as the men needed large-size clothes. Yet, his scent remained in the few sweaters and T-shirts, folded neatly on the shelf above my head. I picked up his sweater, held it to my nose, and breathed in his scent one more time, holding memories close.

I stared into a nearby mirror and looked at myself. What within me needed cleaning? Sorted? Given away? Trashed? Where did I fit? Who was I without Mark? Who was I with him? What do I leave behind? What new role would I choose?

Looking at my hands, I stared at the gold band on my finger. I thought, *I will start here.* I removed the ring and expressed my gratitude with a simple blessing. With a sigh, I put it in the jewelry box on my dresser next to Mark's matching wedding band. We had them designed and crafted by a jeweler thirty years ago with three simple Christian symbols. "Time to let go of a few more things," I told myself, letting go of more than just the marriage.

I had recently left Hope Church to join another congregation in town, an action more difficult than taking off my wedding ring. Before Mark died, he gave me a clear directive to leave Hope Church, the church he had served as pastor.

He and other advisors who studied organizational systems, especially those of churches, described several cases where the beloved widow stayed in the congregation. These congregations remained stuck in their care for her and the remembrance of the pastor. The mission of each of these churches turned inward as they unintentionally placed the widow into a position of covert leadership by watching her actions and seeking her advice.

I trusted and appreciated the leaders at Hope Church and their abilities to understand boundaries and roles. We held significant respect for each other. Yet, I remembered sitting in the annual meeting when the members discussed a critical issue. I felt the pressure of people looking at me, waiting for me to report what I thought Mark might say about the plan. I was not sure if they were, but I imagined it to be so. I could not speak for Mark, nor did I want to. I grew uncomfortable and anxious.

I also needed to find another worshipping community for my own healing. Attending church opened the door to my heart, and I often cried in the quiet and within the melodies of the songs. During Lenten services, as we sang "Holden Evening Prayer," my tears were constant as my mood moved within the music. As I left the church, many greeted me with hugs and words of comfort, their heads tilted sideways in care and sad puppy-dog eyes. The people extended paternal attention, saying, "Are you okay?" "We understand." They wanted to help me, but I longed to remain alone. I felt smothered by their care, and I could not breathe.

I yearned for space to move ahead on my own, to mourn in my own way, and find a new life. Changing congregations was yet another loss for the church and me, but a necessary move for my long-term healing. Symbolically, I said goodbye to the kind and good people of Hope Church on Easter Sunday, seeking a new life.

Yet, I wondered how many losses would I have to experience before life might begin anew? I did not know. I wanted to remember the message I received in South Africa. "You are named Takalani. You will know joy even as you know sadness."

A few weeks later, my friend Sara, a creative woman of spiritual awareness and a dancing soul, shared a gift with me. Several years earlier, Sara had also struggled through a period of grief. While she prayerfully walked along a river, she discovered a stone the shape and size of a womb. As she lifted the stone from the water's edge, she turned it over to see a small hole on the bottom. Inside the opening, a smaller stone rattled like a seed within a pod. Sara danced as she celebrated this symbolic gift, a womb with the seed holding a promise of new life. For months after she discovered the stone, she held it within her hands when she prayed. Sara handed me the stone.

"May it teach you, Elaine. The seeds of new life are for you too."

Both the stone and the name, Takalani, held promises of giving birth to a new life. But giving birth required waiting and struggle. I wrote in my journal:

As Mark's life ended, more tasks were demanded, requiring my attention. With each task, Mark fades into the distance. It is more weary making. Some say that in time grief gets easier. But for me, it is more complicated. Like labor, the contractions swell— back and forth. The energy of my internal muscles increasingly stretches to push through—to push through the funeral, decisions, moving, the clutter, the memories, the cleaning, the giving away, the sorting, the timing, the waiting for the creating. Each push moves me away from Mark. Each releases a pull into a new life.

Like contractions, there is also a pulling back. My gut hurts deeply. With each contraction, the pain brings me to a new place, further away from the knowns, yet closer to unknowns, to more wilderness, more barren land. It demands me to place more attention on something different.

During my own meditation and prayer, I held the stone, longing, waiting, wondering what these contractions would birth.

COMPANIONS – SOME ARE KEEPERS. SOME ARE NOT

I decided to get a dog. But not just any dog. I headed to the local Humane Society, excited to open my heart and my home to another living and loving companion. Carefully, I walked up and down the rows of cages, wondering, searching, trying to trust my gut as to which one to adopt. Feeling a bit overwhelmed and weary, I returned to where I began, the very first cage. I chose a short-haired black mutt with brown spots around his dark eyes, a terrier mix. The dog also seemed a bit tired, too skinny yet eager to connect. Was he just an older dog needing a home? The young woman at the society knew very little about the dog, but she was eager to find him a home. Maybe too eager.

I took the afternoon to think about my choice and then went shopping with new intent and focus. With a checkbook in hand, I bought the best crate, organic food, tasty treats, uniquely designed water and food bowls with a cute paw print embossed on the bottom, a special cozy blanket, a dog harness, and a retractable leash with a poop bag dispenser in the handle. *Having a dog will be fun*, I thought, with a natural eagerness for newness and life.

While shopping, I decided on a name. "Bernie. We'll be best buds."

With the trunk of my car filled with all the supplies needed for a happy dog, I picked "Bernie" up from the shelter in the late afternoon and brought him home, excited for a living companion to love and who would love me in return.

I carried him into the house and sat him on the kitchen floor. He did not appear to be very active. With a treat in hand, I led him to the front door and tried to show him where to go outside to do his business. Bernie ignored the treat but followed me out.

When we returned to the house, I prepared the crate, arranged the food bowls, filling them with fresh water and organic food. Sitting on the floor, I petted Bernie's back and rubbed behind his ears. I wanted to build a friendship, but he just stayed still. Was he calm? Well-trained? Just tired? Suspicious of his surroundings? Or...?

He put his head on the floor, looked at the bowls of food, and spent the rest of the afternoon almost motionless. Bernie stared at me from two large brown eyes.

"Time for a walk," I finally said aloud. "Let's do this." I lived in a small neighborhood on the top of a steep Wisconsin hill with woods surrounding the house. The road outside my door was relatively flat and easy to walk. I looked forward to taking a dog on a stroll around a half-mile loop. My body needed a good excuse to be outside and exercise.

As I put on my jacket, Bernie slowly walked my way. I attached the lease for our first outdoor adventure. We headed out the door, with him slowly following me as I gently tugged the leash. Step by step, we found our way around the road until I reached the far end. By this time, Bernie panted profusely, drooled at the mouth, and ultimately stopped to lie down on the way. I looked around, hoping my neighbors hadn't noticed. *What had I done?* I wondered.

"Come." I tugged at the lease again. Bernie got up, walked only a few more steps, and then stopped to lie down again. I tried it again. The same thing happened, but this time he rolled on his side and stared at me blankly. I picked him up and walked back home, carrying Bernie in my arms and crying.

When we returned inside, I looked at Bernie with a critical eye. He lay on the floor panting, drooling, with blank stares and a warm nose. I realized Bernie was not an old dog. Instead, he was a very sick dog. He probably needed a lot of care—no wonder the young woman at the humane society said so little about him.

Soon I realized something about myself I hated and felt ashamed to admit aloud. I did not have the energy nor the inner strength to provide the care this poor creature needed. I wanted an animal to love me. I wanted life around me. I wanted a dog to help me get out of bed in the morning, help me exercise as I took him for walks, and to show me affection. I knew this was selfish, but I also knew I could not care for him. This dog needed love and care, and I was not able to give it.

Carefully, I placed Bernie on the floor, next to the water bowl, gently wrapped him within the new blanket. Tears ran down my face as I decided I would take him back to the Humane Society the next day.

During the night, I gathered the will to take Bernie back. I knew what this decision would mean for him. I also decided to give the crate, the food, the blanket, the leash, and all the accessories I bought to the shelter. If I did not have the energy to care for him, I would at least give these as a donation. These gifts would be a gift of contrition for my weakness, appeasement for my guilt.

As I carried Bernie back into the shelter doors, the young woman behind the desk looked surprised. My internal guilt saw the judgment in her face.

"I can't keep him," was all I could say. She asked why I was returning the dog. My response was to shake my head back and forth and gaze downward at the counter as I said, "He's too sick." My eyes filled with tears again. I handed her Bernie, whose frail body was shaking more than yesterday. He was as confused as I was.

After carrying the first-rate collection of goods for a dog into the reception area, I turned my back and left.

Disappointment in myself grew. Repetitive messages of self-doubt and regret filled my head.

I needed to make an attitude adjustment, to change this subjective judgment to an external joy. So, I decided to throw a party with just a few friends to celebrate spring and women. For some reason, I imagined drinking martinis, smoking cigarettes, eating good food, and wearing hats. Yes, hats, more costumes to wear until I knew who I was. *Fake it till you make it*, I thought yet again.

I owned the perfect hat. For a "special gift" at Christmas, Sara created a lovely pillbox covered in crimson feathers in the style of Jackie Kennedy. A single peacock plume rose for the side to swish in the air with abandon. The hat represented a phoenix rising from the ashes—a perfect symbol for this party.

The next week, my daughter Sara, along with Carol, Vicki, and Sue (friends from Hope Church), arrived at my home dressed in hats and feather plumes filled with the expectation of a good time. The five of us spanned the stages of being a woman—maiden, mother, and crone. I was the crone, the elder, not so wise these days but seeking the wisdom and love of women I held dear.

We started the evening by tasting a variety of martinis—dry, cosmos, more gin, less gin, olives, no olives. Each drink smoothed the way for much laughter and opened the conversation and our vulnerable hearts. We talked about our mutual love of Mark and our own journeys of grief and discovery of the past few months.

When I brought out the cigarettes, the conversation shifted to stories of being women and coming of age, smoking, drinking, sexual exploration, self-discovery, regrets, and wisdom learned the hard way.

With cocktail glasses in one hand and cigarettes in the other, we gathered in a tight circle around the coffee table. My daughter and I sat on the floor; Sue, Vicki, and Carol on the couch with feet tucked under their bodies. When the conversation moved from first dates to sexual encounters, my daughter Sara often covered her ears and sang "la-la-la-la" with a grin on her face delighting in the "over-sharing," hilarious laughter, and our mutual bonds as women.

Over the sweetness of chocolate and dessert, I relaxed into the mellow affirmation that I was not alone. Yes, I made mistakes, learned from bad decisions, yet love remained through it all. Friends and family accepted me just as I was, even when I did not love as I wanted. This embodied love through the presence of others filled me with gratitude. Their kindness and support helped me rise from the ashes of doubt and be born into myself yet again.

It was too hard to live through grief alone.

A DECISION

Restless energy and the need for action dynamically shaped my walk with grief. I was grateful for the opportunity to study theological coursework in the spiritual direction program. It created the framework for the internal work I longed to explore. Each week of study took me more deeply into the search for a new direction.

Topics included God and suffering, God within other religions, and God examined through the various paradigms of process theology, liberation theology, Biblical theology, and prayer. My world turned upside down with Mark's death. But the academic study of theology turned my understanding of God upside down as well.

I questioned outdated perceptions and expanded fresh insights. I let go of several simplistic interpretations of God and religion that no longer fit my experience in knowing heartache and suffering.

The study of theology intrigued me with the challenge. Exploring the continued notion of a relationship with God energized me. Several professors and mentors opened my understanding of The Divine into an expansive mystery beyond knowing. My suffering and pain as Mark died invited me to recognize God as All-present Compassion instead of All-powerful and All-knowing Omnipotence. My academic study accelerated the exploration of God and the world. I realized that I knew God through the stories of Jesus. Others knew God through different avenues. The study created a thrill of discovery, and yet, more sadness within continued change. Not only did Mark die, but I was letting go of ideas and beliefs that held stability in my thinking for years. The newness was exciting and disorienting at the same time.

When I returned to read theology and write academic papers so soon after Mark's death, I discovered a challenge in another way. One professor confronted me with direct and harsh criticism, returning my first paper of the semester with bold red marks covering each one of the typed pages. He informed me the writing was, at times, inspirational, but was not theological. He judged my work as simple-minded and told me the piece revealed little depth of thought. He questioned my academic endeavors and pushed me to access my brain instead of my heart, to move from feeling into thinking, to shift from subjective to objective, and to step out of emotion into intellect.

I was shocked. Was it too soon? Had I pushed too quickly? Other professors within the spiritual direction program also encouraged, or should I say, demanded me to slow down. They thought I should act less and contemplate more.

Yet, my soul needed to push ahead to escape the dark shadow chasing me, seeking to engulf me with hopelessness and death.

I had to keep moving. I had to find myself. I had to discover "the next," whatever that meant. Was I in denial? Survival? Resilience? Or God's calling?

As I explored the questions, I affirmed what I knew about myself. Returning to school became the one direction I knew and understood. I loved the intentional search for meaning, for God, a place to do ministry, and the church. I wanted to discover at a pace of my own making within the pursuit of my intensity.

I took on the challenge like a woman combatant fighting her way into a new life. I pushed to conquer grief with a fierce intensity. The battle to leave the old behind and claim the new consumed me. The compulsive efforts to win this fight consumed me. My children grew concerned, watching me push so hard.

To encourage me, my son Brent asked, "Why do you have to fight it? Just enjoy it."

What do you mean "enjoy"? I was not sure how to do that. I did not want to remain stuck in grief, in the malaise. I missed the theological conversations I had with Mark. I missed the musing and our mutual give and take. Attending classes filled the emptiness by providing an anchor within the fog of grief. Yet, the academic study also raised more questions.

Questions. Searching. Unsettled longings. Longing to claim life. Leaving past lives. Rediscovering new importance. Orientation. Disorientation. Reorientation. Was I driven? Or called?

Even through the chaos of grief, I recognized my professional gifts. I was a trusted listener and therapist. I walked alongside others, through painful stories to help them discover resilience and new life. I dared to ride the emotional monsters deep because I knew there was life on the other side. I affirmed this truth as I walked with others. I trusted this for my own walk. During the first years of grief, I rode these painful monsters and trusted the journey to the other side.

Before Mark's death, I returned to graduate school for a certification in spiritual formation to enhance my expertise for my work as a psychotherapist in private practice. After Mark's death, I wanted to be known within the church with a voice of authority, beyond that of being a pastor's wife.

I asked, "How will the institution of the church recognize me?"

This question led me to make another decision. I began the process to become a diaconal minister of the church, consecrated into a call to the church in Word and Service. However, the hierarchy of the church did not recognize diaconal ministry as equivalent to the ordained ministry of Word and Sacrament. To gain as much external authority within this role as I could, I decided to enter the seminary to acquire a Master of Divinity. With this degree, my theological training was equivalent to an ordained pastor. This degree would be in addition to my professional background and training as a psychotherapist and spiritual director. Would it be enough? Would I be enough? Would I be enough for others to see me? For others to see me as more than Mark's wife? Would it be enough to finally accept myself?

Knowing how much I enjoyed learning, acknowledging my professional gifts, affirming my attachments to the church, with the encouragement of friends, I decided to enroll in seminary, but not just any seminary. I took what the professor had told me. I wanted to grow.

I also wanted resources to learn how to speak and lead regarding issues of peace, justice, spiritual formation, and affirm the voice of the marginalized. I needed a school that worked with me as an older adult learner. The educational system needed to acknowledge my professional expertise. I wanted to use credits from the master's study in spiritual direction I had already acquired. And I needed to continue my work in Eau Claire. Luckily, United Theological Seminary of the Twin Cities accepted me and all my needs.

Almost two years after Mark died, I walked forward again.

ANOTHER PILGRIMAGE.
MORE MESSAGES.

She walked alone through a threshold and appeared to be looking at me with a face of strength, determination, and persistence. A large ring, given to her on her wedding day, rested on the index finger of her left hand. This statue of Katharina von Bora, the wife of Martin Luther (a seminal leader of the Protestant Reformation in the early 1500s), stood in the courtyard of the estate of Wittenberg Castle and captured her spirit as she walked into another life.

On this afternoon, on a warm summer day in Wittenberg, Germany, I enjoyed a conversation with her. Or at least I imagined it so.

Soon after I started classes at the seminary, I traveled on another soul pilgrimage with several others to Eastern Germany to explore the roots of Lutheran spirituality. Because of past experiences, I trusted I would hear a message intended for my heart. I opened myself to the surprises and insights that interrupt the way. On this trip, Katharina brought me a message.

I identified with her marriage to a strong man and prophet maligned by the church. I admired her strength, authenticity, voice, intellect, and gifts. Katharina worked alongside Martin Luther through the challenges they faced. She alone managed the castle estate and raised their six children. During robust theological debates at their kitchen table, Katie, as her friends called her, shared her own ideas. She brewed the beer, bottled the wine. Together, she and Martin each offered different gifts, focus, and skills as leaders during the turbulent time of the Protestant Reformation in Europe.

On this afternoon, Katie and I bathed in sunlight. A bird in a nearby tree accompanied our conversation. I sat on a bench close to her statue and drew a picture of Katie in my journal. With each stroke of my pen, I listened carefully to what she might say to me.

"Stay strong," I thought I heard her say. I looked up and stared into her bronzed face. "Stay strong, even if things don't work as you plan. You already have what you need to move forward. Be bold. Keep living. Keep loving. God's love will hold on and not let go."

I looked around me and wondered if others heard her voice too. But I was alone.

I paused to ponder the words and remembered the challenges Katharina Luther faced. As the daughter of impoverished nobility, she became a nun, learned and resourceful. In leaving the monastery during the reformation, Katherina and other nuns risked their lives. Eventually, she married Martin Luther. Katharina knew the struggle of difficult transitions. She knew the grief after the death of her children, the heartache of war, and the betrayal of the church. Katharina mourned her husband's death. And finally, she experienced the loss of this grand estate. As a woman of her time, she was not allowed to own land.

I continued to sketch her body and the movement of her feet and hands when her ring captured my attention. Polished by the hands of people who touched it, believing it would bring happiness to their marriages, the ring shone with a bright luster. I saw the ring as a symbol of Katharina's spirit, worn on the hand that led her bronzed body through a threshold.

I closed my journal and thanked Katharina for a helpful conversation. I walked to the statue and studied her face. I breathed in her spirit and then prayerfully touched the ring. I wanted her energy to bring me peace, happiness, and strength.

As I left, I had an urge to go shopping, to look for a jewelry store in the village square to buy a ring. I wanted a gold ring for my left index finger as a touchstone, a reminder of the promise of life she shared.

I walked down the red brick path into town and spoke the name, Katharina. I recognized how similar the cadence was to the name "Takalani" from the trip to South Africa. Kath-a-rin-a. Tak-a-lan-i. Four beats, four steps, promises of hope, assurance, affirmation, and strength. I walked in step with the rhythm of the names.

But the trip did not end there. I heard about the horrors of war on a visit to the Lutheran Cathedral in Dresden. During the Allied firebombing of the city in World War II, many people in Dresden sought refuge in this cathedral. Tragically, the enemy dropped firebombs into it. The bombs pulled oxygen from the air inside the building when the people opened the church doors and ran to the river for safety. The suction from opening the doors pulled the fire inside the cathedral walls and destroyed the supporting structures and all the treasures held within.

A vivid reminder of the evils of war, the rubble remained as a memorial for fifty years. Yet, after the reunification of Germany in 1994, the city's desire to transform the wreckage into a new cathedral took on a renewed energy.

Piece by piece, volunteers gathered and labeled each stone within the debris, noting where it fell. Using the first builders' blueprints and engineers' study of the destruction, builders put the cathedral back together. Like solving a giant puzzle, the contractors used old stones and created new ones to reconstruct the whole building according to the original plans.

I stood across the street, studying the walls of this resurrected church in awe of its beauty. I examined the integration of the old and the new. I listened to the bells ringing, echoing across the city and marveled at the reclamation.

And then I heard the stones speak, ringing in my soul like the bells in the tower. "Elaine, you will also rebuild, stone by stone, integrating pieces of your life before Mark's death with newly discovered gifts and skills." Resurrection is for the living as well as the dead.

I still missed Mark. I missed holding his hand, his gentle rub on my back and neck, the conversation we had regarding Lutheran theology, grace, God, and resurrection. I longed for his help in discernment.

This trip to Germany boldly pronounced promises of God's abiding presence and gifts of new life. But what did it mean? I missed home, a place with confidence and serenity. I kept looking for clues to the future.

Questions surrounded me. I worried about "now." How do I live now? As I traveled, I wondered about home. Where was home? What was home for me after everything changed?

On each leg of the two-week journey, I packed and re-packed these emotions along with the clothes, books, and journals. I pondered and plodded my way through both hope-filled days and days filled with scattered and confusing thoughts.

Carrying this heavy baggage, I walked onto the grounds of Cistercian Monastery St. Mary's at the Helfta Cloister in Halle. The scent of blooming flowers, the warm embrace of the sisters who live there, and a mystical presence of peace greeted me.

Three women mystics, including Helga the Great, established the abbey in the Middle Ages. Through the centuries, the monastery was built, destroyed, rebuilt, used for grain storage in World War II, and rebuilt again.

Yet, no one tore down this ancient structure's walls. Newness grew within them. These buildings, the sisters, the gardens, the flowers each told the story of resurrection.

I stood motionless when I first saw the crucifix in the chapel. Christ's body hung on the cross with very long arms and giant hands. I gazed at its vast expanse. The arms reached beyond the walls, searching to embrace all outside of itself. I wondered at the wideness of God's mercy and compassion, extending outward for the world to know love, reaching out for me.

After dinner, I walked onto the abbey grounds. On my right, I saw the entrance to a labyrinth. Flowers and plants marked the opening with a winding path to the center. I stepped onto the sandy path with a prayer-filled heart, enticed by the garden's beauty.

I walked with two questions, "Do I stay in Eau Claire or move? Or, do I simply ask for a blessing to experience the grace of God and experience serenity?"

At the first turn, yellow roses greeted me, vibrant in the late afternoon light. I immediately remembered the yellow roses Mark received from my brother the day he came home for hospice care. I received their scent as Mark's presence. Green plants and blossoms continued to accompany me as I walked the path winding back and forth toward the center.

At the labyrinth's center, I entered a cone-shaped hut with walls of woven vines. I sat on the ground, hugged my knees to my chest, and imagined being a seed inside a womb, waiting for a new life, a growing embryo within the safety of its embrace.

I saw my life in Eau Claire and the seeds planted there— seeds of vocation, of community, Mark's love. I said aloud, "I have these seeds within me wherever I go. Nothing can take them away." I breathed deeply, grateful for the comforting presence within the hut.

As I looked through this simple shelter's rounded door, I also heard a voice bidding me to step out. "The confines of the comfortable would not allow you to grow."

With just enough room within this woven harbor to stand, I danced and stretched my arms out wide like the arms of Jesus. I touched the gold ring I now wore on my index finger, and I sang a Celtic hymn:

> *"As you go on your way, may God go with you.*
> *May God go before you to show you the way.*
> *May God go behind you to encourage you,*
> *beside you to befriend you,*
> *above you to watch over,*
> *within you to give you peace."*

I touched the sides to the woven cone hut one last time and walked out, blessed for the mystical sense of God's presence and the knowledge that it was time to go, both to exit the labyrinth and to get on with my life.

As I boarded the plane to fly home, I wondered at the insights of travel. I discovered wisdom within history. I saw flowers growing among the ruins. I realized the present is often revealed within the past. The past informed the present. Wonder abided within fear. I was alone in the crowd yet loved within the loneliness. Warmth abided in the barren and calm within the hustle.

I found life in the ruins. It was time to build the new.

ANOTHER STEP

Mark and I wanted to grow old together in our home on the top of a wooded hill on the street called Freedom Drive. The house fit us well. We each mused within our own study. We enjoyed the large, open rooms to provide hospitality for others. The angled walls and central fireplace created a character of warmth and invitation. We loved the expansive views overlooking the woods through the floor-to-ceiling windows on both floors.

For six years, we observed the change of seasons in the woods around us. Deer slept in the backyard and gazed in the windows. Wild turkeys strutted by the azalea plants. The call of birds sparkled into the sounds of rustling leaves.

This home created safety, provided nourishment to be rooted, and offered hope as we wondered about our future lives and past struggles.

Here, we cared for Bette, Mark's mom, as she died. Here, we loved. Here, we wrote. Here we claimed our life as "empty nesters," making love on the living room floor. It was here we continued the journey to be a couple again, learning from our growth and learning from each other. We wanted to integrate our individual stories into a unified whole. I was learning to be less critical. Mark was learning to be more present to me.

Here was the beginning of yet another chapter of our lives, building on a thirty-year history for the long haul ahead. Here we embodied the actions of love within the consistent tending of the daily interactions, of touch, smiles, kind words, mutual sharing, and respect of space. Here we lived the gift and grace of being separate, together.

And here, in this home, Mark died.

One evening as I returned from the commute from the cities, I walked into the house, and I realized it no longer fit me. The thought stunned me. I loved this place. I loved the ways this house fit with my life at one time, like a dress that made me feel beautiful. This house blessed my life with beauty, our experiences with beauty. But like a lovely dress folded in a box in a storeroom because it was too small, this house no longer fit me either. I grew too small. I wallowed within its folds and sank within its walls.

All the work to take care of the house and the yard also exhausted me. During the first winter, I knew the pride of running the snowblower. I remembered walking into the garage after the first big snowstorm after Mark died, bundled in warm clothes, a scarf tied around my neck, and a hat pulled over my ears, looking at the large snowblower. I was excited to prove I had enough strength to handle that machine. I was woman enough to run it by myself. I pulled the cord, and it started immediately. The challenge began. I powered through the first three-foot drift, then pushed into the thick pile of snow at the end of the drive, doubled in size by the snowplow. Empowered, I finished the long driveway and conquered front sidewalks with the fierce fight of my inner warrior.

However, by winter's end, the satisfaction of success was not enough to encourage me through another winter.

"Yes, I can do it," I said proudly, but I had no desire to try.

The burden of the house seemed too heavy, along with the weight of the clutter inside. It was not messy. Instead, the accumulation of stuff weighed on me. I longed to live more simply, to own less, to live with a smaller footprint in the universe. All this stuff built a wall around me, keeping me apart from something more, something else, something in the future. It kept me apart from the freedom of a new life. It was too much.

My life in Eau Claire did not fit either once I changed my church home. When I moved my counseling practice from the office at Hope Church, I lost contact with friends. Since I did not worship at the church, I no longer saw Pastor Skatrud, Sue, Tom, Vicki, or Carol regularly. I traveled back and forth to the Twin Cities for school and had less time to affirm the relationships in Eau Claire. Loneliness echoed within the house's rooms and the space of my own heart.

I met new people in my classes in the Twin Cities, and I liked the larger city's energy. The 90-mile commute seemed longer with each drive. I wanted to linger longer after class and stay to meet a friend for coffee. I enjoyed the coursework and thinking about new ideas. I was less energized by the counseling work and grew more intrigued by spirituality studies. I sensed a pull to move forward.

Each of these realizations became a symbolic contraction in the birthing of new life. With each pull inward, each unique insight, with each turn of events, my heart and mind gained energy to make the next decision. Many avenues of my past life closed; more possibilities of a future life opened.

This house no longer fit me. My old life did not fit here either. It was time to move.

A NEW COMPANION

I made two decisions. One: I would look for a place to live in the Twin Cities and sell the home on Freedom Drive. And Two: I wanted a dog—a healthy dog.

An ad in the local paper described "Barkley" as a middle-aged dog needing a new home because his parents were moving. When I called the telephone number, the woman clearly stated she needed to evaluate the next owner in person and see the home where the dog would live. The new home needed to be perfect for this dog they loved.

As the owner arrived at my house, she carried Barkley like a baby in a quilted blanket. A three-year-old boy ran behind her, trying to keep up with her determined walk. She smiled lovingly at Barkley in the blanket. But she scowled at her young son.

This mom spent an hour in my living room. She sat on the blanket, gently petting Barkley as her three-year-old wildly explored every corner. Her scolding voice interrupted each time his hands reached toward something new. As I tried to pet Barkley and get to know him, I watched the uncomfortable juxtaposition between the woman showering kindness on a dog and pouring criticism on the child. As a licensed therapist, I wondered who needed to interview whom about a loving home.

I explained who I was and why I wanted a dog for companionship and longed for the presence of healthy life to accompany me throughout the day. I passed her test, and she agreed to let me have Barkley.

As she exited the house, she hugged the dog wrapped in the blanket one last time and then harshly took her young child's arm. As I watched them walk down the sidewalk and climb into their car, I thought of Bernie. Perhaps I had made the right decision not to care for an elderly ill dog at one point in my life. I wondered if I would have been crabby with resentment of caring for a living being I did not want? As cranky as this mom with her young son? I shut the door and gave Barkley an extra loving scratch behind his ears.

Barkley and I became quick companions. Barkley loved to sit on the back of the couch, looking out the front windows. He barked at the mail carrier delivering mail and at the squirrels scampering up one of the trees in my yard. Usually, he was very mellow, affirming his nature as a Tibetan Terrier, mimicking the peaceful stance of a Buddhist monk, the mail carrier, and the squirrels being the primary exceptions. We walked the neighbor-hood at least twice a day, circling the block with no need to stop to rest, only to smell and mark each new (and old) patch of earth to make the route his territory.

His grey-haired body was soft to the touch. His dark black eyes peeked through a furry face and calmed my more than occasionally anxious spirit. He walked with a quick gait and a little hop from a back leg, which my daughter-in-law Connie described as a "gip in his get-along."

Barkley cuddled at my feet or curled up next to my body. He provided warmth and care. Many friends told me his spirit reminded them of Mark. I am not sure if Barkley was this spirit presence, but I appreciated his loving and calm nature and the loving look from his dark eyes. Yet again, the company of life around me pulled me back into life as well.

NOW IS THE TIME

After I resolved to move, several more months passed for the process to complete itself. Each day pushed into the next. I continued to study spiritual direction in St. Paul and theology at the seminary in New Brighton. The routine of commuting to school, meeting clients at the new therapy office, and building relationships with classmates in the Twin Cities interacted with downsizing and sorting boxes and books, giving away books and furniture, and sorting more books.

I do not remember any particularities about my life during those months. The specifics became lost in the fog of daily maintenance and the menacing presence of anxiety—the current manifestation of my grief. When panic increased within my body, when my heart beat fast, when I had trouble catching a breath, when tightness grew within my belly, another grief story emerged. Another painful surge of mourning hit me hard.

I missed sitting on the couch with my feet in Mark's lap, talking about the book he finished. I missed the sound of baseball games and golf tournaments on the TV in the family room. I missed the sound of crunching potato chips, even though eating sounds drive me crazy. I missed the smell of the fresh coffee in the morning he made before he went into his study to write.

I experienced a hollow heaviness around my heart. The weight contained a brew of entangled thoughts—a longing for clarity of a future life; a weariness of work, an excitement about something new; the fear of letting go; the hunger for companionship; leaving the past; the discovery of new friends and the absence of intimate love. These burdens echoed into all the losses, creating a restless unease. Anxiety and grief were linked tightly within my chest, one with the other.

Time moved on.

The time proceeded from fall to winter, winter to spring, and spring to summer with the exciting news that Brent and Connie decided to marry. Connie received a full scholarship to the doctoral program at Syracuse University in New York. They planned to move there for her studies. So, they decided to hold a simple wedding at the Minnesota lake home—a holy and humble place filled with family memories and Mark's ashes buried nearby.

Blue skies created a day of joy for their wedding. Brent and Connie hosted games of whiffle ball, pie making, cold beer, and much laughter. The day focused on community connection and the loving bond that held their family and friends together under the understood banner of "have more fun." Brent and Connie knew how to have fun and how to help others have fun too. With them, "Olson Happened."

Mark's brother Rich began at dawn to prepare a gourmet feast with the help of my brothers and other friends. Chairs surrounded a simple table in the backyard under the shade of the oak trees.

And surprises interrupted our well-defined plans. The sewer system backed up with many people at the house using only two bathrooms. My sister-in-law, wishing for a perfect day, worried if the pies Brent's friends prepared in the cabin's kitchen would not be done in time for the celebration. John Ylvisaker found a golf ball at the lakeshore, which he saw as a spiritual gift from Mark. Barkley, usually quite mellow, joined a game of whiffle ball, barking and chasing the ball.

The guests eagerly consumed wine and beer. Connie's four grandparents were divorced and remarried four others. Yet they arrived together and sat at the table for the afternoon, affirming each other's company. Brent's friends from the ultimate frisbee team played a game in the neighbor's yard. A vase placed on a nearby tree stump held roses to remember the lives of Mark, a close friend of Brent and Connie, and Brent's grandparents.

As the hour of the ceremony drew near, we scattered to change our clothes for the celebration. Connie slipped into a dress Sara made for her. Brent showered under the cold spray of the outdoor water hose.

We gathered in chairs placed in rows on the lawn overlooking the lake to witness the vows. To the sound of rhythmic drums, Connie walked in with her parents. I walked with Brent, holding onto his strength and love. Mark's best friend Red presided over the simple ceremony. A call of a loon announced Mark's spirit. Birds gathered in the nearby trees with joyous sounds affirming and blessing Brent and Connie's day.

Time kept moving. Sara planned to live in Moscow for a year as part of her training to be a pastor. I continued to study. Time moved forward. On the very day of orientation at the seminary, I received an offer on my house on Freedom Drive.

It was now time to move.

I found an apartment in St. Paul. Built-in the early 1900s, it had high ceilings, dark woodwork, built-in cupboards in the dining room, and the character of being well established. I loved it. The size and simplicity fit my needs. It was the upper of a duplex one block away from Grand Avenue in a neighborhood made for walking. I saw neighbors sitting on their front porches. Coffee shops, bakeries, and shops were only blocks away.

Along with the anxiety of grief, I hurried to get stuff done. With Sara away at Seminary and Brent and Connie in New York, I pushed to pack all the household belongings on my own.

I gave hundreds of Mark's books to the local library. Yet, more than fifty boxes remained. All were a "must keep." A second "must keep" were the multiple pieces of art Mark and I had acquired over the years. Each piece of art told a story about our lives, our travels, and our beliefs.

Box after box, dish after dish, one memory, and then another became wrapped in paper and packed in boxes. I gave away many things, yet the core of those things close to my heart grew much more extensive in importance than I had initially anticipated.

I worked alone, driven by a radical independent survival brain day after day and into the night. Sorting. Packing. Dumping. Crying. Sorting more. Packing each box. I pushed through—a grasp of anxious tunnel vision held onto me. I frantically worked alone. I lost sight of the importance of asking for help. I forgot about a supportive network of friends nearby.

On the morning of the move, two men and their namesake truck arrived to load and move my belongings to St. Paul. The frantic pace of packing, the grief of moving to a new home, and little sleep exhausted me. Standing in the middle of the kitchen surrounded by my KitchenAid mixer, electric griddle, slow cooker, coffee maker, and all the pots and pans from the kitchen cupboards and a few more large pieces of art laying on the floor in the living room, I wept. I ran out of boxes and energy. I hit the wall of yet another ending.

The doorbell rang, and two burly men eagerly walked into my house through the unlocked door, filled with smiles and vital energy.

Excited to get to work, they casually asked, "Are you ready?"

They were unprepared for a crazed, tired, angry widow ready to explode, "Does it look like I'm ready? Look at all this stuff, and I have no boxes," I shouted into their faces.

I was surprised and embarrassed by my explosive reaction. But it is too late to pull pack my emotional outburst, and I broke down sobbing. The two men slowly backed through the door, heading for the truck to make a quick phone call.

"We'll get the boss," they said meekly.

Within minutes, a tall man with gentle eyes, wearing a baseball cap, grey t-shirt, and jeans calmly walked into the house. He carried several flattened cardboard boxes.

"Let me help," he said as he joined me in the kitchen. After shaping and taping the first box, he placed a pan, then a pot, and then another saucepan into it. He listened as I explained my tears and the saga of the day sitting helplessly on the floor beside him, leaning against the stove.

I am not sure how many crazy women he'd helped move, but he was an expert in calming my frantic pace. Perhaps it was part of the required training a mover received. Or not. But he was kind. And I was grateful.

I then realized I should have asked for help long before this.

The movers secured the final box and drove away. But I attended one last and important task. An empty glass jar hand-blown with an artistic flair and stylized lid sat on the kitchen counter.

I picked it up, took off the lid, and held it gently with both hands. Swooping the jar back and forth, I walked from room to room and remembered stories, conversations, and events. I breathed in the air and gathered its essence into the vessel. I captured a few molecules, particles of breath, cellular remains of Mark's presence to bring with me as I established a new home.

I walked through the entire house and repeated the same ritual in each room—bedroom, study, kitchen, bath. I placed the lid onto the jar, tightly securing its precious ether with a prayer of blessing.

I would carry the jar with me to St. Paul. Imperceptible bits of Mark's presence remained with me.

It was now time to go.

Part Three: The In-between

Someone once asked me,
"Why do you always insist on taking the hard road?"

I replied,
"Why do you assume I see two roads?"

~Author unknown

MOVING LESSON # 1: ASK FOR HELP

After leaving the house in Eau Claire, the moving truck arrived at the St. Paul upper, the top floor of a duplex, late the same afternoon. The leaves on the tree-lined streets were beginning to shift from late summer green to early fall yellow. A few people in the neighborhood walked their dogs along the sidewalk.

Barkley sat at the window, barking his greeting of hello to the people below. Wearily, I sat with him, too tired to do much of anything. I tried to extend a gentle wave to people who noticed as they passed by on the sidewalk. I lifted a finger to point in a direction within the apartment, telling the movers where to place a box.

The glass jar filled with Mark's essence sat nearby. I was not ready to release its contents.

I was exhausted. I should have asked for help both to pack and now to unpack. My profoundly ingrained survival skills returned. The words, "I can do it mine-self," echoed in my brain.

I think these words were the first sentence I ever learned to speak. I always seemed to take the road of doing things myself and never asking for help. I was too anxious, too overwhelmed, or too afraid to ask for help.

Why?

Over my lifetime, I learned a few things about this pattern. First, I was the only girl and youngest in a family of hard-working Germans. As a child, I survived alone. My dad owned a feed mill. The demands of work, teaching at church, and volunteering at the local fire department captured most of his time. Hard work was the family rule. My mom often rested on the couch, unable to function from yet another attack of asthma or emotional despair. She pushed herself to teach Bible studies, play organ, or volunteer at church. My eldest brother Larry helped our dad in the feed mill until he found a job working at a lumber yard when he was a junior in high school. After graduation, he quickly left for college. By participating in sports, my middle sibling Rich escaped the chaos at home and Mom's demands for help. Her words of judgment pierced him deeply.

Secondly, when I was little, we lived in a two-bedroom home on the edge of town across from the railroad tracks. Some would say the wrong side of the tracks. Until fourth grade, I slept in my parents' room. My brothers shared the second bedroom. My grandpa, Dad's dad, slept on the couch. Pretending my bed was a room within itself, I pulled an invisible wall around me for privacy. I slept under the comfort of a flannel-lined, woolen patchwork quilt. Within these self-imposed walls, I survived.

I grew up feeling alone. With the usual childhood explorations of inclusion and exclusion, I remember being the outsider most often. On a warm summer day, a boy in the neighborhood hit me on the side of the head with a thick board. I had no idea why. It hurt—more in my heart than my head. I also remembered looking across my yard at the words, "Elaine Keep Out," written with a black crayon on the walls of the refrigerator box fort. Here was another reason to claim my independence.

As a child, the reality of rejection surrounded me at home too. Some misunderstanding between my dad and his family led to a protracted dispute regarding land and money. A bitter battle exploded as all sides of Dad's family hired lawyers. With several court dates, the other siblings tried to question my grandpa's mental competency. My dad's family connection shattered. After Grandpa left a fifty-year marriage, Dad stuck with him. The other siblings stayed with Grandma. My mother's sister was married to my dad's brother, adding to my mother's pain.

I am quite sure my dad's temper and stubborn attitudes fed the disputes. I never understood the family feud. Most of it occurred before I was born. But I remained affected by the bitterness. Sadly, my dad's mom never held me in her arms.

My parents also faced the judgment of our local pastor, who refused to give them communion because of the disputes. The pastor quoted Matthew 5:23-28, "So when you are offering your gift at the altar, if you remember that your brother or sister has something against you, leave your gift there before the altar and go; first, be reconciled to your brother or sister, and then come and offer your gift."

The rejections were very real. Throughout my life, I tried not to get too close to people, fearing their rejection and judgment. If I kept them happy, I would be safe. An invisible wall protected me from others, as I often kept my distance. Mark was the one person I allowed within my wall. With him, I was willing to be vulnerable.

But Mark was dead. To survive, I rebuilt this protective barrier called "I can do it mine-self." During this process of moving, the old pattern returned to haunt me. *Will I ever learn?* I wondered as I sat, exhausted.

At the end of moving day, I made the bed and grabbed a bite to eat. After finding Barkley's leash on top of an open box, we set out on our first walk in the new neighborhood. The evening sky darkened as the breeze carried an autumn chill. Along the sidewalk, Barkley stopped at every tree, marking his new territory. He helped to slow my pace. I took the time to become familiar with my new neighborhood.

As I returned, I reached in my jacket pocket for my house keys. I pulled out Kleenex, a shopping list, and a plastic bag, but no keys. I tried my jean pockets. Empty. I searched for a second time. Nothing more. I realized I had left my keys inside on the dining room table and my cellphone on the couch. The apartment door locked tight. I had no way to get in. My property owner, who lived in the apartment on the duplex's first floor, left town after the truck arrived. I did not even know her number.

Damn. The aloneness grew large. "Mine-self" was no longer a survival skill. It was a threat.

I walked around the block, trying to figure out what to do and thankful for the tissues I had crammed into my pockets. My tears matched the growing fear. What would I do? I didn't know anyone in the neighborhood. Who could I trust? Will the neighbors shout, "Keep out!" or grab a board to hit me as I knocked on the door? The night sky grew darker. The streetlights turned on. Barkley slowed down and walked close beside me as the wind blew colder. Was he afraid too?

I circled the block, trying to figure out which house would offer refuge, wondering who might help. Cautiously, I stopped in front of the house next door to my upper. Luckily, the front curtains were open. I saw a man and woman inside holding glasses of wine as they turned on their TV.

"They look friendly enough," I said aloud to myself. I wiped the tears from my face. I had to trust someone. I took a deep breath and put on the company face I'd learned from my mom. Even though the porch light was not on, I rang the doorbell. I put on a mask of confidence and an internal protective shield.

The light quickly flipped on. Within its dim glow, the man opened the door and looked at me. Thankfully, he smiled. I smiled back.

"Hi. My name's Elaine," I said. "I just moved in next door." I gestured with my hand toward my house. "I locked myself out of my house. Can you help me?"

He took a step back and introduced himself and then his wife. Thankfully, they graciously invited Barkley and me into their home.

They helped me think and explore my options.

"Is there a key hidden under flowerpots or the doormat?"

"No, I don't think so."

Laughing, we imagined breaking down the front door. Then, the man pulled out the phone book. We scoured the yellow pages for a 24-hour locksmith. I used their phone to call for the truck to come. The kind neighbors offered me a glass of wine while I waited. Parts of my wall of fear broke apart within the kindness they shared.

Within a few hours in my new home, I learned an important truth. Perhaps, it was the same one I was trying to learn throughout a lifetime. It is okay to ask for help.

MOVING LESSON # 2: GROW FRIENDSHIPS

Warm spring breezes filled the apartment's sunroom with the sweet aroma of my neighbor's blossoming tree. I opened the windows to breathe in the newness. On an old trunk I used as a coffee table sat two wine glasses, a bottle of cabernet, a plate of smoked gouda, and fresh fruit. I eagerly awaited Anne's arrival for yet another evening of good food and even better conversation.

Anne and I were both students at the seminary. Within our first brief encounters, I sensed a woman of kindred spirits. Anne stood tall, brown hair around her head, eyes of intellect with goodness, and a heart open to the journey to self-discovery. She engaged others with the same intense spirit she immersed with herself. Not only did Anne know how to fly a plane, but she fixed its engine. She mused with a sense of adventure about Spirit, hope, and transformation. We met within the first days of seminary, but our friendship deepened after a class assignment.

Anne and I both registered for a required integrative studies class. Co-facilitated by several faculty from the school, the course focused on community development. We read articles and engaged in activities exploring how to integrate communities, create conversation among its members, and work together for community transformation.

Rooted within Christian teachings of justice and compassion, the class challenged us to move from words to action. Several activities pushed the class members and me to step outside of ourselves and be vulnerable.

When I enrolled in seminary, I wanted to find ways to engage in progressive Christian values. I wanted to practice what I longed to preach. This class was one example.

The professors teaching this course modeled the way. One professor was from the United Church of Christ in the Philippines and taught Constructive Theology. The other was a woman with a background in education and organizational leadership. Both led educational and immersion trips to Chiapas, Mexico, or the Philippine Islands. Both were bold in their teaching and kind in their challenging.

In one of the first classes, we received a 5"x7" blue card. In the left column, we wrote two to three gifts or skills we were willing to offer to help someone within the class. Perhaps we could rake their yard, help wash windows, or offer help to watch their children.

In the column on the right side of the card, we listed something for which we needed help. Perhaps we needed help to clean a cluttered apartment, needed a ride to class, or had the desire to learn how to use Excel on a computer.

All of us, all twenty students, sat at tables, thoughtful as we carefully considered our needs and our skills.

On the right side of the card, I wrote I wanted to make new friends as I recently moved. On the left side, I wrote, "I like to cook healthy meals and provide hospitality." When the entire class finished writing, the professor asked one of the students to read from her card.

"What is one thing you need help with?" one professor asked.

A student I will call Jane stood, walked to the front of the room, and read from her card, "I need help washing windows for my little house." We looked around the room as Kathy raised her hand and said, "I can help you wash windows." Kathy walked to stand beside Jane.

The conversation continued as Kathy read, "I need help with childcare one night a week."

"I can do that," pipped up Joy, who sat in the back row. Joy stood beside Kathy as they found a connection with each other. They both were raising small children as single parents.

And so, it continued. Joy needed help with her computer, so Tom volunteered to help her. He needed help to use the bus system. Anne stood by Tom because she used the bus as her primary mode of transportation.

And then Anne read from the left side of her card, "I am single and find it hard to eat nutritious meals." It was then I raised my hand. "I can do that, Anne. I like to cook and provide hospitality."

Standing beside Anne in this growing line of connection, it was my turn to speak into my vulnerability. Taking a breath, I said, "I recently moved to St. Paul and would like to meet new friends." Looking around the room, I watched Mickey as she walked forward and stood beside me. She offered the gift of gregarious friendliness. She wanted to help me connect with others.

The process continued until each person in the room stood beside one another, matching the needs of one with the gifts of another, creating a full circle around the room, with no one left out. With this simple dramatization, I quickly learned what should have been obvious—the integration of people's needs and skills build community quickly and easily.

My friendship with Anne grew stronger as we shared many glasses of wine and conversations with the sweet taste of heartfelt reflection. My circle of friends at the seminary also grew. Wine for two grew into dinner for three and then potlucks of shared food and interactive storytelling, laughter, and meeting for Chipotle between classes.

I learned my vulnerability led to connection instead of isolation. I had gifts to share. But my weaknesses invited the goodness of others to join me. Their exposure called forth my goodness to join them.

The motto for my counseling practice became my goal for living: "Some things in life are too hard to do alone."

MOVING LESSON # 3: BLOOD IS THICK, ESPECIALLY WITH COUSINS

"Hello, Elaine," the voice on the other side of the phone spoke kindly. "I'm your cousin John Bringewatt. I talked to your brother this afternoon and heard you moved to St. Paul. Welcome."

John and I met through my brother Rich several years earlier. Rich lived in St. Paul before he moved to Washington, D.C. He and our cousin John found each other through mutual friends who worked in social work. This person linked them together because of the unusual last name, "Bringewatt."

Whenever I heard my birth name, "Bringewatt," spoken, I paid particular attention. This German name is unique. So, when I found someone with this same name, I believed he or she must be a relative.

The three of us—John, Rich, and I—spent hours trying to discern how we were related to each other. The disconnections through the generations of the Bringewatt family defined our history. We thought our grandparents were brothers. We must have been second or third cousins. Or second cousins once removed.

Or...? A shared last name and a genetic link were all we needed to assure the foundation for a mutual friendship.

To reconnect, we met for a couple of hours, talking at a coffee and chocolate shop on Grand Avenue in St. Paul. We soon realized we shared much in common, including 1) a longing to connect with family, 2) a profession of social work, 3) a love of dogs, 4) a mutual sense of humor, 5) our bold German noses, and 6) grief-filled hearts. John's long-term partner, Sinni, had recently died of cancer.

Soon after this first meeting, John invited me to join him and others to be part of a small Christian community group. Sinni was one of the founders. Within their circle of connection, John experienced mutual commitment, friendship, and laughter. Now this small group shared a story of grief.

John graciously asked, "Would you join us on Friday night for wine and dinner?"

The next Friday evening, John came by to take me to the gathering at Pete and Jane's home. As I walked in the door, extending my hand, Pete pulled me toward him with a giant hug.

"Hi, I'm Pete. I'm so glad you can join us." Beside him, Jane beamed in a smile of welcome.

After saying her name, Jane also wrapped her arms around me with a warm hug. Tom and Katie walked into the kitchen, wine glasses in one hand, an open embrace in the other. Tom and Pete worked together at a progressive Catholic Church in Minneapolis. Together with Sinni, they formed this group for thoughtful reflection and active engagement as Christians seeking justice and change.

The small galley kitchen in this upper Minneapolis duplex grew crowded. Mary, Joe, and Ann joined us, each one holding a wine glass, smiling broadly, extending a greeting of hello with a hug, smile, and words of welcome and questions to know me better.

"John told us so much about you."

"Glad you could join us."

"Sorry to hear about Mark."

"How do you like Minnesota?"

"What are you studying?"

Warmth radiated from these people's hearts as they listened with intention. They laughed with bold confidence. They embodied gracious and generous hospitality.

Pete invited us into the living room for prayer. Even with all the kindness I had just experienced, I entered the room with caution. I did not appreciate loud-in-your-face-praising-Father-God prayer.

But this was very different. Pete invited us to find a comfortable place to sit or lie down—on the floor or in a chair for quiet. After placing a lit candle on a side table, he played a CD of meditative flute melodies. We each remained silent, breathing into the calm of the evening and the community of others—still, reflecting, meditating within our thoughts. After 20 minutes, Pete invited us to bring our attention to the immediacy of the room, turned off the CD and said, "Amen." I felt refreshed after the non-invasive, yet mutual, time of prayer.

He then invited us all to the table for dinner. A vase of fresh flowers centered the table filled with steaming vegetarian lasagna smothered in melting cheese, a handwoven basket of warmed home-made bread, and fresh greens mixed with cucumbers, tomato, and olives dripping with olive oil, vinegar, and garlic. Pete opened two more bottles of wine—one white and the other red.

"Which would you like?" he asked, looking at my empty glass.

After passing the food to each other and filling our plates with more than enough to eat, Pete said, "Let's check in." He looked at me to explain, "When it is your turn, light the small candle that sits by your plate and tell us about your day, week, or whatever is on your mind. It can be joys or concerns or frustrations. This is the time to learn more about each other."

Pete asked John to begin to allow time for me to think and observe the process. John took a deep breath, wiped his hands with the napkin, and lit the small candle with the matches that Pete passed to him. After a bit of silence from the people at the table, tears ran down John's face.

"I miss Sinni," he said. "I miss her laughter." John went on to describe the conversation he had with Sinni's daughter during the past week. The people at the table ate quietly but listened intently. Tom and Joe wiped tears from their eyes, and others nodded in acknowledgment of John's hurting heart. Their intensive listening revealed respect. The attention extended care.

When John finished, he passed the matches to the person beside him. Each, in turn, lit the small candle and then shared a story about their life, the painful parts, and the joyous events. I heard about the pain of recent divorces, the difficulty of working within a parish, and the joys and sorrows of being a grandparent.

Because I had observed the respect and dignity offered to each of the people at the table, I was comfortable talking when it was my turn.

After I lit the candle, I said, "Mark, my husband of thirty years died." I then rambled on for several minutes describing my relationship with Mark, my moving from Eau Claire to St. Paul, and attending seminary. The common thread on this night was grief. Each of us mourned the recent death of someone we loved—a husband, a partner, a mother, a marriage.

I ended my time of sharing by raising my glass of wine. Looking straight at my cousin John, I said, "Thanks, John. Thanks for inviting me to join all of you. I think I have found a place to belong."

The dinner conversation grew louder within the spirit of shared stories, wine, trust. We ended the meal with ice cream. Eating sweet desserts was part of the ritual for the evening as well. The meal always ended with ice cream.

I came to rely on the comfort of our mutual worldviews. I grew as we challenged each other to move out of our comfortable inactivity. We discussed the books we read, served meals at a homeless shelter, and debated political points of view. We drank more wine and ate more ice cream.

After John drove me home after the first meeting, I walked into my apartment and sat down within the subdued light of the streetlamp, quietly illumining a darkened living room. Barkley jumped into my lap. My brain was buzzing. My heart was filled with gratitude for good wine, newfound friends, and my cousin John.

Blood connection mattered, too, especially as it led to others.

COMPLETING A BROKEN CIRCLE

As a large man, both in size and presence, Mark read a lot, ate a lot, lived with a lot of optimism, dreamed a lot of big ideas, and even carried a briefcase with a lot of books wherever he went. When my late husband entered a room, the focus turned to him. I often found myself trying to move around him, emotionally and literally. After his death, I was still trying to move around him.

In our marriage, I adapted, forming myself to fit into him, his work, his dreams, his values, claiming them as my own. I became part of him—two circles overlapping in shared experiences, behaviors, and beliefs. When he died, I became incomplete, less than half a circle with an open gap seeking fulfillment, longing to rediscover those parts I left behind thirty years ago. What would fit into this broken circle to become whole?

Part of the search included looking backward into my history. Who was I as a child? An adolescent? As a young woman? What were my passions? My dreams? Who were my friends? What did I do? It was time for a bit of research.

Digging through some boxes stored in the basement of the upper, I found a blue plastic tub marked "Childhood." I sat on the couch with Barkley at my feet and a cup of tea on the trunk. I lifted the lid. A professional black-and-white photograph of my brothers and me lay on top. I was about three years old, sitting on a small chair with chubby legs and arms, curly hair, and a broad smile on my face, holding a stuffed animal in one hand. My brother Richard, dressed in a suit, maybe seven or eight, was standing with one hand on his hip, looking down at me adoringly. My eldest brother Larry, 11 or 12, stood on the other side looking ahead yet with his hand on the back of my chair. I was the only daughter, the youngest, and an adored sister.

I picked up another black-and-white photo with a serrated edge, pulled from a photobook developed by Kodak in the 1950s. I was four, sitting barefoot on a cement porch, holding a calico cat. My bare legs peeked from under a plaid dress. A smile and soft curls created an image of a happy child. I locked this realization into my research.

I knew joy.

Next was a photo of my family—Mom, Dad, my two brothers, and me—taken at a neighbor's home. Their small house was across the street at the end of our quarter-mile drive. My brothers played with the two girls who lived there. I remembered playing on their front porch under a large tree, crying when my leg became stuck in the railing.

Pete, the dad, came to my aid, saying, "You'll be okay, '6-12.'" He called me this because it was the name of the mosquito repellant my mother slathered on my body. As a child, bugs regularly attacked me, and the welts they caused grew half-dollar size. Mom treated bites with Absorbine. So, in the summer, I carried scents of strange perfumes.

For the photo, I must not have smelled too severely as my family sat close to each other on the couch. On the left side, my dad sat with a contagious smile on his face and a mischievous look in his eye. He leaned forward with his arms loosely embracing me. I was about four years old, standing in a buttoned, flannel shirt cradled within his arms. Mom sat beside him on his left. Her eyes were downcast with no smile; her arms wrapped tightly around her thin body as if holding herself together. Richard sat to her left, straight-backed, directly looking into the camera with no smile, folded hands in his lap. Larry, on the far side of the couch, stared straight ahead, now near adolescence as if looking forward to moving on.

Staring into this little girl's eyes, I saw a child adored by a father and a mom who was very afraid, fragile, floundering. This one photograph revealed my father's admiration and the depression and anxiety my mom managed for years.

I realized the weight of keeping my mother happy. When I was thirteen, Rich and I were playing ping pong in the basement. I wore my favorite yellow pants with a flower top, dressed in a perfect 1960s outfit. I felt smart and pretty. Playing a game with my cute, older brother was a big deal for a teenage girl. We were laughing as I just returned a hit with a spike of the ball that bounded in Rich's face. Mom came down the steps.

When she saw us playing, her first words were, "Elaine, I need your help upstairs." In a typical sassy reaction of an adolescent, I ignored her and picked up a ping pong ball and my paddle. Mom moved to the side of the ping pong table and looked at me again. With scolding eyes and a sharp tongue, she said, "Now! I need you now."

"No," I yelled back. "I want to play with my brother."

Mom started to yell at me. "How dare you mouth back!" Crying out of control, she fell to the floor, curled up in a fetal position, and began to rip her dress from the neck to the waist. I was shocked. I knew Mom was having a tough day, being more nervous and anxious than usual, but something broke inside her. I had seen her collapse at other times, but this was the first time my actions and words caused her to fall apart. My brother and I ended the game, carried Mom upstairs, and put her into bed, where she stayed for several days. We never called the doctor when Mom fell apart. We hid this from others and ourselves because of the shame of mental illness in our small town.

For much of my life, I believed my smart mouth wounded her in some way. Something broke inside me when Mom broke. I thought, mistakenly, that my assertive voice was the cause of Mom's emotional breakdown. The image in my head was that my boldness could injure another, wound them to the point of falling apart. This belief stopped me from claiming my voice and interfered in the leadership roles. I needed to keep people happy. If I challenged them, they might fall apart. I had power, and power hurt others.

I also wondered in my adult life whether my mom ever looked at me with adoring eyes the way my dad had. I remembered a picture that I had placed in another photo album of my children and my parents. The colors faded within the dated image. But within a white-edged border, the photo showed my daughter Sara lying on a blanket crocheted by my mom, who was sitting on the floor looking at Sara's face with an adoring smile. Sara appeared to be giggling in delight. If Mom could look at my children with such warmth and love, it indeed was there for me too.

I noticed a smaller box within the blue tub marked "grade school" in the bold writing of a child's hand. I opened it carefully, curious. On the top was a yellowed newspaper clipping reporting the honorable mention I received for a poetry contest in grade school. I had forgotten how much I liked to write. I wrote poetry in high school and college. Yet, I abandoned it when I married Mark. He was a good writer. In bold assertions to help me, he gave negative critiques of my attempts. But these comments hurt and silenced me. This criticism stopped my efforts to write, though I do not believe Mark intended this to be the result. In this way, I lost another part of my voice.

Even though I wrote pages and pages in journals over the years, I never considered it "writing." I did not believe my writing was good enough for anything other than my musings. Maybe, just maybe, I was good enough. Maybe, just maybe, I could write—good enough.

Next, I pulled a long string of wooden beads, varied in color and shape from the box—honor beads from Campfire Girls. Each bead represented an accomplishment in some area of service. "WOHELO" was the word standing for Work, Health, Love. I began singing the song as I remembered from 45 years earlier:

"Worship God. Hmm.
Seek beauty, give service,
and knowledge pursue.
Be trustworthy ever in all you do.
Hold fast onto health, and your work glorify.
And you will be happy in the law of campfire. "

I loved Campfire Girls. I loved the experiences and the process of earning beads. As I held a brown bead, an honor for outdoor activities, I remembered experiences I would have never had in my family. I remembered the smell of cooking bacon on a cold spring morning, kneeling in front of an aluminum-can hobo stove. Early in the morning on a spring day, the girls' group hiked to a nearby park and cooked breakfast on our makeshift stoves. We cut a three-inch square opening at the rim of an empty gallon-size can and placed it upside down on the ground. This opening created a way to build a small wood fire under the can. Near the top, we cut another smaller space on the opposite side to let out the smoke. The top of the upside-down can became a griddle to cook bacon and eggs. Cooking breakfast was not an easy task as the hot bacon grease ran down the side of the can into the fire. The cooking eggs burned on the lid because of scorching heat. With each attempt, we received another honor bead. I received a different colored and shaped bead for various adventures and projects regarding home, health, nature, business, patriotism, and spirituality. I proudly sewed the colored beads on my Campfire Girl's vest.

I took a breath, and tears came to my eyes as I saw the colored construction paper design for my Campfire Girl name. The specific Native American name was gone, but the red and blue intersecting triangles and the yellow flames that represented a desire to pray and to search for God remained. My child-crafted symbol of a Native American name affirmed a spirituality I longed for—a spirituality I knew intuitively. Even as a young girl, I searched to understand God and the mysteries of life.

I rummaged further inside the box. A dark blue folder caught my eye. As I pulled it out of the box, another picture fell into my lap. I was a junior in high school, standing in the front row of a large group of teenage girls under a banner with the words, "Cornhusker Girls State." I stood smiling with a blue beanie on my head. The local women's auxiliary chose me to attend Girl's State that year. This week-long camp in the Nebraska state capital taught leadership skills and state governance in the hope of empowering young women to be local leaders. To be the one chosen from my class was an honor and a privilege.

Yet as I studied my smile, I remembered how hard that week was for me. I remembered hanging back, watching, and not getting engaged. I was afraid, afraid of doing something wrong, afraid I was not enough. I feared that if anyone at the camp found out the truth about me, I would be a fraud. The leaders at the camp pushed me to be bold, to run for office, to set up an election campaign. Being from a small town, I felt outside my comfort zone. I ended up running for some county office. I think I won because I was the only person running. As I looked at the picture, I remembered the shame I felt. I disappointed myself. I wondered if I disappointed the women who sent me. This fear became and remained part of my identity.

Toward the bottom of the tub was my senior high school yearbook with the award for being the editor with distinction. I paged through the pictures remembering the varied activities I enjoyed: 1) Head of the pep club (I was not popular enough to be a cheerleader); 2) Alto in the chorus; 3) First chair trumpet in the band; 4) The witch part in the senior play; and 5) Editor of the school newspaper and yearbook. I was a leader in high school, and many adults and teachers affirmed my leadership abilities. But I also remembered how often my internal self-doubt grew like a balloon filled with hot air. Whatever confidence I managed to obtain eventually popped and blew apart with any challenge. I second-guessed myself, my ideas, my voice, and my choices. Then I would pull away, sometimes quitting in the middle of a project.

I remembered practicing the art of dwelling on what was wrong with me. I pulled away quickly to avoid this truth of myself. I often felt like an outsider, uncomfortable, and different. I spent hours wondering about my true self. How would I make a difference in the world? I longed to be important in some way but judged myself as a fraud.

Being told what to do made me feel vulnerable. I hated it. I could figure it out myself. I learned to sew from a pattern, cook from a recipe, play the piano and trumpet, love music, and create stories in my head. I wrote poetry. I fantasized about becoming a beauty contest winner, a teacher, or someone with a moral code better than others. Being a beauty contest winner was not going to happen because I was short, flat-chested, and had chunky legs and German facial features with a big nose. So, instead, I worked hard on the moral code to affirm I was better than others. I could teach or preach at others, depending on who was receiving my self-defined "important" information or judgment.

One boy in my high school class told me I was too strong. I looked at his picture in the yearbook. At the time, I saw him as a friend. He told me that I would never find a husband because I scared the boys away. As a girl, I was just too strong, too opinionated. He said I needed to soften up. I found it curious that from the outside, I appeared assertive, but inside, I was afraid. I assumed I did not fit. His statement confirmed yet again that I was an outsider, the odd one out.

As I dug more deeply through the artifacts of my adolescence, I found the sermon I preached at my home congregation using the hand gestures for "Here's the church and here's the steeple. Open the doors and see all the people." I laughed. I read handwritten prayers in large printing, journal entries, and poetry reflecting on the warmth of God's presence and the wonderment of God's love and the absence of God's justice for the poor in paved cities and the violence of war.

An image of sitting on the low-hanging branch of a cottonwood tree that stood beside a creek at my dad's farm filled my memories. At the tree, I mused of the quietly flowing water, the safety within the old tree's arms, and the connection I felt with all of creation—a prayer beyond words. Meditations beyond liturgy. Deep contemplations for a young girl.

I remembered being a youth leader in the church was the one place I stayed active in, even when the self-doubt raised its voice against me. Within the church organization, I was able to maintain some sense of personal authority and successful follow-through. Two pastors from local churches became my mentors. Both were younger clergymen who recognized and supported my efforts. They believed in me even when I did not believe in myself. As a youth leader in the church, I led with an appearance of confidence. The church accepted me for me and gave me a place to find my voice.

In front of me were a few pieces to add to my broken circle. I wrote this list:

1. *I grew up adored and deeply loved.*
2. *I knew joy.*
3. *My continued relationship with God was not just my imitation of Mark's story. These longings are mine too. I am spiritual.*
4. *I am at home in the religion and the institution of the church.*
5. *Others see me as a leader.*

6. *I have an authentic voice. When I write my thoughts, musings, and reflections, I am heard.*
7. *I am strong. This strength can scare or hurt others (and me, too). But not always.*
8. *I get afraid and doubt myself.*

At the bottom of this box was a large black-and-white photo of me the summer of my first year at college. In it, the director of the college choir placed a kimono on my shoulder in front of a Japanese Airlines banner. We were leaving for a three-week choir tour of Japan. I was eager with anticipation, excited to see the world, open to adventure, filled with hope and trust. I placed this picture on my refrigerator, inviting this 19-year-old woman to bless me and pull me forward into wholeness. She would be part of the circle, too.

9. *I am a woman open to adventure.*

PLANETS IN RETROGRADE

The confidence of moving into wholeness shattered to pieces yet again. Since Mark died, the most intense waves of grief occurred in the autumn, the season of the year Mark died. Rustic smells. The sun's lowering angle. A morning's chill. Sweet and sour bites of a Granny Smith apple. Each scent opened the door to grief spasms. But ten days into November of the third anniversary of Mark's death turned into "what the hell?"

It began with grocery shopping. Pushing an empty cart, I meandered through the store. My mind focused on the memories of Mark instead of what was in front of me.

CRASH.

I looked up in time to see a tall display of Kleenex falling around me. The tumbling boxes rolled into a nearby Snickers candy display. Then it fell.

Surrounded by candy bars and boxes, I asked aloud. "Who did that?" as I stood on top of the "for sale" sign lying on the floor.

My face flushed in embarrassment as I realized I was the one who caused the crash. I looked around and saw no one was nearby. I quickly knew what I needed to do. I turned my cart in the opposite direction, hurried down the next aisle, and moved to the front of the store, leaving my empty cart at the flower department. I found the front door furthest away from the scattered Snickers and walked outside, leaving the piles of Kleenex boxes far behind.

Two days later, I drove to the airport in St. Paul to fly to Chicago for the fall meeting of a seminary board. I quickly parked my Running late, I grabbed the parking ticket. Pulling my suitcase, I dashed to the parking lot shuttle. I threw my briefcase and purse over my left shoulder with car keys in my right hand. I sat impatiently in the back of the bus, fidgeting with my bags. I put the parking ticket in my billfold. When we arrived at the airport, I gathered my belongings. Or so I thought. I ran inside to check the departure flight board. "Canceled" appeared to the right of my flight number. *Oh, shit*, I thought. *Why did I hurry?*

I went to the ticket counter and arranged for the next flight, which was also delayed another two hours. *Of course*, I thought. It fit the negative character of the day.

I had time to kill. So, I went shopping to buy a gift for my cousin John. He was dog-sitting Barkley.

I tucked my briefcase and purse close to my body, pulling my suitcase behind me. The small airport gift shop had little room for shoppers. I tried to make myself as small as I could, remembering the grocery store disaster. I stopped in front of the Minnesota souvenirs—loon-droppings candy, cardinal-shaped salt and pepper shakers, and Twins baseball coffee mugs sat on the glass shelf. It was the Minneapolis skyline shot glasses that caught my attention. *These are interesting*, I thought. John enjoys Canadian Crown Whiskey. When I moved my hand across the display to examine one of the small glasses, my bags fell from my shoulder, jerking my arm. My hand hit the shelf.

Crash.

Then another. Crash.

Two shot glasses fell to the floor, shattering at my feet.

"Shit." Swearing was becoming a frequent companion. This time, I was not out of earshot. All the people in the shop turned my way to check out the noise. The person next to me jumped. The cashier looked up from her phone, surprised. I shrugged and tried to smile.

The cashier waved her hand in a friendly gesture, grabbing a small broom from under the counter.

"It happens all the time. It's crowded in here." She scurried close to me to clean up the broken glass. I picked up a shot glass, sheepishly gathered my bags, and walked to the counter to pay for three glasses, the two broken ones, and the whole one in my hand.

I opened my purse to retrieve my billfold. I looked inside. Then I looked again.

"Where are my keys?" I panicked. My car keys were not where I usually kept them. I dug into the bag, pushing its contents back and forth, searching for them. The cashier returned and watched me dump my purse's contents on the counter. My car keys were not there. "Shit," I said yet again.

The cashier, now impatient, waved the shot glass above the clutter and asked, "Cash or credit?"

After paying and gathering my belongings yet again, I walked back and forth in the airport hallways, pacing, racking my brain. "Where are my keys?" I retraced each step of the day in my mind.

Then I remembered. The keys were on the shuttle. I left them on the seat when I hurried out the door. I had enough time before the next flight to make a phone call. I pulled out the parking ticket from my billfold and called the number listed. Luckily, the operator connected me to the central booth at the parking lot. The attendant reported to me that the bus driver found the keys on the seat in the back of the bus and returned them to the booth. She would have them waiting for me upon my return. I sighed in relief.

When I arrived in Chicago late in the afternoon, the board meeting was in full swing. I entered the boardroom as they were breaking for supper and an evening on the town with dinner and the Broadway show, *Wicked*. I enjoyed the meal, delighted in the play, mused with colleagues, and received condolences from the board members who had known Mark.

As the day ended, I promptly returned to my room, where memories of Mark flooded into my mind, and stress-filled tears soaked my pillow.

I returned home in time for a preaching class the next day. I was one of four students invited to preach to my classmates in the sanctuary of a nearby church. We were to experience what it was like to preach from a large pulpit. Luckily, I had written the sermon before I left for Chicago and had time the morning before class to practice my delivery in front of a mirror. Feeling confident, I tucked the six-page, typed homily inside my bag, along with my Bible, notebook, pen, and a filled water bottle.

I gathered with my classmates in the church's front pews, ready to listen to the other three presenters and write a critique for each one after their turn. The church was modern in design, with pews in a half-circle around a sturdy, wooden pulpit boldly standing to the right of the altar. The placement demanded a confident presence and a bold presentation. The professor invited us to order ourselves to share our sermon. I volunteered to be last.

After the first person completed his presentation, I reached in my bag for a pen to complete his evaluation. My fingers felt cold dampness. As I searched deeper toward the bottom, I felt a soggy mess. I pulled out a wet notebook, a water-logged Bible, a water-bottle lid, and a half-full bottle of water. Finally, I grabbed the six pages of my sermon, dripping wet.

I looked at the papers in stunned, wide-eyed disbelief. My environment forced me to squelch my internal desire to swear. I turned to the classmate on my right and saw a grin slowly and slyly develop on his face as he watched the papers fold into themselves. His eyes twinkled as he covered his mouth to muffle a chuckle growing with intensity. His amusement broke my stress, and I began to smile with him.

As others turned our way in the commotion, I held up the pages of the saturated sermon for all to see. They understood the conflict of the building pressure of this staged presentation and the breakdown of well-made plans into a sappy puddle. The laughter grew throughout the front pews.

Internally, I experienced the building of this absurdity. My laughter grew along with my classmates' kind support.

I excused myself to go to the bathroom to fix what I could. I pulled the pages apart and patted them dry with paper towels, so I could hold them without tearing. Luckily, the type was clear enough to read.

When my turn came to climb the stairs into the pulpit and preach, I knew I would be okay. These classmates had my back. They got it. Our shared laughter affirmed a holy hilarity needed for survival as a pastor in the church. The professor encouraged me to go for it and work through the problem, reminding me of a favorite saying of one of Mark's mentors, "This is good preparation for the parish." This was most certainly true, mainly when preaching through a soggy sermon.

The ten-day chaos, however, did not end here. When I came home, my computer would not boot up.

There was a note from my landlord that the tank with oil to supply heat for my upper apartment was near empty. The cost would be just over $500.

I drove home from class the next day to discover a large tree branch flat on the ground.

The car engine light on my Beetle turned red.

This repair cost $600.

The storm continued. The electricity went out.

On the weekend, I tried to gain some control of the chaos by deep cleaning my apartment. I stood on a ladder to clean the antique light fixture, only to drop it, shattering it on the floor.

I climbed off the ladder and sat on the sofa, staring at the broken glass. I felt broken, too. I had pushed through three years, putting a new life together. I accomplished a great deal—moving, new friends, going back to school, growing in new ideas, changing paradigms, learning more about myself.

But this month, this November, this year, all the work, passion, and process fell into frustration, breakdowns, and obstacles. It was like the planets had stopped and turned in retrograde.

The anniversary month of Mark's death had always been challenging. Yet, each year, it seemed to get harder. The first year we buried his ashes in November. In the second year, I experienced profound loneliness. I thought this year would be better, but instead, the universe turned on me as if to say, "Stop. Slow down. Wait. Let the grief pass. Give yourself time for the planets to re-right themselves."

Give yourself time. Your inner planet needs to realign too.

I swept up the glass, took Barkley out for a long walk, called Anne to vent, and poured myself a glass of wine. I wrote several pages in my journal. And I tried to remain still.

Waiting for November to pass, waiting for grief to pass. If only it could.

CLINICAL PASTORAL EDUCATION –
(OR A CRAZED PERSON EVOLVES)

The hard work of self-discovery continued. Although CPE, Clinical Pastoral Education, was a seminary requirement, I fought to get out of this eight-week intensive chaplaincy training at a hospital. My argument included these points: 1) I was a therapist for years with a successful private practice; 2) I worked with a supervisor throughout those years who continually pushed me to explore my own issues, specifically as they interfered in helping others; 3) I paid for hours and hours of personal therapy; 4) I met regularly with a spiritual director; 5) I traveled the world, having been on several immersion trips to developing countries; 6) I had lots of training and practice in listening and being compassionate to people in stressful situations; 7) I had a unit of CPE when I first practiced pastoral counseling at a center in Denver 15 years earlier; 8) I wanted to be a diaconal minister integrating Word and Service, not ordination; and 9) I had worked through my issues.

Or so I thought.

The seminary held firm. Graduation required one unit of CPE. Ordained or not, the candidacy committee affirmed this seminary requirement. The purpose of Clinical Pastoral Education was to discover one's pastoral identity, internalize, affirm one's gifts and strengths, and explore the limitations and challenges regarding one's personal power.

With a chip on my shoulder, growing anger, and an exasperated spirit, I gave in. I completed the application for CPE, and a St. Paul, Minnesota, hospital accepted me.

The CPE program began in the middle of June, four years after Mark was initially diagnosed with cancer.

I had not set foot into a hospital since Mark spent seven weeks confined to a hospital bed with tubes pulling green bile from his belly, and with different IV tubes pushing antibiotics, nutrition, and painkillers into his body. There with the beep, beep, beep of the heart monitor, I sat alone with him surrounded by the smells of disinfectant, bright white lights, the blare of unwatched television, uncomfortable chairs with plastic cushions, and the deafening spirit of death. Memories returned.

As I entered the hospital on the first day of CPE, the glass doors closed behind me. A wave of shock took my breath away. The fluorescent overhead lights glared into my eyes. The too-clean smell burned my nose. The echo of squeaking shoes bounced off the brick walls and pounded into my head. A taste of old bitter coffee soured in my mouth when I remembered the touch of Styrofoam on my lips. The air chilled my skin, drawing goosebumps on my arms from beneath a summer sweater. Sensory memory from Mark's stay in the hospital overwhelmed me. I had not expected this to happen

I swallowed hard, pushing down a need to turn and run. I put my focus on the task at hand. After all, it was only eight weeks, five days a week sitting with a group of other seminary students reflecting on pastoral identity. I had been a therapist for years. I tried to put on my professional hat and identity.

"I can do this," I said aloud.

There were the words again, echoing in my head from a long time ago. "I can do this."

I rode the elevator to the fifth floor. I think it was on the fifth floor. Or at least the one with the office of chaplaincy. It was hard to remember because much of those eight weeks were a blur.

But so much was not.

As I entered the chaplain's office, William, the internship supervisor, and his intern, Julian, from Norway, greeted me kindly. The intern would sit and observe the process.

William was a solid man in stature and heart. He laughed easily and had ears that heard what was deep inside others. The kindness of his eyes held my attention. Compassionate energy emerged from his large hands. I sensed I could be safe, vulnerable with him.

I had not thought I needed safety.

He spoke in a calm voice, gentle and supportive. He stood tall. When he sat in his desk chair, he eased himself into a shared level of connectedness with a comfortable presence. His office had just a metal desk on a side wall with a few bookshelves holding notebooks above. A black phone sat on the right side of the desk, and the red lights bleeped, often warning of incoming phone calls and messages. A framed picture that appeared to be his family sat opposite the phone. And there he was, standing with them in a leather jacket, a smile radiating from behind his motorcycle. Nearby, several file folders and a yellow legal pad with several pens spread across the desk.

William pulled his chair beside an empty armchair and invited me to sit down. To my left was a side table with a single lamp, a candle, and a box of tissues. The lamplight was the only light in the room, yet it filled it with a bright and warm glow. The office was dull yet welcoming; stark, but pleasant.

After a bit of small talk about the weather and the busy summer, he invited me to tell a bit of my own story, list my goals for the eight weeks, and my expectations of the program. I told him I had not wanted to do CPE, but that I would do my best to meet the

227

expectations and follow through with the requirements. He nodded with a knowing smile.

What did he know that I did not?

After this brief meeting, I walked into the larger lounge area of the chaplain's offices to meet the other CPE students—Nancy, Joe, Joan, and Tony—all students from various seminaries. After greeting each other and sharing our names, we each sat on the too-low, soft couches along one wall. Just opposite me was a bank of four computers and telephones on a continuous desk stretching across the narrow, long room. A black swivel desk chair stood at attention at each station, along with pencils, pads of paper, and a hospital directory. As we waited for William and Julian to arrive, I looked around, trying to size up my colleagues, all much younger than me.

Of course. Duh? What more will be expected of me because of my age?

The day of orientation proceeded with a growing cloud of irritation that followed my every step. When we had to choose a floor assignment, I went with neuro-epilepsy, orthopedics, and overflow surgical, assuming it might be less demanding than the Birth Center, Heart/Lung, and Medicine. I did not want Oncology.

Why would I go there?

I wrote three goals: 1) Development of pastoral identity; 2) Cultivate the skills of self-care and boundaries; and 3) Initiate helping relationships and assess spiritual concerns.

I did not write the raging thoughts echoing in my head: 1) I am sick and tired of transformative experiences; 2) I will keep this experience on a superficial level as much as possible to keep it all at a distance; 3) I do not want to be here; and 4) Anger? What is anger? I am not angry.

Weeks one and two passed uneventfully. I met the nurses in neuro-epilepsy, joined the morning rounds to gain an understanding of the hospital routine, and observed the activities in my assigned department.

I observed my own discontent.

I made a couple of short visits to patients. However, with each step off the elevator and into each hospital corridor, my anxiety stirred. The lights were too bright. The smell of hand sanitizer too pungent. The supposedly quiet conversations outside hospital rooms too intense. I longed for a peaceful place. I always felt incompetent in a new work setting. "Stupid all over again," as one person described. I was surprised there was so much to learn as a chaplain.

At the end of the week, I sat in the hospital chapel. There were no windows in this simple space, only light wooden panels, cushioned chairs, a kneeling rail facing an altar with a cross, and two candles. The lights dimmed in a soft invitation to stillness. In this small, cornered room, I breathed in peace.

I had not realized the learning curve at the hospital would be so hard for me. I did not expect the anxiety and growing intensity of the anger.

On Tuesday of week three, the day after Mark's birthday, I walked into Daniel's room. Daniel was a 56-year-old man who would go on disability after recovering from a second surgery for posterior fluid collection on his brain. Daniel explained his concern for his wife.

"Could you speak with Mary?" he requested in an anxious, quiet voice.

"Sure," I replied.

After the visit to Mary, I went back to the chaplaincy offices and wrote the following verbatim, a CPE requirement.

Conversation for Verbatim	My Internal Reflections During the Conversation
Chaplain E: Hello M. (stretching out my hand). I'm Elaine Olson, a Chaplain. I talked to your husband yesterday. D: This is the woman I told you about. She is also a counselor. (pointing to me) M: Nice to meet you. Yes, my husband told me you would be coming today.	I was aware that M looked very tired. Yet, she greeted me with a smile. It seemed essential I was a counselor. I wonder where all the additional information I shared with her husband, including that I was the wife of a pastor for 30 years and a widow, fit into this conversation. I found a place to sit on a nearby chair. M sat on the bed with her husband.
D: I was really hoping that my wife had someone to talk to. M: My husband does not want me to share my feelings with him. It is just too hard.	The counselor in me wanted to check out this need. What were the dynamics? Why didn't he want to hear her feelings? My internal anxiety grew.
Chaplain E: M, let us talk a bit.	I walked with M to a nearby private family room. My heartbeat grew.
Chaplain E: How is all of this for you? M: I do not have any anger or questions at God. God is just	I am very aware of how I also knew this feeling.

silent, distant. There are lots of prayers from family and friends. I am tired. I have been trying to read this book, but it does not make a difference. What am I to do? How do I get through this when I cannot talk to my husband about how I feel? What do I do?	Mark was also unavailable to me. I remembered the loneliness of this experience. I worked to stay present and focus on M.
M: I've been reading this book on healing and spirituality, but it does not seem to help. Chaplain E: It is hard to do this alone. M: (Weeping) No one understands. They try to talk to me, but they do not know how hard this is to do by myself.	I know all too well. How do I let my feelings inform me, but this is NOT about me? Focus. I have a strong urge to connect to her. To hold her. To tell her I understood her. I felt pressure to engage with her but needed to keep a reasonable distance as a chaplain. She wept deeply. I just listened. I worked hard to hold back my tears. Ghosts were haunting me from afar. It was all too familiar. Anger grew within me.

M: What do I do? How do I keep going?	Holding onto my growing rage, I finally answered.
Chaplain E: Breathe. Sometimes all you can do is breathe. M:(sighed as she wiped her tears) Chaplain E: Sometimes, God is in the breath we take. M: I can do that.	We talked about self-care and the need to rest. I held on to my emotions until she left the room to go back to her husband. I hurried out of the room, walked quickly to the elevator, pushed the button for the fifth floor. When it stopped, I exited with a run to the chapel. Sobbing.

Immediately, as I finished writing the verbatim, I knew why I held so much anger. I knew why I did not want to experience CPE. The ghosts of my past found this time, this experience to haunt me. My anger tried to hold them at bay. But my visit with Mary invited them in. The ghosts were the trauma of spending six weeks in the hospital, silently sitting beside Mark's bed. The ghosts remembered. The ghosts of the past swirled around me with vivid memories. The ghosts of the past screamed from their loneliness with a message. They demanded me to listen.

The ghosts reminded me my personal suffering needed a place and time for resolution. When I focused on Mark during his last weeks in the hospital—his pain, then his death, I pushed aside my distress. I denied the strain of sitting for hours and hours, alone, helpless, afraid beside his bed. I hid it inside.

Something broke inside me during CPE. These ghosts followed me as I walked through the hospital corridors. They came to remind me of my broken heart.

During the past years, I worked through many levels of grief and pushed to claim a new life, a new vocation. I traveled. I moved. I made new friends. I rediscovered parts of myself. I was resilient, moving ahead boldly and confidently.

The ghosts used the hospital as the platform to speak with a message I needed to know. I was angry because I was required to do CPE. But I realized the real issue was that I was mad at Mark. I needed Mark's love. I needed someone to hold me. Why did he not talk to me during those six weeks? Why did he die? Why had I given so much of myself to him only to be without him?

I realized the anger protected me from more grief. I had lost so much—Mark, my friends, my home, my private practice, a life vision. My children moved on with their lives and lived far away. Many personal losses built one upon the other after Mark's death. Many were of my own choosing. Yet, the long shadow of deep grief finally consumed me. When the weeping began in the hospital chapel, I could not stop it.

The interns had not seen me all afternoon and began looking for me. They found me in the back of the chapel. Worried about my weakness and crying, they called William to come and help. William came to sit with me in the chapel.

I sobbed from the depth of my being. The tears burned my eyes, and the wrenching hurt my gut. But waves of deep grief eventually engulfed. It had no words.

More importantly, I did not try to escape. I felt safe. Finally, I was safe. Safe enough to let go. Strong enough to face pain directly. Sheltered enough within William's gentle presence to cry without shame. Secure enough to take off the mask of survival.

I invited the ghosts to join me. Together we surrendered to the truth of pain. Together we remembered the constancy of the weeks with Mark when I sat alone within his silent presence, surrounded by machines beeping, nurses talking. The ghosts helped me remember my feelings during Mark's extended hospital stay.

William permitted me to take the time I needed. I stayed home for several days, crying. I walked around the Minneapolis lakes. Anne and I talked often. I cried more. I shouted at Mark. I yelled into the universe for letting me down.

"Why did you not tell me you loved me one more time?"

"Why was learning a prayer more important than me?"

"I sat alone for days. Alone. I needed someone with me."

"I trusted you to give me life, and you gave me death instead." I screamed at God. Where was God now? Where was comfort? Where was peace?

After I returned, I often spoke with William, sitting in his office. He listened patiently. I allowed the pain to move through me until the raging subsided, its energy spent. The crying stopped, emptied of its power.

In time, I finally returned to the neuro-epilepsy floor to continue the work as a student chaplain. The smells of disinfectant remained; the corridors were still illumined in artificial light. My shoes again squeaked on the floor, announcing my presence, but I was not alone. The ghosts of the past were with me. I had made peace with them and invited them to come along. They had much to teach me. Together, we knew pain, despair, death, and loneliness. Together, we survived. Together, we knew resilience. Together, we were strong.

AN EXPLORATION ALWAYS BEGINS AT THE BOOK STORE

The neon lights above my head dimmed again and then again in a slow rhythm. A shadow cast by the overhead fan's slowly turning blades of the overhead fan passed across the floor. It added to the spell, holding me captive. I stood in front of the shelf of books in the back of the store at my favorite independent bookstore marked, "Sexuality—Women." I looked around to be sure I was alone. I was embarrassed, maybe even a bit ashamed. Would someone I know see me? My heartbeat increased; my hands grew sweaty. My muscles tensed, and my vision narrowed. Would I ever make love with a man again?

As a middle-aged woman whose sexual urges screamed for attention, I stared at the books. I was not sure what to do or how to proceed within my current narrowly defined rules for sexual expression and exploration. Mark and I were both virgins when we married more than thirty years earlier. I was supposedly part of the sexual revolution of the '70s. Before we married, we explored our bodies, touching, kissing, heavy petting, spending nights together. But we did not have sexual intercourse until we married. Our wedding night was the awkward exploration of this new reality, made even more uncomfortable as Mark was 6'5" and 250lbs, and I was a petite 5'3".

Most of the time, during our thirty years of marriage, our sexual life was satisfying. We occasionally had what we thought were exotic escapades. We made love on the living room floor. One afternoon, we lay in the woods off the main trail on a mountain hike. When the church was vacant after a wedding one Saturday afternoon, we made love on Mark's office couch. I was delighted when we shared a Sunday afternoon "nap." We bought the book, *Joy of Sex*, and read it together, curious. Even as we explored various places to be sexual, our sex life was never a central part of our marriage. We got much more excited about an in-depth discussion of a book we'd both read.

Our sex life dwindled to almost nothing during the last three years of our marriage when Mark experienced a profound depression because of the national church's rebuke. He showed no interest at all, even on Sunday afternoons, which had been a regular event after the kids left home. Our sex lives completely stopped when Mark received the diagnosis of cancer, five months before he died.

During the first years as a widow, I shut down any sexual desire. Instead, I turned most of my energy toward figuring out what was next. I did flirt occasionally and longed to marry again. I knew love once, and I wanted to love again. I missed being in the company of a man.

I wondered if I would ever have sex again. Then this long-dormant state returned to life like a bear seeking food after a cold winter's hibernation. This hunger led me to this stack of books.

What did it mean to be sexual as a middle-aged widow? I developed into a sexual being in my marriage to Mark. I enjoyed sex, and I missed it. Would masturbation be enough? How would I meet a man and develop a relationship committed enough to be sexual, intimate beyond a goodnight kiss and holding hands? Or was a commitment even necessary? What were my values about sexuality now?

Mark had been precise in his understanding of sexual ethics and the importance of being single and celibate. But I was now alone and not married. Older. Wiser? Perhaps. What were my ethics? My values? My desire? What did I want to believe?

A set of external rules also set boundaries around me. I knew I would not date a parishioner or client. Following these expectations was very important to me. But because I was in the process of becoming an ordained pastor, the church required me to sign a paper stating that I intended to refrain from sex outside of marriage. They expected me to be celibate.

How realistic were these rules for me, or anyone for that matter? I enjoyed being sexual when I was married. I had passions. My body longed for human contact—male contact to be specific. As a single woman, I desired touch, attention, warmth, and intimacy.

Being celibate may have been my intention, but what was my desire? I wondered how I would follow the church rules and explore these sexual questions about myself at the same time. What was realistic? What truths did I need to learn about my body? My passions? Was sex outside of marriage that bad? Was it as awful a sin as the church and my childhood training suggested?

As a young woman, the church taught, "Sex is dirty, so save it for the one you love." My mom lectured me as a teenager about the dangers of being sexual. I believed in saving sexual intercourse for marriage into my early adulthood. I followed the understanding that the level of commitment in a relationship determined the extent of sexual activity, equating marriage with sexual intercourse. These rules meant holding hands in dating—heavy petting when going steady. And sexual intercourse only after marriage. As a therapist, I taught this to others in classes on sex for adolescents. My life with Mark fit into this neat package of religious and moral teachings. They were the values I lived for many years.

I stood in front of the books, overwhelmed with internal urges I could not explain. Who was I as a sexual being? Would God strike me dead if I tried to find out? Would my friends see me as a "slut"? Shun me? Judge me?

The fan above me kept spinning slowly. My brain turned faster as I bought three books. One about self-pleasure and masturbation for women. A second exploring sexual desire. And a third on how to please a man. I hurried to the counter, blushing, trying to look calm as I placed the three books on the checkout desk and paid with a credit card.

Perhaps reading these books might help me find a man.

In time, I began observing men, studying their faces to discern kindness, and then quickly looking at their left hand to see if they were wearing a wedding band. Was this man available?

Many men caught my eye, but no one appeared available. No one seemed attracted to me. I prayed to find the ideal mate. I heard from a friend that if I let God know I was ready, and I prayed specifically for the qualities I wanted, God would place that person in my life. I prayed. I made lists. I prayed harder. God never answered these prayers. Not for me, anyway.

It was a friend of Mark's who first caught my heart. He had been widowed and recently remarried. He and his wife invited me to many dinners in their home. I held a deep fondness for him and looked forward to being with him. I tried to catch his smile, sought his thoughtfulness, and intentionally engaged him in theological conversations. My fondness for him grew more deeply into a heartfelt love with each visit. I longed for his company and his attention.

But I also respected his marriage and appreciated his wife's company. Out of the need to protect my own heart and self-respect, I pulled away, finding excuses not to visit them. I distanced myself from these dear friends out of the fear I might cross a line and embarrass myself. The friendship slowly drained of life through lack of attention. I set a boundary to protect my heart, but it only left my heart sadder. I had lost another friend. No, two friends.

Not one man appeared interested in me. I was not a go-to-the-bar kind of woman. I thought I made myself available and open during seminary classes, workshops, and church gatherings. I told friends I wanted to meet someone. But there was no one. No one seemed to notice me. It had been a long time since Mark's death, and no man appeared in my life.

Not being noticed by men fed a growing concern about my personality. Was I too strong? Did I scare men away? Was the warning I had from a friend in high school correct? Was I a prude? Did I send off vibes that I was a cold fish? Was I sexually attractive? Did I need to loosen up?

No man showed any interest.

Yet.

LEARNING TO BE NEIGHBORLY

Then I met Louis. It was a late summer morning, and I was worshiping at a nearby church. I stayed for a new member orientation in the fellowship hall and was talking with another acquaintance. I noticed him as he stood across the room, getting a cup of coffee, standing alone, and looking around the room. Louis was a small man, not much taller than me, dressed in a white, button-down shirt, no tie. He stood confidently, with sad eyes and a friendly smile. I set my mind to start noticing men more intentionally. I studied him while he stood by himself. He looked close to my age, worn, tired, and did not wear a ring on his left hand. I was not enamored but curious.

"Look at him," I told myself. "Give it a shot." When I caught his eye, he walked toward me.

He reached out his hand and said, "Hi. You must be new here. My name is Louis."

"Hi, I'm Elaine." Returning the gesture. We chatted about the warm weather, the worship service. I told him I was studying in the city, widowed. Louis spoke in a compelling voice, with intensity and directness. Then he surprised me with a blunt revelation, saying something like, "I know we've just met, and I'd like to get to know you better. But before we can continue, I need to get the truth on the table. I was once a wealthy farmer and traveled the world, working to shape farm policies. I challenged the government, big business, questioned farm subsidies. As a Christian, I wanted to find ways to distribute excess grain to feed the hungry in the world."

Louis added, "But, I made some bad decisions, and I spent two years in prison for choices I made regarding my use of government money and challenging the system. I'm a felon and broke."

I did not understand what he meant precisely, completely surprised by this revelation that came out of his mouth so quickly. Yet, he seemed like a fascinating man. Maybe my loneliness blinded me to look beyond the obvious. I became intrigued by him, especially about his desire to feed hungry people.

He continued, "My wife divorced me. My children no longer talk to me."

I had lots of questions. Do I follow my first instinct in the judgment of Louis and approach with caution? Or do I continue forward? Yet, I saw Louis as passionate, intense, and with a strong desire to make a difference in the world. He was willing to go to prison for his principles. And he was interested in me. What could be better?

We met each other again the next Sunday at church when he invited me to brunch for corn pancakes at my favorite South American restaurant. The following week, he asked me to a movie and dinner. He came to my apartment for wine and dessert. I was joyous. This man was interested in me, though most of the time, he talked about himself.

He listened to me, a little. But he told his story again, and then again as if rehearsing it to affirm its truth. He talked. I listened, smiled, flirted. He asked if he could kiss me. I did not refuse. I remember it was not a great kiss, but it re-awakened something I had shut down when Mark died. Like Snow White, I received a lousy kiss from a weird prince, woke up, and reconnected to the feeling I had missed. I felt aroused.

Louis's passion for changing the world with farm policy was not mine. I grew bored with his repeated stories. I realized I was embarrassed to introduce a felon to my friends and family. He did not make me a better person, and I did not want to be his helper or healer. This relationship only lasted a few weeks when I told him I would be his friend, but I did not want to date him. I was grateful for the attention and kindness.

Yet, I was confused by the sexual energy igniting within me. The questions returned. What did it mean to be single in my 50s? Was it a sin to have sex outside of the marriage vow? How did I date? When do you have sex within the process? What was morality for me now? How did this fit into the expectation of the church?

I wished I had explored these questions as a younger woman. Here I was older, widowed, confused, working for the church, and sexually eager.

In December, I went to a neighborhood party and met Jon. I walked into the house and looked around the darkened living room. Small groups of people stood together, chatting and laughing. Jon was standing beside the decorated tree, dressed in a black turtleneck with a wool sports coat. He was small in stature, but I mostly remember a quirky smile and generous laughter as he spoke with several people, all holding a glass of wine. As I walked in, he looked straight at me, excused himself from the others, and introduced himself.

"Hi, I'm Jon. May I get you a glass of wine?"

"Hi, I'm Elaine. I would love a glass of wine. Red, please." We spent the rest of the evening chatting, just the two of us standing beside the decorated tree. He listened when I spoke. I was surprised and excited that yet another man noticed me. I grew more interested when he said he was single, divorced with adult children.

After a few days, Jon called and invited me to lunch at a nearby café. He seemed eager to introduce me to the neighborhood, show me the best parts of St. Paul, and be a friend. Over coffee and chocolate cake, I learned Jon loved music, saw himself as a tragic romantic, was an active member of a progressive congregation, and had kind and compelling eyes. Jon announced he recently ended a "passionate relationship" with a woman who he said was abusive toward him. Together, we laughed at the difficulty of entering a world of being single. Jon listened to me and my story about Mark's death. He said I was charming. Did I mention he was good-looking with blond hair, blue eyes, and a boyish grin?

On a sunny Sunday afternoon in early February, he invited me for a walk at a nearby park along the river. The sun reflected through the oak trees, illuminating an amber glow within the barren branches. His company was as sensual as the day. I relaxed as I walked and experienced the company of a kind, sensitive man. Later in the week, he sent me a poem describing the walk in the park. Being with Jon sparked a romantic interest within me. I glowed with a smitten heart like the trees from the Sunday before. Then he kissed me.

Jon gave me mixed "cues." He invited me for walks, dinner at his home, wrote poetry, played music for me, and kissed me. Yet, Jon continued to tell me he only wanted to be a friend.

When I asked him about his behavior, with a boyish smile, he said, "All these actions are my compulsive spirit to be with women, especially interesting women. Yes, I am passionate," he continued. "But other women have hurt me. I am not ready for anything other than being a friend."

I was confused but captivated by Jon.

We continued to date. Often, in fact. We rode bikes, took walks, shared meals, drank good wine, and shared philosophical conversations about the meaning of life and God. Jon was a gifted musician and often played the piano for me. One Sunday afternoon, he composed a song for me on the keyboard while we watched the rain outside his window. I met his family.

When I was with Jon, I felt pretty, smart, and engaging. He called me vivacious. On one level, I intuitively recognized his desire for me, but I also felt his unwillingness to be close.

I flirted with him. He flirted back. On Easter Sunday afternoon, Jon came to my home for a glass of wine. We sat on my couch for most of the afternoon, talking, holding each other. The intimate talking moved to touch. I invited his touch, and he responded in kind. I relaxed into a loving experience. I sighed into his warm embrace, surrendered into his gentle, slow easiness. He told me I was beautiful. I felt beautiful, whole, satisfied. I was someone other than "widow."

We often laughed when we were together. Jon prepared romantic French-style picnics with wine, cheese, and kisses. We drank too much wine, surrounded ourselves with music, laughter, and philosophical conversation. We sat on his porch and read books as we soaked in the southern sun. The more time we spent together, I believed the relationship was growing.

One day in June, I heard a knock. It was late morning, and the sun warmed the living room with brightness. As I went to the door, I looked through the small viewing window and saw Jon.

"What are you doing here? I thought you would call later."

Jon shifted his stance from one foot to the other, looking at the floor. "I have something I need to talk about."

I tried to greet him with a kiss, which was the usual routine of the past several weeks, but he turned his head to the side and barely touched my arm as he walked by me into the apartment. A hint of alcohol lingered in the air.

Jon walked past the couch where we often sat with his arm around me and my legs across his lap. He kept walking into the dining room where he sat on a single wooden chair, against a far wall with the dining room table between us. I stood dumbfounded, trying to figure out what was going on. A wall of a wooden table, chairs, his crossed arms, and legs separated us. It looked like he tried to make himself as small as he could, as far from me as he could get.

Jon began to speak in a quiet, cautious tone in words that sounded rehearsed.

"I am sitting here because I am afraid of what I have to tell you and how you will respond," I remembered that his past girlfriend had hit him during arguments.

"Okay," I said. "I will be okay. What do you want to say?"

"I am no longer interested in being in a physical relationship with you. We can be friends, but I want nothing more. I have lost total interest in being in a close relationship."

"What changed?" I asked.

"Me. I've changed." Then he stood up, walked past me, and out the door. The conversation ended abruptly.

I tried to understand but felt brokenhearted. I did not want to be a hysterical woman, but I was confused. I could not figure out what happened.

He did remain friends with me. We tried to meet a few times for a friendly afternoon picnic or a swim at the beach. I respected the physical boundaries he had established, but internally I hurt. My heart hurt. He was my first love after Mark. When Mark died, I knew I wanted to love again. Jon was someone I loved.

But Jon was different now. He built an emotional wall I could not break down. He was distant and restrained. The friendship ended entirely by the end of the summer. Jon did not want to see me anymore.

An internal obsession about Jon grew like weeds in the front lawn after a rain. This preoccupation overtook the garden of loving I had just planted. While we dated, joy consumed my spirit. Jon saw me, and I thought he had loved me. Now, the need to be with Jon devoured me.

I became a stalker. I woke early each morning to walk Barkley in the hopes I could catch sight of Jon boarding the bus on his way to work. I walked Barkley by his house in the evening, so I could see him as he read the paper on the porch. I longed to at least see Jon, sneak a glimpse of him as I walked by his house. Later in the evening, I walked past his home again. But this time, I stood on the edge of the walk, straining to see into the lighted windows. Was he playing the piano? Was another woman visiting him for a glass of wine? Or dinner? Was he alone? Breaking up was what he told me he wanted, but was it true? Had he gone to bed? Was he reading?

I became fixated on the past months we'd spent together. I tried to pull the obsessing weeds from my heart and brain, but they only grew back more robust. I added the word "focus" to my self-talk, repeating the word aloud to get my mind again.

"Focus."

"Focus."

But images of our relationship interrupted the study of theology or conversations with my kids on the phone. How could I win him back? I schemed, looking for various ways to see him. When did he shop for groceries? Would he be in the backyard this afternoon? What bike trail would he be riding today? Could I "accidentally" run into him when I took a ride?

I acted 13 years old, a young girl crushed after her first breakup. I thought I was mature, smart, and resourceful, but emotionally I behaved like an immature adolescent refusing to admit the reality of a broken heart. I think I overwhelmed my friends with the litany of laments. To help me move forward, we all agreed Jon was a jerk.

But was he a jerk? Jon was passionate and romantic, perhaps naive in his flirtations with me, a lonely woman.

I was the naïve one.

IT WAS ONLY A SIMPLE LUNCH

Once I started down this path of dating, I realized how much I wanted to be in a relationship. It interrupted any intention to focus on other parts of my life. None of my usual behaviors to get re-centered worked. No amount of study, time with friends, writing in my journal, talking to my spiritual director, or even prayer stopped the pining.

It was no surprise when a radio commercial describing a dating service caught my attention. It promised a matchmaker would do all the work to make a "real connection," so I could have all the fun. Was there a catch?

The experience began with a personal meeting with a matchmaker to review the contract. For a certain amount of money, a representative interviewed me to gain an understanding of my values and desires in a man. The Matchmaker would review the profiles of many men and find a match with someone who had similar experiences, hopes, and values as me. She would arrange a lunch date for us to meet at the local restaurant. After we ate lunch and talked, the "date" and I could mutually agree to see each other again or say a kind goodbye and go on our way without a messy ending. After the date, the Matchmaker would call to see how we connected, what part of the match worked, and what did not work. She then looked for a closer fit for the next date. The terms of the contract promised six lunch dates over two months.

She promised, "I'm sure someone will catch your eye."

The "certain amount of money" required to work with my Matchmaker was a couple of thousand dollars, equivalent to the tuition I paid for one four-hour course at seminary. I was lucky enough to have extra funds set aside for school and decided to proceed. *It's all part of the learning*, I thought.

Eagerly, I arranged an appointment with Matchmaker (the name I called her). Her office was on the top floor of a high-rise in downtown Minneapolis. The floor-to-ceiling window behind her desk revealed a view of the Minneapolis skyline overlooking the river. She stood as I entered and shook my hand, motioning to a leather chair for me to sit down. I looked around the room, at the artwork, and the plush furnishings. Matchmaker appeared to be wearing an expensive business suit. I assumed the clientele of this service matched this environment—wealthy businesspeople eager and able to pay for what they wanted.

Would I fit? I wondered, second-guessing my decision to pay for what I wanted as I sat down. She sat across from me with her legs crossed, high heels extending the length of her legs, and a kind smile on her face. Holding a questionnaire and pen in her hands, she began asking me many questions. With the skill of a good therapist (or soothsayer), she put me at ease. I sat tall, straightened my skirt, and rambled on.

"I'm a widow. I have loved well and want to love someone again. I have two adult children. I like to travel, especially to parts of the world that are different from my European background— South Africa, Guatemala, Russia, Eastern Germany. I want to meet people and learn about their culture. I grew up in a small town in America. I am religious, so I want someone who understands spirituality. I'm not athletic but enjoy watching football and baseball. I like to read novels." I answered questions for more than an hour. She took my picture for the files.

Matchmaker explained there were many more women than men among the profiles, so I needed to wait for a man to become available. She needed a couple of weeks before she could arrange the first lunch.

Several weeks later, Matchmaker called with my first match. Jim was a widower, loved to travel the world, and grew up in a small town in Minnesota. She arranged for us to meet at a lovely restaurant in downtown St. Paul for lunch the next week.

I dressed in a suit, wanting to appear sophisticated and feminine without being too sexy. Anxiously, I walked into the restaurant and told the host I was here to meet a man from a dating service. He smiled, slyly, knowingly, and led me to the table near the back of the restaurant covered in a white cloth, holding crystal wine glasses and a simple vase of fresh flowers. A man with dark hair was sitting there and looking out the window.

Jim stood as I approached. After we shook hands, we sat across from each other at a small, white cloth-covered table. He appeared calm, but I sat on my hands to stop them from shaking. The lunch started with wine. I ordered a house white while he ordered a glass of Italian red, explaining its nuanced flavors and how it paralleled his travels to Italy.

Strike One. My choice of wine outclassed me.

We briefly talked about our families, the death of our spouses. The conversation moved to travel as the meal arrived.

"What was your favorite experience?" I asked.

Jim described the helicopter ski trip in the Alps. Dropped at the top of a mountain, he and a friend experienced the thrill of a lifetime as they skied down in fresh snow. Second, antique and modern art shopping in Spain. And the third, staying in an exquisite hotel in Paris.

"How about you?" he asked. I told of the travels to South Africa and staying with the people in the townships. I explained how honored I was to listen to their stories and wonder about justice in the world. Strike Two. Jim's eyes glazed over. His interest seemed to fade.

The conversation waned. I explained I was in school to study theology. Jim was a Christmas/Easter Catholic. Within an hour, he asked for the check and paid for my lunch, though we both understood the rule that we were to each pay for our own meal.

At the end of lunch, we both stood. Shook hands, thanked each other for the time. Jim turned to walk out the door.

Strike Three. No exchange of business cards. No, "let's talk some more." No second date. I remained uninterested but was disappointed that neither was he.

Matchmaker called the next day, eagerly asking, "How did it go?" I tried to explain what I meant by travel and the importance of learning about other cultures. I did not imagine traveling with such expensive tastes. I tried to explain what spiritual meant for me. It was a lifestyle rather than just attending church. Matchmaker agreed to look through her profiles of men and find a closer match from my more explicit descriptions.

I think Match Two was also a widower, a financial planner, but was moving to another state to be near his son. We just had lunch.

Match Three? I do not remember. The areas of connection were even less noticeable than in the previous two matches. Like the other lunch dates, the food was tasty, and the café's environment was inviting. But the guy? I do not even have a journal entry to remind me of who he was.

Match Four, another widower, seemed to be the most open and honest. He cautioned me from his experiences with the lunch-dating service.

Over a glass of wine, he said, "The process of arranging lunch dates is like filling out a dance card. Each consecutive match grew less like the description I shared about what I wanted in the person I was to meet. But the arranged lunch fulfilled the promise of six dates. Perhaps it worked well for others, but it does not work for me."

I agreed, it was not working for me either. We were cordial but recognized there was no spark between us.

Then came Match Five. Matchmaker was confident about this one. He was quite religious. As I walked into a restaurant and followed the host to a table, I glanced over my shoulder and saw a man who appeared to be shorter than I walk in the front door. He wore white pants, a black satin shirt unbuttoned to mid-chest, and a gold chain at his neck. His body was well-tanned, and sunglasses tilted upon his forehead. I laughed to myself as I sat down, hoping he was not my match.

As I looked up, he stood, extending his hand, saying, "You must be Elaine." I restrained myself from laughing aloud.

I will call him Flex though I do not remember his name. Flex sat next to me at the table, picked up the menu, and began telling me he was a bodybuilder, a champion in his field, and wondered if I had seen him on the cover of some obscure magazine. I tried to imagine him with a greased body, muscles tensed, and almost naked. In my mind's eye, I was not impressed. As he explored the menu, he scrutinized each item, finding just the right food for its nutritional value and his current body needs.

Other than saying my name and a bit about my family, I spoke very little. Flex filled the time with his stories about body lifting weight, proper nutrition, and competitions. He presented me with his business card.

With pride, he said, "This is my ministry. I give my Christian testimony and play the accordion in senior care facilities. God has blessed me with this mission."

I cringed.

I continued to listen as Flex spewed forth. I grew more impatient as this silliness transformed into insensitivity. At some point amid his pontificating, the server took our order. Flex continued to describe in detail his battle with cancer. He prayed to

God, and with proper nutrition, God completely cured him. Flex pointed to the heavens.

Stunned, I interrupted him, and politely asked, "Could we please change the subject? This conversation is not helpful. My late husband died of cancer. Even as we prayed, God did not cure Mark. Even though he was a faithful man, Mark died."

Flex tilted his head, smiled, touched my arm, and said: "Oh, but let me finish."

I had enough. Offended and cheapened within Flex's presence, I stood up, picked up my purse, and said, "Thank you, but I need to leave now."

I began walking out the front door when I realized my lunch had not yet arrived. I stopped at the front register to pay for my order. I did not want the waitperson to be stuck with the bill. Flex lifted his head high and walked out the door behind me.

The person took one look at my face and asked, "Are you okay?" Her kindness broke the tension within my body, and I began to cry. The manager soon came and led me into the back of the bar. I tried to explain what happened. The manager ordered a glass of wine and delivered my lunch to me at the booth.

"It's on me," he said.

I cried because I was angry—angry at Flex's selfishness, angry at the program's lack of understanding of what being a religious woman meant to me, and at myself for being so vulnerable and spending so much money on a plan that did not reflect my values.

I cried because I missed Mark; because God did not cure him, and he died; because I hurt; because strangers showed me compassionate care. The waitperson filled my wine glass again and sat at the table. She listened attentively to the experience with Flex.

As she stood to go back to work, she patted me on the arm and said, "No man's worth this, honey."

When I returned home, I called Matchmaker. I reported the experience at lunch, expressing my disappointment and frustration about the disconnect between my desires and the matches I was getting on the "dance card." She extended her sympathy and told me she would try again, reminding me I had one mark on the punch-card left. I never heard back from her.

I felt like a fool. A fool for trusting a system so unlike my life experience. A fool for spending so much money. A fool for working so hard to find love.

LOOKING FOR HARMONY CREATED DISCORDS OF REGRET

Six months after obsessing about Jon and spending thousands of dollars on a matchmaker and eating lunch at fine restaurants, I remained "single."

I already had great friends through school. We ate together with home-cooked meals and drank glasses of wine. I enjoyed walking Barkley for fresh air and exercise, and he provided unconditional love. The course of my theological study neared completion. My life seemed settled and focused.

Sara's experience at seminary also blessed her with many friends who challenged and supported each other. But one young man from this cluster of colleagues attracted her heart. Sara and I often talked during this time, and one new point of interest changed our conversations. Clark. They dated some before Sara studied in Moscow for a year. When Sara left for Russia, she wanted her independence, so she stopped seeing him. I think she has a bit of her mother's nature in her.

But after Sara returned for the last year of seminary education, Clark became the person of interest. As he captured her attention and time, Sara called me less frequently. She did not need me to process a problem. She found another for that.

I affirmed this change in our relationship, knowing that if Sara and Clark were to have a good relationship, they did not need me to interfere. But this change added to my loneliness and my search for love.

Sara and Clark graduated together in the spring four years after her dad died. They married on Pentecost weekend. Pentecost, for church people, is the day to celebrate the active presence of God's Spirit, the fire of love let loose in the world.

Clark and Sara gave all who attended the wedding T-shirts with the words, "Come on baby light my fire." Sara was born on a Pentecost Sunday, so to celebrate their marriage on this Holy Day seemed perfect. Mark would have been proud. I believe his spirit hovered nearby.

Both Sara and Clark received invitations to work in separate churches in New Jersey, and they started their lives together far from me. After they moved to the East Coast, Sara and I talked less frequently. They did not need a mother-in-law to interfere. I backed away.

I felt her absence, and my loneliness grew deeper.

I started work at a congregation in Minneapolis, leading a ministry of community and faith formation. This work combined theological studies, my career as a spiritual guide, and a counselor, integrating issues of faith and life. I bought a house located within a walking neighborhood in Minneapolis, close to the church, and moved again. Much of my life was good and satisfying.

Yet, I missed being in love. I wanted to love someone again. I prayed. I told my friends to "keep an eye out." My own eyes saw no one.

After dinner one evening (and maybe too much wine), Anne and I worked together to complete a profile for another online dating service. My cousin John had good luck on this site as he met a woman who shared a worldview with a faith orientation.

My heart began to beat with the possibility of meeting someone with a similar perspective on life. Various profiles appeared on the website. I clicked past the motorcycle-leather-jacket photos. I deleted pictures of men smiling as they stood by a beloved pick-up. I made quick judgments based on my own assumptions, for good or ill.

I used a pseudonym for my profile but stated that I was a minister and wanted to find someone who shared in this faith understanding. I soon discovered the men who reached out to me had a very different experience of "Christian" or faith or what it meant for a woman to be a leader in the church. I had not expected the patronizing, protective, and pontificating exchange within the initial emails through the server. Each man who connected to me needed to gain an advantage over me and my religion in some undefined competition. It appeared to me they tried to prove their piety, devotion, doctrine, prayer, or charitable actions to be worthy of my attention. Or they needed to convince me they were better than anything I could ever do on my own. I deleted many profiles who wrapped themselves in Christianity.

Then, one man caught my eye, Jacob, an ex-Catholic priest. In his profile, he listed books from spiritual writers I admired, including Henri Nouwen and Richard Rohr. As we exchanged emails, I wondered why he left the priesthood. I knew several progressive Catholics whom I admired and was curious to see if he might be of a similar vein. We agreed to meet over coffee at a nearby coffeehouse.

Arriving early, I had bought a cup of coffee and took a seat at a table near the door, wanting to watch as he entered. Jacob, tall, thin, and dressed in jeans and a button-down shirt, carried himself a bit hesitantly. He held a large bouquet wrapped in a ribbon and appeared too eager and too earnest.

Yet, I knew I had grown accustomed to making rapid assumptions about men and decided to give him a chance. We discussed our histories. I was a widow attending seminary, working in a congregation. He recently left the priesthood and was in therapy to rediscover his identity and purpose. We talked about the authors we both read. I appreciated his intellectual insights. Yet, he seemed young, almost boyish for being a man in his 50s. After walking along the river for the rest of the morning, I took the flowers. We agreed to meet again in a week or so. I remained curious.

When I left work at the church the next day, I found a note on my car's windshield. It was from Jacob. The message, written in child-like printing, said he liked me and included a school picture of when he was in fourth or fifth grade. It felt creepy. As I looked around, I saw no one and stuck the note in my purse. My curiosity transformed into waving red flags.

On Sunday, Jacob showed up for church where I worked. He walked in with a prideful gait, greeted me with a silly grin, wrapped me with a hug in the entrance hall, and took a seat near the front. Appalled by this intrusion into my church, I thought, *How dare he invade my space!*

I tried to focus on the congregation as I led the liturgy for the next hour, yet my anger grew, and my focus narrowed. Jacob stayed after the closing hymn, talked to several people as they left the church, and brazenly signed up for a book group I was leading. When he asked me to lunch, I told him I was busy. He left with a sad expression, shuffling his feet.

Later in the afternoon, I wrote an email to Jacob describing my experience and feelings regarding his actions and inappropriate connections. I did not want to see him again. I told him he needed to work out proper adult relationship behavior with his therapist. After I hit send, I took a long shower.

A few days later, I tried again. This time it was the profile of a man I will call Chuck. In his site profile, he said he had traveled the world with philanthropic adventures. We emailed a few times. I was open to meeting him because he seemed to be someone with a generous spirit. We met for coffee in a crowded café. Chuck and I spoke loudly, trying to hear above the noise. My intuition made quick assumptions about his character. He seemed too charming, and his hands moved across the table to touch my arm too quickly. Chuck talked too much about his money and the influence he had on others.

I decided within the first twenty minutes after meeting him to leave. As I stood to excuse myself, Chuck gathered his coat and said he would walk me to the car. As he did, he put his arm around me, rubbed my shoulder, and pulled me close, matching his gait to mine. When I arrived at my car, I quickly opened the door and said goodbye from inside the vehicle. I drove a very roundabout route to my house, making sure he did not follow me.

Later in the afternoon, I turned on my computer only to discover a note from Chuck, sent through the dating site's server. Luckily, I had not given him my email. He wrote, "I was so glad to meet you today. You are a lovely woman, and I want to spend more time with you. When I walked to the car, I was so excited that I had a hard-on while I caressed your breast. When can we meet again? Love, Chuck"

Yuck. I felt sick. Chuck touched my shoulder, not my breast. Yet I still felt invaded. What kind of man was he? Were all available men so immature? Were they all perverts?

I quickly wrote to the dating website's management to report Chuck's inappropriate behavior, deleted my profile, and took another shower. Trying to find someone to date was becoming a total disaster.

IS THIS A MATCH? A MISTAKE?
OR A MESSAGE I NEED TO LEARN?

The work at the church was going well. My self-confidence grew. My leadership skills blossomed. I developed enough willpower to lose 20 pounds of the stress-eating weight I had put on my body during the years after Mark's death.

As my body grew thinner, a desire to find a lover grew larger. So, I tried another dating service. I must have been crazy because crazy is repeating the same behaviors expecting a different outcome than the one that always occurred. I spent another large amount of money with yet another dating service, trusting their promise to meet a great man. As part of the process, the company provided a photoshoot. I felt pampered and affirmed. I looked great in the portfolio photos—healthy, confident, and pretty for someone in her mid-fifties. I met a few men through this program, but no one measured up to my expectations. I spent more of my savings than I should have. But this project of finding a lover also failed miserably.

What was wrong? Perhaps I was crazy. Was it the men? Did I want to find a clone of Mark? During this time, the men I looked for had to meet a high standard to fill the hole left after thirty years of marriage to a soulmate. The man had to be as charming as Jon. He needed to be smart, well-read (meaning he read what I read), progressive, good-looking, funny, religious in my way, and interested in the same things I wanted. Because I made quick judgments, the man needed to make it past the first 20 minutes.

I had forgotten the long, complicated process of growing friendship, then dating, and then developing a committed relationship. I ignored the fact love took time to grow. I became more impatient. Time was slipping by.

After I lost so much weight, a growing obsession with being sexually close to someone surprised me. My body ached for touch. I missed the sweetness of kissing. I yearned for the warmth of a hug and being held with a man's arms. Touching my own body for sexual release was no longer enough.

Acting on this desire meant I had to push a professional edge as well as a personal one. As a single woman working in the church, the church expected me to be celibate. The internal messages from my mother about being "too loose" with men echoed in my head. I believed Mark would be disappointed in me, for he also expressed stringent guidelines for the sexual behavior of clergy outside of marriage.

Yet, even with negative self-talk, the desire for sexual closeness did not go away. The curiosity for sexual exploration and a sense of adventure only grew with each internal rebuke. Perhaps I was too closed, too puritanical, too pious. When I was a young woman, these words defined me, but what about now as a woman in my 50s? I had been sexually active in marriage. As a single woman, was I to be asexual? The messages of the past no longer seemed realistic or even helpful.

So, I returned to another dating site, yet again. This time it cost me less money. I completed a profile, but I did not say I was a pastor. I experienced enough piety from well-meaning strangers. In the site profile, I acknowledged I was religious, spiritual, and stated I worked in community development. All of which was true.

But I was a bit smarter. I scrutinized the men's profiles. When I met someone for coffee, I called a friend for backup and to process the experience. But this time, sexual longing and a desire for physical connection became one of the primary reasons to meet someone.

First, I met Anthony. He moved to the United States from Poland several years earlier because of some issues that he kept secret. My intuition told me it was something illegal. His foreign accent was a turn-on, and his mysterious history was exciting. We met for coffee, then dinner. Several days later, he joined me on a long walk along the Mississippi River. After a couple of dates, I invited Anthony to my home for dessert. The pleasure of touch set free a desire to be with a man, beyond dating a man. The search for sexual freedom exploded within me.

We were together only a few times after that. He would set up a date and then cancel after making excuses. Thankfully, I was able to recognize this was a dead-end street and returned to the dating site to find someone else.

I met a few other men. I didn't know how to date and invite sexuality. Often, I was too quick to act on the lust to become intimate and get past the confusion—not a wise idea, but a real one for me at the time.

And then there was Jeffery. Jeffery was a devoted Catholic man, a retired coach from a college athletic program at a Catholic university. He was divorced, working as an insurance salesperson, and had a sister who was a protestant pastor. Jeffery played jazz piano, knew how to tell a good story, and drank too much beer. He lived beyond his means in an expensive penthouse in downtown Minneapolis.

After connecting through the dating site, Jeffery and I met for lunch at an Italian restaurant and talked a long time over wine and food. We walked in the park by the river most of the afternoon, and I invited him home for dinner. We dated for several weeks, enjoyed dinners and Valentine's Day, attended baseball games, enjoyed some conversation, and were often intimate.

Yet one question haunted me. Was being sexually free the physical adventure I was seeking?

I lost interest as I realized he had many issues to address before I could take him seriously. Drinking too much was one of them, along with being self-centered.

Within a few weeks, these escapades led me to a doctor's office to be tested for an STD. I made an appointment with a therapist. I needed to talk to someone about the guilt I experienced after each sexual episode. I needed to reconcile my religious and strict sexual history with the sexual expression I currently named as freedom.

I did not feel free. The idea of needing sex held me captive and distanced me from myself. As a young woman, I had not explored my sexuality and my own sexual attitudes. I took others' opinions as my own—my mom's, the moral teachings of a conservative church, Mark's narrow view. I thought I knew all the answers in the smooth transition into marriage. Now, in my 50s, I had to define sexuality for myself. The work of self-identity seemed never to end.

Thank goodness the STD tests came back negative. I thanked my imaginary guardian angels for working long hours to keep me safe, both from disease and from dangerous situations.

And thank goodness for a good therapist. She held a non-judgmental bucket for me as I verbally upchucked the stories of the last several months. I judged each situation through the lens of Mom's eyes, the discipline of the church, or Mark's opinions. I felt shame.

The therapist then invited me to reflect through a different set of lenses. She turned it around and asked, "What do you think?"

"Holding on to those old ideas is not helping you."

"What do you believe?"

With her help, many long reflective walks, and conversations with close friends, I developed a more detailed understanding of sexual freedom that integrated into my values and moral code.

Freedom meant I trusted the goodness of God and God's desire for me and all people to live with delight and joy. Freedom said my body was good and beautiful; being sexual was good and beautiful. Freedom meant that I chose. I chose to be discrete and discerning in my sexuality. I decided when to have sex and with whom. Being a woman who enjoyed being naked, being sexual, feeling pretty was not a sin. I need not be ashamed.

Freedom also meant I needed to be smarter and safer.

I removed my profile from the website for a while.

Just for a while.

Part Four: Proceed as the Way Opens

"And suddenly you know:
It's time to start something new
And trust the magic of beginnings."

— Meister Eckhart

CROSSINGS

Where hearts meet
at crossings,
few dare to journey,
love grows strong along paths
least traversed.

t. teruo haru

THIN SPACE

My widow's walk stretched forward almost six years. I discovered a renewed identity through intention and attention, making new choices. Some were helpful. Others not so much. I was fully aware of how privileged I was to have the financial and community resources to take several years to figure myself out. Most are not so lucky. My dad often reminded me of the privilege of choosing a profession. He wanted to be a pastor, but the poverty of his family of origin and the push to support his children denied him this dream. During this time, I embraced the gift of exploration.

When Mark died, I experienced God's presence in a clear and comforting assurance. Earlier in my life, many decisions I encountered seemed led by God's movement, especially when I started Covenant Counseling Center, a private practice as a psychotherapist in Eau Claire. I believed God opened the way with clarity of thought and planning. I achieved success quickly. I received affirmation and trust of many people around me with direct referrals and many invitations to speak and present at workshops. I lived my vision to teach, counsel, guide, and affirm others as they integrated issues of faith and life. I confidently trusted this venture. The practice met its five-year goals within three years after it began.

But in these years as a widow, my understanding of God changed as much as I did. I no longer experienced God as the guide to answer questions about my profession or things I wanted. God did not answer my prayers to find another husband. God did not explicitly tell me, "Be an ordained pastor." God did not cure all illnesses. Mark died. God did not stop my suffering or others' in the world. Many know injustice at the hands of the greedy or the pain of disease. I suffered through long loneliness. I did not believe in God as an all-powerful protector. I experienced God shielding some lives, but not others. I did not think God was the great fixer of problems nor the generous Santa in the sky, offering prosperity to the faithful.

My growing understanding of God was more mysterious, beyond my grasp, beyond words. Instead, God was Spirit. A Spirit of peace and Spirit of churning. A Spirit of hope and a Spirit of challenge. A Spirit of Oneness. A Spirit of compassion lived through the presence of others.

As I continued my theological studies, some of the church doctrines and dogmas no longer made sense to me. My understanding of God grew more transcendent, mysterious, and more imminent, an unknown presence. I knew God as the force of Love set loose in the world. I cherished moments when Love surrounded me. I treasured the compassion embodied by friends and family. I prized visions of hope and moments of internal peace. This was God's presence. There was Love—imminent and immediate.

I experienced serendipitous moments of blessings and holiness. Celtics described these as thin places where the Holy and the world gently kiss.

As seminary classes were ending, I traveled to the family lake home to reflect and wonder about the next steps for my career, relationships, and loneliness. We buried Mark's ashes there. On this holy ground, I wanted to pray, to be quiet, to ponder, to be.

The early summer sun shone brightly, reflecting sparkling light on the water's calm surface, inviting me to come and stay a while. The lake home's backyard was perched on top of a high bank several feet from the water's edge, secluded by trees, a privacy fence on one side, and a tall retaining wall on the other. The view of the lake opened wide. When Mark was alive, we sat on this bank overlooking the water. Together we were quiet, read, wrote, or just watched. We did not need to talk. Our mutual presence was enough.

On this day, I sat on the bank in the sun. I wanted to feel my body's freedom of my body. I desired the day's warmth to soak into my whole being and engage my soul. I sat cross-legged for several minutes, breathing in and out, resting in the warming light. I grounded my being into the earth as I listened to the echoes of my past and wondered about the expanse of my future.

Mark's grave sat on the bank to my left, surrounded by trees. I gave thanks for Barry, grateful for the time he took to nurture the surrounding trees that reached into the sky. Barry and his family kept the area around the granite marker of Mark's ashes clear of debris.

I watched the water in front of me. The surface remained still even as a delicate breeze blew against it. The sun's full energy reflected in the vibrant dancing of glittering light flashing to me on the shore. I took a deep breath to cherish this extraordinary glimpse of calm. Peace. I experienced a thin place, a gentle kiss, Holy Presence.

As I watched, two loons swam into my view, gliding slowly on the water's face, interrupting the smooth surface. Each bird formed a "V" in the trailing water as they swam forward, side by side. They took turns leading as they moved in a mutual rhythm. First one. Then the other.

One of the loons dived into the water, seeking food. After staying under for a seemingly long time, its head rose through the surface a small distance away. The other paddled to join him. Back and forth, the loons played, enjoying the sun's warmth. The black and white feathers glistened. I delighted in their oneness, a mutual dance of life.

After a time, one of the loons dived deep into the water and did not reappear in my sight. It must have found some morsel to eat from far away. I waited and watched. Nothing. The loon did not return. The second loon swam alone, circling the water, quietly moving here, there. After several minutes it swam alone, off to my right, the wideness of the trailing "V" melted into the movement of the water as the loon swam away. Their togetherness ended.

I knew this story, the mutual swimming with a mate and then one leaving the other, disappearing into the waters of the deep. I felt sad. But I also experienced a promise: I would be okay. I wondered what kind of trail I would leave in my wake as I moved forward.

I felt whole, firmly grounded through my sitting bones that connected to the earth; beautiful in my nakedness under the light of the sun; one with the universe under the open sky. God was present within me, within the stillness of the moment, and in the world around me. We were one.

The glimpses of calm and presence stayed with my soul through this time at the cabin. The memory remained as a blessing.

However, I did not receive any direction about what to do next. There still was no clarity of God's call or any answer to my specific prayers. It was as vague as the melted "V" in the flow of the water behind the loons. And like the loon swimming off into the lake to explore something more, I wondered what was next.

A CHALLENGE AND A CALL

While attending school, I also worked in a congregation in south Minneapolis, leading a ministry of community life and faith formation. A church grant-funded this three-year position focused on connecting people to people and people to God.

As I understood God as the Spirit of Love embodied within the world, I created opportunities for people to interact with each other. I believed the closer we got to each other, the closer we got to God. And the closer we were to God, the closer we became to each other. I trusted the care, conversations, empathy, and joy the people within the congregation embodied. By creating a hospitable environment, God's love did its work for compassion, reconciliation, and peacemaking.

In my work, we planned Wednesday evenings for families for a time to eat, sing, and study. We organized a mom's (and a dad's) morning bible study once a week. As the children played, the parents found camaraderie with other adults. With other leaders, we planned quiet times to pray in silence and breathe in peace. The congregation members and I worked together to affirm and bless each other. We found various ways to learn and guide each other in faith development and service for others.

When I preached sermons, I discovered my passion for publicly proclaiming God's love. I found it affirming and rewarding to do more than only listen. I had stories to tell and wisdom to share. And to my surprise, I also released the anxiety and second-guessing that challenged me over the years.

In response, many friends and church leaders encouraged me to pursue ordination. The seminary professors assured and affirmed my public voice and the gifts I had for ministry in the church. My faculty supervisor was quite insistent.

Discerning what to do was ever-present. I believed in God. I thought Jesus revealed God's character of compassion and justice in a particular time and place; I understood the presence of God's Spirit active with Love for the sake of the world. I did not accept the strict interpretations of Lutheran doctrine and dogma. I wanted to bless, affirm, guide, and teach others to know of God's love that surrounded and embraced our lives. I wanted to remind people God called them "beloved."

I wondered if I was seeking ordination to be close to Mark. I asked if I should remain a therapist and continue the work I had done for years. I sat just inside the edge of a religious box. I sometimes had one foot in and one foot out.

My daughter Sara, who was finishing her seminary studies at the same time, became the one person who questioned my ordination. We stood in my apartment's front yard when a tense conversation grew between us.

Sara said something like, "Mom, you have so many gifts as a therapist. I watched you grow in confidence alongside Dad and how he trusted your wisdom and guidance. He listened to you and what you knew about how people lived and interacted. Other leaders in the church told me what a difference you made in the lives of many people. They referred clients to you for therapy and asked you to lead workshops and teach classes. I saw your practice grow in Eau

Claire before Dad died. You are successful. Many bishops referred pastors to you for care and counseling. Mom, many people can be ordained. But how many have the skills you have to transform people's lives?" Sara loved me enough to speak the truth.

Sara also understood the vocation of the pastor in a more complex way than I did at the time. She experienced being pastor as a call of God for her, a call from others, and a call from deep within her soul. Since she was a child, she wrestled with discerning this vocation for herself. Yet, I did not fully understand her challenge to me and what the commitment of ordination meant for her. I proceeded, anyway.

Mark often said amid challenging times, "Given this reality, how do you make Love known?" Given the reality of this time in my life, what did I need to make Love known for others? I was good at my work as a therapist and spiritual director. And I could also work as an ordained pastor. Both fulfilled this mission.

The title "Pastor" would give me a voice of authority in the church. The people in the church did not always recognize a layperson in the same way. As an ordained pastor, I had the power to baptize, name, and bless and affirm God's love for another. As an ordained pastor, I had the authority to preside at communion, to consecrate bread and wine with God's forgiveness and covenant, and feed others with this love. I longed to nurture others with God's compassion and care. Ordination gave me the authority to be with others for the sake of God's love in a broader and more acceptable and professional way than in the work of private practice as a therapist.

Something inside of me kept pulling me toward ordination even with the doubts and challenges. Was this God's call? I was not sure. But I chose ordination. *I can do this*, I thought as an internal voice of empowerment spoke from the past yet again.

I waited for Sara. The call to be an ordained pastor was well-defined for Sara since she was a young child. I wanted to honor her and her call from the church and God. Sara walked in her father's path, but with the eyes of the next generation. Sara embodied the truth of this call deep within her being and claimed her right as a woman of vision, wisdom, and courage.

In time, Sara grew to accept my reasons and supported my efforts to become an ordained pastor. Yet, she remained wish-filled that, at some point, I might return to work as a therapist, which she saw as my true calling. We both knew the Lutheran church's expectation. I needed to serve three years in parish ministry before I could do the work of specialized ministry.

Six years after Mark's death, the Bishop placed his hands on my head in prayer as I was ordained. Pastors and my family gathered around me to bless my spirit, and friends gathered with me to bless the day.

These actions changed me. Not so much because of the title "Pastor," but because of the blessings. Being blessed with God's Love always changes us.

The blessings confirmed my future, but more importantly, these blessings affirmed my past. Blessings claimed my life lived in love—my life as a daughter, sister, aunt, friend, wife, pastor's wife, mother, teacher, weaver, therapist, and spiritual guide.

Blessings proclaim the reality of God's presence.

ENTERTAINING ANGELS UNAWARE

We normally functioned well together, working in mutual support and care to meet the needs of an urban congregation in south Minneapolis. But on an early spring day, Helen, one of my colleagues, said something that unintentionally hit a hidden nerve within me. My internal residue of anger attacked me instantly, shutting down my thinking brain to the point that I do not remember the specifics of the argument. But I do remember how angry I was. I remember feeling misunderstood and questioned.

I tried to breathe and excused myself, slowly walking back into my office.

"I need to take a minute." I steadied my hand to stop myself from slamming the door shut. Sitting in my office chair, I turned my back to the door and stared out the window into the parking lot. "Think. Breathe."

Nothing worked. The anger erupted in me like a blast of hot lava, fiery red, spewing from my core, flowing into my body. I experienced the heat of a conscious burn, buried deep within, yet fueled by just a few words from a coworker.

I struggled. "What happened?" I could not figure it out. I needed to escape before the confusing anger devoured me.

Without saying a word, I slipped into my jacket and walked out the front door for fresh air. I hoped to find a way to calm this flare-up.

A park covering most of a square city block was across the street from the church. It appeared inviting. The trees were budding shades of fresh green. Daffodils and tulips pushed through the ground in closed pods, eager to open in bursts of yellow, reaching toward a deep blue sky in scattered patches through the park. A smooth breeze hit my face, bidding me come.

But I usually did not walk here. Drug dealers made their deals on the basketball courts, and the homeless hung out on the benches. I stayed close to the church in my comings and goings, especially at the end of the day.

Yet, on this day, the sun shone brightly. My raging mind made it unsafe for me to drive. So, I walked across the street and began pacing the sidewalk around the park's perimeter.

I pulled the jacket tight around my body and the collar close to my ears. I jammed my hands in my pockets and walked, pounding each step, pushing forward to break free of my anger. My jaw clenched. My eyes glared ahead. My forehead pinched into my nose. My brain rehearsed what I wanted to say when I returned. I practiced in my mind the words I would use to win the disagreement with Helen. In the anger, I imagined how I might slice my opponent with the sharpness of my tongue and then stand over the defeated body with a victory, my fist thrust toward the heavens. My brain ruminated with anger. The walk did not release any of the tension. Each step forward and each quarter turn around the park reinforced its power.

As I moved with a fierce pursuit, I turned the third corner. Down the block, a woman walked toward me, approaching in an ambling gait. The breeze blew an unpleasant odor my way. A quiet fear grew, replacing the anger with caution. I moved to the side, grateful that I left my purse behind.

As she came closer, the brims of her enormous hat flapped in the wind. The tails of the red and orange scarves wrapped several times around her neck floated behind her like wings. A single button held a brown, woolen coat around a bulging belly as the layers of skirts billowed around her in various colors and prints. She carried a plastic bag stuffed with many things in one hand close to her body. She walked with confidence and held her head high.

This strange woman slowed as she approached me and my intense movement. I slowed to walk around her when I heard her say in a quiet, calm voice, "Let it go, girl. Let it go." I looked up, and she smiled at me through crooked teeth. Her eyes carried a softness of quiet peace and met mine directly, peering deep into me. For just a moment, she paused. I hesitated and then stopped walking. She nodded and walked on.

This odd woman saw me in my angry ugliness and blessed me with her wisdom.

I slowed. And let out a long sigh, "Let it go."

I walked around the park a second time, at a much slower pace, breathing the intention to let go into each step. As my brain began to work again, I knew this anger did not help me or the situation in the church office. I thought about my reaction, my defensiveness that undermined my colleague's concerns.

I slowed to walk with gentler steps.

"Let it go."

I thought about ways to engage the situation with kinder words. I did not need to win. I softened my face and allowed the brightness of the sun to reach into my heart's unease.

I did not see the woman again. Yet, I felt as if I heard a voice from an angel.

"Let it go."

Peace cooled my angry internal fire.

When I returned to the church, I walked into Helen's office. Greeting her with an apologetic smile, I said, "I'm sorry. Let's talk." It was time to let it go.

A DECISION

Within months after my ordination, the pastor of the south Minneapolis church took a call to another congregation. The funding for my position ended soon, and the church worked with a deficit budget. The church could not afford to keep me in my job and call a senior pastor at the same time. Several people approached me to see if I might seek the position to be the senior pastor.

The leadership thought I had the capabilities and skills. But I was not convinced this was the best choice for me. The congregation's president and I met weekly, seeking to discern what was best for me and the parish. He listened to my concerns about budget, my ideas of what needed changing, and my fears of changing my role to be the senior pastor.

I was afraid and cautious. Within three years, my role at this church changed from a lay associate to an ordained assistant pastor. The possibility of being a senior pastor loomed large in the options that lay ahead. I realized this was too much change for me. It was too big of a jump.

The regional church office's leadership also informed me that it was not a good idea for the assistant pastor to move into the role of senior pastor. I thought I would use up my goodwill too quickly as I implemented my ideas. I would balance the budget and organize the church in a way that made sense to me but would also challenge the status quo. I did not hear a clear call from God to step into this new role. I questioned my abilities to lead. I also knew needing to be liked interfered with the actions I needed to challenge others.

At the same time, I talked with the leadership of a counseling service that worked with clergy at a nearby hospital. The administrator knew of my work with clergy and the church in my private practice in Eau Claire and was very interested in finding ways to bring me on board to work with pastors at the hospital. They wanted to expand their work with the clergy, especially those who were angry, depressed, and overwhelmed with the pressures of ministry. I was very intrigued and curious about this work. It was a perfect fit for my history and my innate skills, and I could remain in Minneapolis. However, all of this was in the development stage; no definite plans were in place.

Then a third possibility interrupted this discernment. A call to be the campus pastor at the University of Illinois became available. I always wanted to work with college students. The Lutheran campus ministry national leadership heard of my background in therapy, spiritual formation, and ordination and told me I was a perfect fit for the call. After an interview on the campus, the campus ministry extended an invitation to take the job. I took it.

Why? Because it sounded fun. Because others told me it was perfect for me. Because it was another chance to try something new. Because I thought I could make a difference in young adult lives.

"Proceed as the way opens." Campus ministry seemed like an opening into the next part of my life.

But was it the right choice?

After I moved, I realized it might have been an unfortunate decision. I should have paid attention when my flip phone fell in the toilet and died during a break in the two days of interviews.

THE WAY DID NOT OPEN WELL

Home. The two-story Tudor-style brick home sat on a tree-lined cobblestone street. A large, covered front porch with hanging ferns and a red door bid me welcome. I loved it as soon as I walked in, the high ceilings, wooden floors, sleeping porch off the upstairs bedroom, and the flower gardens in the backyard. Built in the early twentieth century, it carried a character of welcome and warmth. The repainted interior artfully embraced the rooms with colored ceilings and soft colors. The upstairs bathroom had an old-fashioned tub. Most importantly, it would be mine.

The home was big enough to house all the things I loved—books, the art Mark and I collected, the grand piano, and yes, more books. Even after I donated several boxes to the library and the seminary before my move to Illinois, I still owned more than 40 boxes of books, Mark's plus my own. It appeared Mark moved with me even though it was seven years after his death.

I was eager to create a home in Champaign for Barkley and me. We arrived in town the same week the students moved into the dorms. My emotions fit the campus energy—uprooted, confused, excited, and filled with both anticipation and dread.

And I was alone. Alone with no friends. Alone, as my family was far away.

Alone and very frustrated by the run-around of my realtor and the mortgage company. The moving van with all my belongings was to arrive a few days later. The mortgage broker had not yet approved my loan. The realtor was not sure it would be accepted in time to move in.

So, instead of moving into the house, Barkley and I rented a room at the Red Roof Inn. We made ourselves at home with my computer, two large house plants, one suitcase of clothes, my private files of essential papers, and anything else that fit into the 2002 Volkswagen Beatle (the one Mark bought for me before he died). This room at the Red Roof Inn and my car were to become "home" for much longer than I anticipated.

The academic year began in a confused state. I attempted to find my way around the unfamiliar university campus. At the same time, I struggled through the complex process of the mortgage application, hoping to speed it up. I re-sent several records the mortgage company lost a second time. They discovered an unpaid bill for a 30-dollar pair of pants I bought on a credit card soon after Mark died. The clothing company did not forward the statement to the address in Minnesota after I moved. As a result, I owed almost 200 dollars with accrued interest on the bill. The mortgage company wondered if I was a bad credit risk.

The company went through the process one question at a time. One step. Then the next. Only after I addressed and settled one concern did they decide to go to the next question. One. At. A. Time. Efficiency was not part of the company's process. Disappointment grew as part of mine.

When the moving van arrived, the drivers stacked my furniture in a storage unit instead of arranging it in the home as I imagined. I piled boxes on boxes of books and art in my office at church, creating a maze of cardboard leading a path to my desk. My meals were fast food at best. In the morning and at night, I cautiously walked Barkley around the motel parking lot, scooting around the trucks, vans, and cars, concerned for my safety.

Most nights, I locked the door behind us, and I cried myself to sleep. Or on the nights when I was not sobbing, I was screaming mad. Mad at the mortgage company. Angry at the realtor for making promises she could not keep. Mad at myself. What had I done? Why did I leave Minnesota? I had friends, a home, and my family there. Why did I leave Minneapolis where I walked safely and lived within the familiar and good?

Six weeks into the semester, the mortgage company finally discovered that I was a "good" risk. They granted me a mortgage at a rate higher than I initially planned because of that 30-dollar pair of pants with interest. Luckily, I still had the pants and wore them on closing day. That pair of pants was now the most expensive piece of clothing I owned.

This time as I moved into the house, I was lucky enough to have Brent and Connie with me. They were driving through Illinois on their way from one coast to the other and stopped in Champaign to help. They unwrapped the dishes and stacked them in the cupboards, carried boxes of books up to the attic, made the beds, and placed furniture in the various rooms to create an environment of hospitality. On the last day of unpacking, Connie pulled a handbell from her backpack.

She held it high above her head and rang it boldly, "Let's get rid of all the bad energy in this house." She brought the bronze bell with her from India, where she had studied for the summer. She saw it as a way to bless my home. Brent and I followed her from room to room as we laughed. She rang the bell, dancing around the room. With each ding, the spirit of joy entered my heart and my home. With each clang of copper to steel, Brent and Connie gifted me with a blessing of hope and fun.

Campus Ministry was not what I expected. I enjoyed the students, their stories, and their energy, but they were busy with classes, work, and social life. They were not ready to talk to their pastor about their private lives, which was part of why I applied for the position. They had friends for that. And trust took time to build.

I was unsure of what to do and how to do it. This ministry was so different than parish work. I met with students in small groups for dinner and worship. We planned fun events and service projects. But I did not trust what I was doing. I felt like I was swinging a bat at a piñata called "campus ministry." I knew when I finally made a "hit," it would be sweet and bring a great reward. But I felt like I was blindfolded. I wondered if I was even in the same room as the piñata, much less close by, making it impossible to hit.

The idea that I could integrate being a pastor and the work as a therapist/counselor proved disappointing. Being a pastor was public work. I was open about myself to help build community and to preach with authority. I was public. I sat in coffee shops to be available and accessible to others. However, doing the work of the therapist/counselor was personal work, which meant keeping confidences, sharing little about myself, and keeping my focus on the other.

Because I was busy most weekends when others were not working, I also found it challenging to make friends like I did when I was a student at the seminary. Other professionals around me were married and had little available time to include me. There was no cousin John in Champaign to connect me with other adults. I was lonely. How did I fit into this new place? I thought campus ministry would be fun, but the reality was not what I imagined.

The one thing I did enjoy was college football. I grew up cheering the Nebraska Huskers, so cheering for the Fighting Illini was a natural fit. On a Saturday (after I finally moved into my home), a member of the center's board offered me a ticket to see a game in person. She gave a second ticket to another woman, Rhonda, for a blind date.

On the day of the game, Rhonda planned to meet me at the Campus Center and park her car there. The Center sat on the corner of two one-way streets. Rhonda said she knew exactly how to get there. I waited for her at the Center's main doors when I received a call from her.

The one-way streets around the venue complicated the directions to the building. After several miscues and confusing phone calls, we finally met in the Center's drive.

I was not quite sure what to expect as Rhonda opened the car door. The phone conversations had been intense. She was as headstrong as I was in describing the driving directions from our different perspectives. Graciously, we both laughed as she stepped out of the car.

With bags in hand and curiosity about the other person, we walked down the street to the game.

Within the first block, Rhonda stopped and said, "I need to make something clear before we spend the afternoon together. I want you to know what we will and will not talk about during the game. Your 'pastor gig' is not one of them." I agreed. The religious talk would come later as we learned to trust each other.

We headed to the football game. In time our friendship grew with intellectual intrigue, challenge, mutual respect, heartfelt passion about those we love, many lunches, glasses of wine, and Rhonda's love of "bling."

OPENING DOORS

The friendship with Rhonda was needed and helpful but was not enough to fill the void of the friends I missed in Minnesota, nor soften the hard work of campus ministry. Though it kept me busy, I was alone. I wondered why I moved. The pricey mortgage on a house I loved made it too difficult to move back to Minnesota. I missed my past, the life I created there.

So, what did I do? By the end of the first semester of campus ministry, I decided to try an online dating service again. Yet again. Was the third time the charm? Or was I just crazy in the repetition? I missed being in a loving relationship. But this time, I revised my profile to describe my work as "director of a campus center." I did not say the word, "Pastor."

Scrolling through the profiles of men in a 60-mile radius around Champaign, "AutumnsEagle" caught my eye. His tag line, "Good conversation—expands vision, deepens understanding and is emotionally enriching," hooked my brain. His favorite book, *The Artists Way: A Spiritual Path to Higher Creativity*, attracted my spirit. The last book he read, *Picking Cotton: a remarkable and unusual memoir written by two people about injustice and redemption*, engaged my desire for social change. The last line of his profile, "If you also enjoy spontaneity, laughter, and meaningful conversation, perhaps we could explore this further," became an invitation. I read this profile several times. Perhaps there was someone in this faraway place in which I found myself who might become a male companion. To meet him, I "winked," the first-level method to let someone know you are interested in their profile.

To my surprise, "AutumnsEagle" sent an email response. He took the time to write a thoughtful note through the dating site in return. We began to email back and forth. He was half Caucasian and half Asian and grew up in California and Hawaii, a world very different from my own. He had a doctorate in sociology and wrote about world hunger when he was a professor in a small liberal arts school. As a trained therapist, he had led workshops on personal growth. He currently worked as a chief compliance officer at a comprehensive behavioral health center in a community an hour from Champaign. In the emails, he wrote about his desire to establish a genuinely compassionate, respectful, empathic, and caring relationship with others. He asked questions about me. His name was Terry.

After several emails, we exchanged phone numbers. After talking by phone a few times, Terry and I planned to meet in person by having lunch on the Saturday of the Martin Luther King holiday weekend.

The second semester would begin in a few days. In preparation for programs at the center, a student and I scheduled to paint the campus center's main lounge area on the same day. I thought it would be no problem to break away for a little while for lunch. I excused myself at noon, promising I would be back within an hour and a half, at most. I believed this to be plenty of time to meet Terry and check him out. Especially since I had left other first encounters within the first twenty minutes.

I arrived early at Biaggi's, an Italian restaurant, and sat in a booth where I could watch as Terry arrived. When I saw him, he was a bit shorter than I imagined, but he carried himself with dignity and was well-dressed in a red crew-neck sweater. He shared a genuine smile. When he approached, I saw a twinkle in his eye, looking directly at me with kindness and attention.

Hmm? So far. So good.

We ordered food. Terry told me about himself, as I usually asked questions first. But then Terry became curious about me, which surprised and enchanted me. This well-educated and charming man showed interest in me. He looked, smiled at me, and even flirted a bit. Twenty minutes extended into an hour.

After an hour and fifteen minutes, I grew anxious as I needed to get back to the center. This lunch date was taking longer than I had assumed. I had promised the student I would return within 90 minutes. I was preparing a way to excuse myself when Terry ordered dessert.

Dessert? I did not have time for dessert. This first "date" was going well. But I had another commitment. A student was painting walls at the center by herself and expected me to return soon.

As politely as I could, I told Terry I needed to return to the campus center for painting. It sounded lame, but it was the truth. Terry looked surprised but asked for the check, paid for our meals, and walked me to my car. As directly as I could, I told him I wanted to meet again. He said he would call. I got in my car and drove back to the center, wondering if I had lost a chance yet again.

One thing was different, however. I was smiling, and my heart pounded. My stomach flip-flopped each time I remembered Terry's smile.

When Terry called the next day, he invited me on a date for the following Saturday, outlining a detailed plan. After picking me up at 3:00 p.m., Terry planned to visit the campus museum, dinner at an Asian restaurant, a movie, and then dessert. I laughed as I realized he allowed no room for me to make an early escape.

More than an hour before Terry arrived, I stood in front of the mirror in my bedroom. I tried on several outfits, each piled one on top of the other on the loveseat. I could not decide what to wear. With each set of clothes, I wondered, *Does this outfit make me look old? Fat? Too sexy? Not sexy enough? Was it too dressy? Too casual?* I wanted to make a good impression.

Just as the clock marked 3:00 p.m., the front doorbell rang. Barkley let me know I had a company. Terry arrived right on time. I could not change again. So, wearing a blue skirt and sweater, I walked to the door. When I saw Terry, a kind smile greeted me in return. I relaxed. I would be okay.

Terry helped me with my coat. He walked me to the car and then opened the passenger side door. I was surprised. When was the last time someone opened a door for me?

We drove to the museum parking area. Terry parked the car and then parked it again to make sure it was precisely straight between the lines. He walked to my side and opened the door. We walked to the museum. He opened that door.

As we meandered among the art collections, our bodies began moving in a mutual connection. Now and then, our hands touched as we mused about a painting we liked or examined an unusual sculpture. Each time we encountered a closed-door throughout the museum, Terry opened it for me.

At dinner, he invited me to try sushi as he told me more about his Japanese grandparents. At the movie, we laughed or sighed at similar times. When we got to the restaurant for "Death-by-chocolate-cake," they were preparing to close. We were both disappointed. Terry excused himself to use the bathroom before we were to leave, and while he was gone, I ordered two pieces of cake to go.

When he returned to the counter, I said, "Let's have dessert at my house."

When we walked to the car, he opened the car door. After he parked at my house, he opened the car door again. When we walked to my home, he opened the door.

Dessert was in my living room with conversation into the early hours of the next day, as he opened yet another door—the one to my heart.

TRUSTING AGAIN

At first, I did not tell Terry I was a pastor. In the online dating profile, I reported I worked with college students as director of a campus center. I remembered the assumptions several men made about me when I included information about being a pastor in previous profiles. The title "pastor" placed me in a box. Some men assumed I was "super-pious." Others thought they needed to reform me because I was a woman with too much authority. I did not want to explain this again until I could discuss it in person. I wanted a man to meet me as an individual rather than a title.

When we saw each other the following week, I shared with him I was an ordained pastor. However, Terry was not surprised. One of his married female friends who took an interest in his love life had researched my name on the internet and told him what she discovered. I was an ordained Lutheran pastor serving Christian students at a campus center. Terry was waiting for me to report this to him myself.

When I told him about my profession, Terry asked many questions about my beliefs, the Lutheran tradition, worship, the Bible. Terry's curiosity was never judgmental. He described himself as agnostic. He was not a Christian or even religious, but he accepted spiritual realities, serendipitous events that were beyond understanding. Native American spirituality intrigued him, so he acknowledged the Great Spirit, but not the concept of a personified God.

Terry and I continued to see each other regularly. We enjoyed movies, music, plays, good food, and always a glass of wine. He listened as I talked about my kids, Mark, his death, and the complicated process of rebuilding my life. Terry talked about his kids, his childhood, and growing up in poverty living in the projects in California. At the age of ten, he cooked for his three younger siblings because his mom was too ill. She died at the age of 33 when Terry was 13. An unsupportive stepdad then raised him and his three younger siblings in Hawaii.

Terry went on to tell me of his three previous marriages. He described himself as being a self-absorbed, selfish, and insensitive younger man. I was impressed that Terry was open and forthright about the issues and mistakes made in past relationships. He said he was in his mid-fifties before he realized how to love differently. Terry was reflective and honest. He often noted that I was the lucky beneficiary of whatever wisdom he gained from those mistakes.

Yet, I remained cautious. Much of the time, I was calm and open to the relationship. However, when I thought too long and hard, I grew terrified. My brain flooded with many questions, doubts, and statements of judgment. What would others think?

The fact that Terry was not a Christian was of great concern, added to my internal fear, and shamed me in judgment. When I told a few of Mark's friends about Terry, their first question to me was, "Does he love Jesus?" If my mom and dad were still alive, what would they think? Would they ask the same question? Dad refused to do business with anyone who was not Christian. I was married to a pastor for 30 years. While Christianity and the church rooted my whole life, both public and personal, Terry had no connection with the church.

Terry invited me to see beyond the institution of the church. He affirmed my desire to understand and live in a more pluralistic world of differing ideas, differing cultural perspectives, differing reflections on God. He lived with integrity and gave from his heart in service for others from his code of morality, not the strict demands of religion. It grew from a well of wholeness and love that I longed to understand in my constant search to find meaning and a more profound spirit of truth about a bigger God, one I had not encountered before. But this search also frightened me. The unknowns overwhelmed me.

When I remained mindful and present to Terry, I was happy. Whenever he touched me, held my hand, felt the core of my back, or put his arms around me, I experienced warm energy—spiritual and healing.

Several weeks after we met, Terry invited me to a party to meet his co-workers and friends. Most of his good friends were women. At the party, they huddled around me, asking questions about my work as a pastor. I immediately sensed their love and respect for Terry. Like many men's female friends, they wanted to protect him from some crazy woman who might hurt him in some way. After this initial interrogation, his co-worker Gloria pulled me aside. She explained she was very active in her church and worked with Christians every day.

"Terry may not be a believer or engaged in a church," she said, "But he is the most Christian man I've ever met. He lives it."

A few days later, I asked Terry what loving someone meant. He believed it meant "a willingness to give up your life for the one you love." *That is Christ-like*, I thought. Jesus asked his followers to lay down their lives for another. Although only half-Asian, Terry also identified as Japanese. For him, the samurai warrior modeled the path of respect. The code of the samurai meant to live in total service to another. The values of honor, courage, and loyalty paralleled Christian morality.

In my journal, I wrote, "Terry's so respectful. He is bright. He is kind. If he were a Christian, I would have fallen for him immediately, hook, line, and sinker."

Why was I so hung up on this Christian identity? I was a pastor. I was supposed to model a Christian life. I grew up in a Christian home. The church defined my whole life. I lived by the liturgical calendar of Advent, Christmas, Epiphany, Lent, Easter, and Pentecost. Yet, Terry had no idea what any of this meant. Church language was utterly foreign to him.

In the past, I believed it was essential to be in a relationship with only a Christian. Was it still? Could I be with someone who did not feel as I did? Did I need Terry to articulate the words, "I believe in Jesus"? With all these questions, my brain smothered in a fog of "should." I should date a Christian. I should put Christ first. I should follow all the church rules. I should date a believer. But I also knew a pluralistic world affirmed God beyond all-knowing, beyond my knowing.

I was falling in love with Terry. He drove me crazy, sometimes with long stories and a multitude of details. Or when he insisted on a precise explanation of some concept we tried to discuss. Or when he peeled away layer upon layer of an idea with peppering questions. Or when he exemplified the stereotypical absent-minded professor forgetting details of things we talked about many times. Or when he spoke to himself aloud.

We were good companions and friends. We talked about important things. He was a gentle lover, and I felt whole and feminine when I was with him. Terry admired me, encouraged me to be me. I knew love.

During one of the many phone calls we shared throughout, I told Terry I had to fly to Albuquerque for a conference. Terry offered to meet me at the airport and bring me home. I instantly broke into tears, my heart deeply touched. I had forgotten how lovely it was to be greeted with love and welcomed home.

During the past seven years, my radical independence demanded that I make life work alone. I longed for a real relationship. Someone to call at the end of the day. Someone to talk with me about life. Someone to think of me, to make me dinner, to make love, to listen.

A few nights later, Terry invited me for dinner at his condominium. He made a simple meal of salad and salmon, lit candles, turned on romantic music, and started a fire in the fireplace.

When we sat down to eat, he poured glasses of wine and asked, "Will you pray?" I broke into tears again, deeply touched by his heartfelt respect for me. Praying at meals was never part of his life, but he invited me to share a prayer at dinner and have prayer be part of his life now.

As we talked, I mused aloud that I was trying to trust again. I wanted to trust someone who would not leave me or hurt me or use me. Terry responded with a surprising answer. I thought he was going to say, "You can trust me."

Instead, he said, "Trust yourself. Trust yourself to be able to manage whatever the challenge."

My growing love for Terry invited me to trust myself. It was like walking through a high-ropes course. God-revealed-in-Love was the safety harness. This relationship asked me to jump into falling in love, to enjoy the beauty of present reality. Love was unfolding around me.

And yet, my brain-fogged-in-fear kept returning.

OBSESSION COMES TO PLAY

As the spring semester ended, my relationship with Terry grew. I did not run away. During the summer, I met Terry's family at a reunion in California. Terry met Sara, Clark, Brent, and Connie on a three-day excursion in New York City. Both of our families supported us. My kids liked Terry and accepted him graciously. They saw that he treated me respectfully, provided a calming influence, and affirmed my happiness.

I prepared for the second year of campus ministry, but I did not feel rested after a busy summer. In directing the center, being pastor, connecting with students, and dating, I was tired. I had not spent enough time during the summer to be quiet, reflect, read, and plan. Usually, this was part of my routine.

Overwhelmed with what to do at the center, I struggled to find my way to lead as a campus minister. What do I teach? How to raise money? What do I do to engage students and be relevant? How do I talk about the Christian call to seek justice and peace?

I worried about others' perceptions as I dated Terry. What would they think? (Mostly as we traveled together.) Would others negatively judge me? Would I lose my job if people asked too many questions about our relationship?

When Terry and I were apart, my anxiety grew. I made assumptions about him. I dwelled on the contrary idea that we had nothing in common. We were interested in different kinds of books. We grew up differently. When he talked about some issues that interested him, I could not relate. At times, I selfishly judged this as boring. I criticized him when he told me he played the lottery. I could not connect. I believed it was below me.

The fear inside morphed into a critical monster filled with judgment of both Terry and me. This angst became an obsession. My brain began repeating the words of my past harsh religious training filled with condemnation. Did my relationship with Terry distract me from being an effective leader in campus ministry?

I drew a picture of Obsession in my journal as a hairy character with a large head, tiny feet, no arms, and wide-eyed with a shouting voice, and spikey hair spreading out in all directions, covering its whole body. At other times I drew Obsession with the hair flattening around its shapeless mass, sad eyes, and a frowning mouth looking troubled. Obsession never had arms to reach beyond itself.

When Terry and I were together, this obsession disappeared. The anxiety went away as I relaxed with a single sip of wine. The spirits (Spirit?) helped me settle into being present with him. The concern to share spirituality and find a common background did not seem important at these times. Judgment disappeared within the love we shared. We had fun together. Terry's care and admiration wrapped around me. I truly enjoyed his company.

By the end of the summer, the internal dilemma, the crazy push-and-pull, became too much. The polarization of the inner Obsession and the present external joy exhausted and overwhelmed me.

One evening of an incredibly hot summer day in early August, I abruptly told Terry I needed to end our relationship. It was complicated because he had no idea that I was struggling with any issues at all. I never shared any of the destructive thoughts with him. I was too embarrassed and ashamed by the internal critic that grew within my brain fog. It was particularly challenging because I announced it after we had a lovely evening together and had even made love.

I remember telling Terry I missed being with someone who understood my spiritual reflections and faith commitments. I needed someone who knew about the church and church life. I did not think our relationship could grow any further. I was grateful to him. I appreciated who he was.

We left on friendly and mutual terms, though both stunned by the words I said aloud, which were alien to our experience together. The internal Obsession calmed for the moment.

Two days later, I sent him a card expressing gratitude for the nine months we had together. I was beginning to miss him. Did I miss Terry or the idea of Terry?

Two weeks later, my brain was racing again. I thought I would feel free when I ended the relationship. I remained bound by the shame I experienced from the internal critic. This time it judged me for letting go of a good man. I missed Terry and missed the fun we had. I longed for Terry's company.

The work at the campus center took on a new challenge, as well. A board member confronted and chastised me for a decision I made. In front of the whole board, he mansplained how the board was my boss, and I needed to do what they told me to do.

"Everyone has bosses," he said, "and we're yours. It is like running in the pack of dogs pulling a dog sled. There is only one lead dog. Like every other dog in the pack, your nose is in the butt of the dog in front of you. Get used to it." He laughed as he spoke, but it did not feel like a joke.

These words seemed abusive to me and shook my spirit. His actions deeply hurt me. I needed help from someone who understood leadership to help me discern what to do. Terry was the only person I knew who could help. The only person I trusted to help.

Terry's experience included leading workshops about the principles of servant leadership. Being a chief compliance officer of a large institution, he knew about power and its effects. Terry led investigations when others used their superiority against employees in hurt-filled ways. I believed Terry would have insights I trusted to figure out what to do.

I called Terry because I needed a friend. (Or at least this is what I claimed.)

"Could you help me think this through?" We talked on the phone several times in the next few days and discussed how to be a leader as a woman. We explored ways to regain my place of authority.

Terry's non-anxious presence and non-judgmental help soothed my anxious spirit. "Obsession," a thing in my brain that blew up like a balloon, now attacked me as an inept leader with its screaming voice. Terry's acceptance helped quiet Obsession's judgment.

By the end of the week, I invited Terry to dinner to say thanks for his help. As we talked in person, I confessed that I had been unfair when I ended the relationship too abruptly. We agreed to grow our friendship. I needed and wanted his company.

We affirmed this new understanding by going to his home for a glass of wine. After the wine, we danced. With dancing, we kissed. The next morning, we agreed to be "friends" until either of us found someone else or if the relationship no longer made sense.

How long would that take?

FINDING HOME

During this next year, I found my footing in my work as a campus pastor. I trusted my pastoral skills, preached well, and was an engaging teacher and Bible study leader. The attendance at church on Sundays and the mid-week dinners grew significantly.

Announcing the blessing of God's love was work I cherished because I needed the reminder of God's love as much as everyone else. A significant donation to the ministry helped stabilize the center's financial needs. A few students came for pastoral counseling, seeking my advice. They began to trust me.

But I still missed the transformative work I did when I was a therapist. I struggled with being a leader.

Obsession engaged me regularly and kept me from seeing love, receiving love, and giving love. She also criticized my leadership skills.

I decided to seek the help of a therapist to stop the internal angst. I wanted to find a path through the resistance to commit to Terry. I needed to understand why I had a difficult time exerting my power and authority as a leader. I needed reminders of the goodness of God, to remember the shame and angst I experienced were my internal judgments, not God's. How could I stop Obsession from consuming me?

I met weekly with my therapist Joan. Her office was in the basement of a building on the edge of campus. Whenever I walked down the stairs and entered her office, I felt safe. A cocoon of protection and wisdom surrounded me.

I waited for change and transformation. We began each meeting with an offering of a cup of tea, but it often cooled as it sat half-full. Words poured out of me, making it difficult to swallow anything down.

As we explored this fear of personal power, memories of my mother flashed in my head. Again, I remembered the one wounding scene—when I was 13 years old, playing ping pong with my brother Richard. For most of my life, I had put an internal check on my strength and voice because I mistakenly believed my power often wounded others.

After I remembered this story, I knew why I was afraid to show leadership. My power could hurt others. But just knowledge was not enough. How could I stop the unconscious reactivity?

Joan introduced me to EFT (Emotional Freedom Techniques) tapping. Tapping various parts of my face and body provided a calming message sent to the amygdala in my head that allowed my thought and body to feel safe, dissipating my anxiety. Obsession found a challenger. By tapping the significant points in my body and speaking the reason for my concern, my mind and body would align.

While tapping each part of my body, I added the words, "Even when I get afraid to lead, I deeply and completely accept myself."

The words, "I deeply and completely accept myself," were the ones I most needed to own. These were the words I needed to lead and to love.

I wondered about using these same words for Terry. "I deeply and completely accept you." Whenever Obsession began to criticize him, judge him, or judge me about loving Terry, I started to write affirmations. "I love Terry because he adores me. I love Terry because he is honest, fair. I love him because he has done his work of transformation and growth. I love Terry because music is the language of his heart. I love Terry because he helps me see a world bigger than my own."

"I deeply and completely accept you." These words were a different kind of tapping—one for my heart.

My friends, family, and even my therapist seemed to understand Terry was a gift to me. Whenever they listened to me talk about him, they heard the joy in my voice and the affirmation of his love and presence in my life. Whenever I questioned or doubted, they took his side. They all seemed to believe he was right for me.

Anne said, "God gave you Terry as a gift."

Terry's tolerance and staying power allowed space for me to push through yet another layer. He stayed near as I worked through the long loneliness of the past years after Mark's death, much of which was self-imposed. The angst and self-doubt I carried since childhood created much of the isolation.

I loved Terry and longed to commit to him, but something more stood between us, like bricks in a wall. Terry remained patient, grounded within himself. He did not always know what I thought and explored in therapy, but he remained present even when I was not open or transparent. His presence was an anchor, a rock, an embodied steadfastness of love and care.

I began talking more with Terry about my fears, the push and pull for being in a relationship, my sadness, my loneliness, and my mistrust.

In time, Terry asked, "What does any of this have to do with me?"

I stopped. Terry was right. This struggle was about me and my obsessions. When was I going to let him know who I was? When was I going to let him meet Obsession?

In my journal, I drew another picture. I drew a picture of me, looking down, hair tangled, a line for my mouth, hands at my side. I drew Terry standing on the other side of the page with a smile and arms open extended toward me, reaching out in acceptance. Between us, I drew a wall, with several boxes representing the bricks keeping me apart from him. Each block had a label. Mark. Judgment from others. Expectations of others. Independence. Fear of losing myself. Widow's identity. Fear of making a mistake. Some bricks had no name. There were just there.

The word, "Mark," labeled the most massive brick on the top of the wall. I realized it would be impossible to accept and love Terry if I always saw him through Mark's paradigm. Terry was worthy of honor and respect on his own.

As I looked at the picture, I said aloud, "I will not let a dead man get in the way of my future. To receive the love, I need to completely let go of Mark and my identity as Mark's wife. I will not be married to a dead man."

I went through my house and took down all of Mark's pictures. I put away various mementos and reminders of him.

I took other actions in the next months. Tapping. Time. Words of affirmation. Letting go. Talking more about myself with Terry. Listening to my friends. Going to therapy. Trusting myself. Trusting Terry and cherishing Terry as a gift. Remembering God is Love, not judgment. Tending to love allows love to grow. Love grows. It does not just happen. It needs attention and care. It required a home. The imaginary bricks building the wall were crumbling away, a bit at a time.

In the spring of the academic year, I took several students to Nicaragua for a cultural exchange trip. I had done this the year before as part of the center's outreach ministry, but this time I took several more students.

Before I left on the trip, Terry held me and said, "I want to come home to you." These words hammered through the brick wall. At the end of each day on the trip, I realized how much I wanted to talk to Terry about what I learned. I wanted to hear his ideas. I longed to listen to his voice, his perspectives, his insights. I wanted to come home to Terry too.

When I returned home, I gave Terry a brick and the following poem:

Through the bricks, you said, "I want to come home to you."
Simply spoken, calmly shared, within the routine of daily connection.

"I want to come home to you."

These words seeped into my heart as gentle waves of grace.
I stopped thinking. Inside, I felt your love.

"I want to come home to you."

Come home. Home.
Where love grows, shares, affirms. Where love welcomes. Forgives. Accompanies.
Home is where love trusts. Home is one with another. Not alone.

"I want to come home to you."

Your words flowed like honey over bricks of fear,
Crumbling the mortar with kindness.

Now from behind the bricks, I say, "I want to come home to you."
Words simply spoken.

I want to come home to you
Where bricks no longer protect a heart alone but
build a home together.

Several weeks later, on Palm Sunday, Terry asked me to marry him.

I said, "Yes."

My friends and therapist cheered.

OBSESSION HAD MORE TO SAY

We sat at the counter in my kitchen on tall chairs, surveying the clutter of dishes and the remains of dinner. It was my birthday. Terry and I drank more wine than should be allowed to remain sober. He handed me a small white box wrapped in a yellow bow with a wide grin and a twinkle of compassion in his eyes. I already had an engagement ring, so I was not quite sure what to expect. I felt the warmth of his hands as he gave me the box, penetrating deep in my body as it always did whenever his touch connected to mine.

Earlier in the day, I had experienced another bout with Obsession. But something about this box challenged all its apprehension. I wanted to relax and accept this gift, receive it with the same love Terry had given.

As I lifted the lid, I saw a delicate, simple golden cross, with several small diamonds placed in the bars. My head hurt with a pressure of bewilderment; my heart pounded with an affirming, knowing the truth of Terry's heart.

My eyes met Terry's. I broke into tears and wept. Obsession had spent the day judging my choice to marry Terry. It said Terry was alien to my history, a betrayal to the thirty years of marriage to

313

Mark, disloyal to my work as a pastor. This gift defeated Obsession again. None of what it rumored into my brain was true.

I sat in the loving presence of a man who showed deep respect for me with his words and actions. On my birthday, he gave me a gift symbolizing a religion he did not understand and affirming a spiritual life he did not practice.

When we talked about marriage, Terry said he needed three things from us. We needed to be great friends, enjoyable and satisfying companions, and have shared mutual passions and sexuality. I needed a fourth—spirituality. I had asked God for a man who knew religious doctrines and practice. God gave me a man who lived love instead, a much broader spiritual truth than I could have imagined.

We talked about living together, but I knew it was impossible because of the pledge I took as a pastor. We needed to be married. A fall wedding seemed fitting for a man who introduced himself to me as "AutumnsEagle." We were both in the autumn of our lives. The fall filled the world with color, crisp air, and Thanksgiving. The fall had been a time of death for me. A wedding would transform it into a time of life.

In the summer, we took a trip to the Olson lake home. I missed the water. The call of the loons. And the quiet reflections. I wanted to share this experience with Terry.

However, Obsession decided to come along on the trip. As soon as we arrived at the cabin, it started to talk in my head. Memories of Mark grew large. I knew Mark's love in this place, and his presence was everywhere. In the chairs where we sat. In bed when we slept. In the conversations I heard in my head.

The memories echoed with the judgment of myself and the criticism of Terry. My head ached with over-analysis. Obsession separated me from Terry and his love for me. It kept me away from my love for Terry. It took over any notion of present reality and mindfulness of love.

314

I panicked and could not breathe. I needed to escape. Obsession told me I had to flee from Terry.

On the second day at the cabin, I sat with Terry on the couch overlooking the backyard. I knew I had to talk to him.

Through my head fog, I finally found the words to say, "I can't do this anymore." He thought I meant I did not want to be with him anymore, to end the relationship ultimately, not to get married. I probably sounded that way. That is perhaps what Obsession wanted me to say. But I could not. I did not want to break it off completely. But I could not find the calm to go forward. Terry asked me what I wanted. I said I did not know.

We stumbled through the next hours, gingerly engaging the situation. I was afraid of what to say or not say. Terry pulled away. Quiet, guarded. Introspective. We decided to drive home.

We called the wedding off. I asked Terry to wait as I wanted to sort it all out. But we continued to see each other, to affirm our love, to proceed as the way opened.

Before we drove home from the Minnesota cabin, I sat at Mark's grave. I needed time to think. While I sat, two hummingbirds came near. I breathed in their presence.

"Take time," I heard them say into my being. "Take time. It will be revealed."

When I got home, I searched for the spiritual meaning of hummingbirds. Native Americans see them as healers, as signs of love, as bringers of love.

What did I want? I wanted to heal from the damage of Obsession, the grasp of fear. I wanted to move into a new life. I wanted to love others.

But love revealed itself to me. Love was Terry. I just needed to see it.

REVELATIONS

I still had internal work to do.

On our way home from the cabin, we stopped to see my friend Anne. We told her we decided to postpone the wedding. Anne looked at me, knowing that this was my idea and not Terry's.

"Don't forget Terry is God's gift to you." These words reminded me of what a pastor from Minnesota told me earlier in the summer, "Don't let Terry go."

When we returned to Champaign, I walked through the rooms of the house I loved. The porch and sunroom were my holy places where I wrote and prayed and wondered. The art on the walls told my life story. I loved it here, for the house reflected all the good in being single. This house symbolized that I made it through. It proclaimed the resurrection. This house revealed I moved through death and transformed my life into something new, a new career, a new life. I changed my life to the point where I loved again. It was hard work, and I wanted to celebrate and remember what I had done.

But Terry did not fit in this place. There was no room for his stuff, for his life, or even our life together. To marry Terry, I would need to create a home with him. We would buy a place collectively where we each had a room of our own. Selling this house was yet another loss. I was not quite ready to leave. I did not want to lose myself.

But I did not want to let go of Terry. Marrying Terry did not mean I lost my identity. It only said we shared in our mutuality. Marrying Terry invited me into an opportunity to grow larger. Terry walked beside me. He did not need to walk in my way, but he found ways to open my path. Neither of us used the other or consumed the other. We were whole people walking side by side.

I began to prepare my house to sell. I wanted to come home to Terry. Our home would be different and shared. We would be together in our home, not mine.

I also had a strong urge to tell my parents about Terry. Even though they were both dead and I was sixty years old, I wanted them to know Terry. I longed for their blessing. I wrote to them in this way:

Dear Mom and Dad,

I would like you to meet Terry. You may disapprove, but Terry and I both agree we probably would not have given each other a second look forty years ago. But we've both grown.

Dad, you will be disappointed Terry is not a Christian. Mom, you will worry about his soul. But I love him. This love has grown through my fears, too. I will leave any judgment up to God.

It was long loneliness after Mark died. Not only did I survive, but I was also resilient. I formed a whole new life for myself. I have another degree. I am an ordained pastor. I have new friends. I believe this journey led to Terry and his love.

I know God as Love, a transforming Love. God is not only about life after death, but for bringing life now. I know God as love. Terry helps me live in that reality. I believe he is a gift God sent.

Terry is love for me. He holds me, listens to me, and cares for me. He dances with me and makes me laugh.

And most importantly, he makes me think. He matured through his pain and told me I am the recipient of all he learned. He can be a bit of an absent-minded professor and is a poster child as an INTP in the Myers Briggs. He loves his children. He adores his grandchildren. Terry forgets where he left things. He can get deep in thought and into his brain and fail to connect with me or others.

Yet, Terry's colleagues admire and respect him. He is a trusted friend. Integrity guides in decisions. And he is deeply spiritual in ways I am just learning to understand and appreciate.

Terry carries warmth and passion within his own body.

And Mom and Dad, I love who I am becoming when I am with him. His love pulls me outside of myself and helps me imagine a bigger world. He does not overshadow me. When I am with him, I have room to be myself, to live with my own life, beliefs, and leadership. He encourages me to create. With him, I can live a more balanced life with health, play, work, spirit, family, and friends. He asks me to be open, to play, to live large.

I sometimes get afraid, but I love the person I am becoming when I am with Terry. I think you would like Terry, too, and grow to love him. Everyone who meets him does.

I love you. Elaine

My mom and dad could never give me their blessing. But my eldest brother Larry did in their stead. In the early fall, Larry and his wife Kathy came to visit. Larry wanted to know Terry better. After they spent the weekend asking Terry questions and seeing his integrity and his love for me, Larry and Kathy both responded that Terry was a good man. They could see he was right for me. They gave us their blessing. Larry and Kathy expressed their Christianity in similar ways as my parents. I believed their consent represented the grace and love of my mom and dad. Like everyone else, they began cheering for Terry also.

My brother Richard never met Terry before we married. But with each phone call I had with him, he listened to my stories and my heart. He longed for me to be happy. Rich heard it in my voice and gave us his blessing as well.

And then Barkley died. As he grew older, his body stopped working. Terry was with me when I took him to the vet. As Barkley looked at me before he died, he seemed to know what was happening and appeared to know it was time to die. Barkley had been a companion after Mark's death. He got me out of bed in the morning, made me laugh, took me on walks in the fresh air, and sat with me when Obsession overwhelmed me. Barkley's "gip-in-his-get-along" always made me smile. His eyes saw deep into my heart as if it were God's gaze. When Sara was a teenager, she wrote a report for church saying that God is like a dog offering unconditional love. Barkley gave this Godly love. Many had told me he held Mark's spirit. Perhaps Barkley's dying opened the door wider for Terry's love.

I also needed to call Red, Mark's best friend. I needed his blessing, too. Perhaps if he affirmed my relationship with Terry, I would accept it as approval from Mark. Red had not met Terry, but he watched me grow through the years since Mark's death. He saw the confidence I carried. He saw the joy I reflected. He saw how Terry's love created room for me to be me, fully me. Red wondered with me if Mark would love that about Terry. Red also knew I was seeking to know God and God's Love within the diversity of the world. Red realized Terry helped me understand this, too.

Terry and I just kept moving forward together, one step after another. There was no dramatic reconciliation—only the constancy of togetherness, stability, respect, kindness, and trust. And a little wine, good food, laughter, lovemaking, and just plain fun. We set a date to be married in the spring, right after Easter. We found a church for the ceremony because the chapel where I worked was too small. I wanted to invite many family and friends. As they grieved with me, I wanted them to celebrate with me.

We began looking for a place to live as a couple. We both agreed that we each had 100% veto power. Terry wanted something more modern. Modern was okay with me if it had character. We had to decide together what "character" meant. We found a condominium we both liked—high ceilings, a room of our own for our books and belongings, as well as space for family and friends to visit, walking paths, and open green space to breathe.

One more difficult step presented itself—the wedding ceremony. Just as we had absolute veto power in deciding on a place to live, we agreed that it was also necessary to have complete affirmation of anything read or spoken in the ceremony. I looked for Biblical texts that Terry could affirm. Terry found Native American readings I could claim.

It took time, patience, and lots of willpower to keep Obsession's judgment at bay. The teaching from my church when I was a child and the continued influence of my parents' attitudes toward non-Christians was hard to silence. With much dialogue and commitment, we found the words that spoke a truth we each could claim on our own and affirm together. The ceremony would close with this benediction:

> *Creator God, Jesus Christ, The Great Spirit,*
> *Make you strong in faith and love,*
> *Defend you on every side*
> *And guide you in truth and peace,*
> *Now and forever. Amen.*

DO NOT OVERTHINK IT

Several days before our wedding, my brother Richard sent a card. It ended with the words, "Don't overthink it." It reminded me of a quote from Mark Nepo, a spiritual writer, in the devotions I read the previous year.

"No amount of thinking about yourself will give you confidence, just as no amount of thinking about the sun will warm you, just as no amount of thinking about love will hold you. Confidence and love and the light of the world wait below all the labors of our mind." After the reading, Nepo invited the reader to breathe in practice, stopping your thinking in mid-thought. And then to breathe out, dropping beneath your reflection into your being.

Obsession often held my brain in the months as I found love. Overthinking caught my mind and made me afraid. I feared love. I feared losing love again.

But Love lived within my being and around me. I knew it. I trusted it. Terry embodied it and invited me to embrace it. God claimed it.

It rained on the day of our wedding. Squirrels played in the church courtyard while friends and family gathered to celebrate with us. We filled the altar with candles to announce life, the power of light, and the promise of new beginnings.

Terry and I stood together in the back of the church holding hands. I breathed out a long sigh and sank deep into my being to hold fast to the confidence and love and light below the labor of my mind.

I breathed in Love from its very Source.

I took Terry's arm, and together we walked into life.

A FEW FINAL THOUGHTS...

"Someday," I mused aloud with Sister Michaela, my spiritual director at the time. "Someday, I would like to be known as wise."

She smiled in her reply with heartfelt compassion, "Be careful for what you pray. Wisdom grows through great suffering."

Just a few years later, my husband, Mark, of thirty years, died after a five-month ordeal with multiple myeloma, cancer forming in one's bone marrow.

My family and I lived with sorrow and suffering. Not as deep as others whose pain is so much worse, more long-lasting, or caused by the injustice of greed and power, but enough suffering to wonder about its meaning and purpose. I wondered what I learned. Perhaps it even made me a bit wiser.

Mark also used to say, "Why waste a good suffering?" It was part of Mark's understanding of Christianity and the theology of the cross, where God joins the pain of the world to show His compassion for those who hurt, being at one with the suffering.

Yet, I pondered this quote for years. What did it mean for me? Could it mean that through the resilience of sorrow, one can find transformation and hope?

Or it could be that our pain teaches us about the suffering of others, opening our hearts to their hurts in ways we could not otherwise understand?

Or it could be that the suffering created wisdom—just a bit of wisdom?

I am not sure if this memoir is wise or just a revelation of what I experienced in my ten-year journey as a widow.

Mark and I were married for thirty years before his death. I would describe our marriage as very good. Yes, we had our share of disagreements, but we always found our way through. Mark dreamed of being a pastor since he was a small boy, and I had visions of being a pastor's wife. Seventy years ago, my Christian tradition did not ordain women.

When I fell in love with Mark, our visions intertwined, and I supported this mutuality wholeheartedly. Walking alongside him, I claimed his dream as my own. We mutually shared common ideas, read similar books, and worked together. Because of his work as a pastor, many people invited us into the intimate parts of their lives. I met leaders and great church theologians through his leadership and connections.

Mark loved me and respected me. He encouraged me to develop my hand-weaving. And with this backing, I created woven vestments for pastors and art for churches throughout the United States. He cheered for me as I went back to school for the MA in counseling. With his encouragement and financial backing, I opened a private psychotherapy practice.

Toward the end of our marriage, I worked with him to lead workshops for pastors and other church leaders. When he died, someone told me, "Not only will I miss Mark's words and thinking, but I will miss the two of you and your work together."

Still, throughout this shared mission, I pushed hard against him with my independent spirit. I saw myself as someone who kept Mark honest, challenged his self-absorbed assumptions, and fought for my voice to be heard as clearly as his.

As he died, I grieved who we were together. I cherished our marriage. Yet, I had to rediscover myself beyond this knowledge. In so doing, I pushed even harder at his memory. I needed to name the disappointments, the hurts, and what I lost of myself when I married him. I needed to do this to grow and transform.

For those of you who read this book and cherish your memory of Mark, please recognize the negative stories about Mark are also vulnerable parts of my story. He, like all of us, was "saint and sinner," as Martin Luther would say. So am I.

This memoir is my story. When Mark died, part of me died too. For thirty years, I lived in his shadow as a pastor's wife. Unimpeded as a widow, I searched obsessively for identity and love. This journey pulled me into soul struggles, grief, world travel, disastrous dating, dog drama, spiritual surprises, and eventually, marriage with an agnostic who, to my surprise, embodied God's Grace.

The week my husband died exposed the internal conflict between my public role as a pastor's wife and my personal needs as a spouse. In the following ten years, I set out on a circuitous journey to rediscover myself, God, and new love as a middle-aged woman.

I wrote this memoir to uncover meaning for myself. I wrote it for others so I might not waste a good suffering. Although the book includes reflections on the week of Mark's death, it is mostly about the struggle to find me again in the years that followed.

In my work as a psychotherapist, my brand was "some things in life are too hard to do alone." This statement is also true for the journey of grief. This writing uses my own story to reflect on the four steps I experienced in my own path toward a new life. These are 1) The Loss; 2) Survival; 3) Finding a new identity; and 4) Now what? I long for my journey's stories to be helpful to others in theirs. Through this journey, I sought God and spiritual meaning.

There are so many who cherished us both and supported us through Mark's death. I have named only a few in writing. Please forgive me if I have forgotten parts or not written about others. Please know how grateful I am for your compassion. This gratitude is for the members of Hope Lutheran Church and the staff: Pastor Skatrud, Marilyn, Tom and Carol, Sue, Vicki, Ann, Audric, Peggy, and Kyra. Thank you to friends, Wayne, Red and Susan, Tom and Sara, John (deceased) and Fern, and others in the community like Father Frank, Natalie and Paul, Ruth and Randy, and too many to name in this small space. To my family: my deceased dad, my late brother Larry and his wife Kathy, and my brother Rich and his late wife Valerie. To Mark's family: Barry and Diane, Joanne and Tim, my late brother-in-law Rich and his wife Denise, and our nieces and nephews. Thanks to the bishop and the pastoral colleagues who loved and challenged Mark and his big ideas. Thanks to the followers of "Notes to Eli" and those who were part of the Center for Congregational Leadership.

Many loved me through my transitions and mistakes. I especially appreciate the love of both Mark's family and my own. And friends: Anne, Mickey, Vicki, Lauren, Chris, John, Pete and Jane, Tom and Katie, Ann, Joe, Peggy, Terry, Dave, and Rhonda. Friends, pastors, and professors at United Theological Seminary; the Lutheran School of Theology at Chicago; Peace Lutheran in Lauderdale, Minnesota; Our Saviour's Lutheran Church; and St. Andrew Lutheran Campus Ministry. Thanks to Sister Michaela and the other spiritual directors who listen with their hearts to my own.

If I have forgotten to name someone specifically, please forgive me for there are so many who showed compassion and care during this grief walk. Some things in life are too hard to do alone.

Thank you to my son Brent and his wife Connie, to my daughter Sara and her husband Clark, and my grandchildren, Amos and Susannah. I love you tons and tons. We still miss your dad.

Yes, our stories are different. This memoir is mine. Thanks for your love along the way.

And thank you, Terry. Early in our marriage, you wrote:

Where hearts meet
at crossings,
few dare to journey,
love grows strong along paths
least traversed.

This journey of grief is a daring one. The meeting of hearts in love is always daring. For, loving means growing. Loving means losing. And loving means life. Perhaps this is wisdom, after all.

I am grateful.

Elaine

FOR REFLECTION

(Lynn Batcher Robinson wrote these questions for reflection. She is a retired hospital chaplain who has worked with grieving individuals and support groups for over 30 years. She has also grieved the deaths of two husbands and continues to be amazed by the transformative power of grief, tenderly engaged.)

Loss is a given in the life of anyone who loves. Just as each person is unique, so is every relationship and every grief journey. This book is the story of one person who lost her life partner in particular circumstances and how she mourned. It is not intended to be a road map, a kind of "how-to-do-grief" manual.

However, one person's story can be a way into understanding our own grief as we search for meaning in the experience and eventually find healing. These questions are tools for reflecting on your life during and after a loss. Not all of the questions will seem relevant to you. Some may be too painful to explore at this time. But you are invited to use them in any way that may be helpful to you.

The Loss

1. How would you describe your relationship with the deceased before the events leading up to the illness and death?

2. How did your loved one's response to the illness or coming death affect you?

3. What do you think you needed most in the last days of your loved one's life? What was it like for you to need help for yourself?

4. Who were the people who were incredibly helpful to you as your loved one died? In what ways were they helpful?

5. What hard choices did you have to make regarding visits or offers of help?

6. What comments did people make that were less than helpful? If so, how?

7. Did your loved one make requests of you that caused you pain or resentment? Or great joy?

8. How did your loved one say goodbye, in words, or in other ways? If you remember his or her last words, how did you feel about them? How has it changed?

9. How did you experience the visitation/funeral/memorial events? What pleased you? What disappointed you?

10. Look at the quote at the beginning of Part I. How does this statement relate to your experience of watching someone you love die?

The Impact

1. What were your predominant feelings in early grief?

2. What physical effects did your loss bring?

3. What other losses came with the loss of your loved one?

4. Elaine writes, "When he died, I became incomplete, less than half a circle with an open gap seeking fulfillment, longing to rediscover those parts I left behind." In what ways might that sentiment reflect your own?

5. Are there losses in your past that might be affecting how you grieve this one?

6. Do you think your childhood might influence how you deal with loss?

7. Have you struggled with regrets about actions taken or not taken before the illness, injury, or death?

8. How did others' grief affect you?

9. What expectations did others (family, friends, colleagues) have of you? What did you expect of yourself? How did you react to these expectations?

10. Were you ever disappointed in yourself as you grieved? If so, what did you do with that disappointment?

11. How did the need for physical touch affect you both before and after your loved one's death?

12. Have the arts (music, visual arts, literature, etc.) played any part in your mourning? If so, how?

13. Can you describe any "mystical" experiences you may have had as you grieved?

14. What were holidays and anniversaries like for you, especially the first year? What became essential for you?

15. Restless energy and the need for action shaped Elaine's grief walk. What do you think is shaping yours?

What's next?

1. Are there parts of your grief experience that you dreaded that turned out to be a blessing?

2. Are your beliefs and values regarding physical intimacy consistent with your experience as a single person?

3. What life lessons have you learned that helped you grieve? What do you need? What do you have to give?

4. At any point, have you found joy within great pain? How would you describe it?

5. Have you recognized any signs of new life even as you grieve deeply? How would you describe them?

6. Have you ever experienced an "angel unaware"? What happened?

7. As a partnerless person, how would you describe your desire for physical intimacy? Are they consistent with your past?

Spirituality in Grief

(Please note that spirituality embraces the meaning of life with something bigger than yourself and your being. Religion is more often associated with an institution and a practice.)

1. If spirituality is about a relationship with the divine and finding meaning in life, how would you describe your spiritual journey as you grieved?

2. Has your understanding of, or relationship with, the divine changed since this loss.?

3. If you are usually a person of prayer, what has your prayer life been like through this illness/injury, death, and mourning?

4. What does the phrase "…resurrection is for the living as well as the dead" mean to you?

5. Given the reality of your life at this moment, how do you make love known?

ABOUT THE AUTHOR

 Elaine Olson is a retired ordained pastor of the Evangelical Lutheran Church in America, a certified spiritual director, and a Licensed Clinical Professional Counselor. She has been writing reflections and narratives in personal journals for most of her life. In the past five years, she has written to inspire and encourage others. She is a mom and gramma, and her life-long passion is to wonder, teach, guide, and affirm others; and together integrate issues of life and Spirit. She writes a blog called "g'amma gazing" at elainekolson.com.

The ocean feeds her soul...

Made in the USA
Monee, IL
22 March 2021